Approaches to Organizing

Approaches to Organizing

Edited by Robert T. Golembiewski, University of Georgia

Published by The American Society for Public Administration

PUBLIC ADMINISTRATION LIBRARY

Published by the American Society for Public Administration

PAR Classics Series

1. **Professional Public Executives**
   Edited by Chester A. Newland

2. **Perspectives on Budgeting**
   Edited by Allen Schick

3. **Approaches to Organizing**
   Edited by Robert T. Golembiewski

The American Society for Public Administration
1225 Connecticut Avenue, N.W.
Washington, D.C. 20036

Library of Congress Catalog Number: 81-70133

International Standard Book Number: 0-936678-03-8

Price: $11.95

Contents

Approaches
to
Organizing

Three Basic Approaches to Organizational Phenomena: Insularities and Interfaces

This slim volume seeks to encompass a treacherous and ill-defined domain —that associated with "organizing" and "re-organizing." Simple definitions can help us get started—e.g., organization is patterned cooperation, which may be defined as that class of acts where several people working interdependently can do more (or better or faster or different) things than the same individuals working separately. But beyond the simple metaphors of two persons together lifting a rock which neither could manage alone, things get complicated fast. For some, management and organization theory is a "jungle."[1] Others, like Waldo, titilate us when they speak of an "elephantine" problem,[2] with several intended implications: that there is a lot of "it": that what one perceives depends on what one has a "hold" on; and that most or all observers perceive only smallish parts of the total beast, thus being poor communicators not only about the beast's essence but even in being poorly understood by observers holding fast to other parts of "its" anatomy.

This introductory essay has two ambitions within the context of providing a general map for explorers of "organization" and "reorganization." First, hopefully, this introduction will provide a useful perspective on why the area poses such intellectual and practical challenges. Second, this opening piece also will imply a way to cope with such challenges—it will sketch the kind and quality of integration of disparate approaches that will eventually generate a serviceable set of organization theories to guide research and praxis.

A Generic View:
Three Approaches to Organizing/Reorganizing

Let us simplify in the service of highlighting the complex interplay of three basic approaches to organization that eventually will be part of a satisfactory theory but which, at times, have been zero-sum competitors intolerantly neglectful of mutual strengths or wedded to individual weaknesses. So our task is not an easy one, and cross-currents can be treacherous. Thus, the three approaches sometimes stand out in bold relief, only to blend ineluctably into one another at points. At times, the three approaches feed contentedly at the same

1

trough; at still other times they snap and snarl for their fair share of attention, or even the ever-greedy monopolist's share. Periodically, one or another approach gets emphasis, while interest in others fades, only to be energized for later reappearances. Finally, specific individuals have sometimes played roles in more than one of the approaches, which complicates separating the sheep from the goats.

So our targets are moving ones, and protean. Yet, the present view is that three basic approaches to organization phenomena can usefully be distinguished in terms of some significant central tendencies.

1. *Organization Analysis and Theory, or OA & T.* At the very beginning, in this version of Genesis for a theory of organizing, there was what will be called organization analysis and theory—or, far more conveniently, OA & T. OA & T does not constitute a homogeneous literature, except in its basic systemic ambitions. Work in this tradition always sought to encompass whole organizations, which constitutes a very large agenda even today, given the lack of detailed supporting observation and empirically-rooted theory.

Beyond this basic commonality, at least three distinct tracks of OA & T work can be distinguished. Some of the work—early on, as well as more recently—had a very detailed descriptive character, and sought to root its analysis in the enshrouding socioeconomic-political environments. Such work was empirical, but its observations at best generated only rough and tentative classifications of reality. Exemplars of such work include summary efforts such as that of Fayol,[3] as well as studies rooted in specific organizations such as Selznick on TVA and Kaufman on the ranger in the U.S. Forest Service.[4]

Even more of the work on OA & T can be said to have a "general-system sociology" orientation. This includes the substantial volume of work in both Marxist and Parsonian traditions, which was often deliberately armchair theorizing or even defiantly antiempirical; and it also encompasses the work of people like Barnard[5] and Thompson[6] who built on experience and (in the latter's case) sought to facilitate testing that experience.

But most of the work that can reasonably be classified as OA & T sought universality and comprehensiveness *via* that variety of simplifications embodied in the "bureaucratic principles." Scientific management constituted the most profound and pervasive expression of this approach to organization.[7] Overall, the bureaucratic principles dominated in OA & T, even though it also included comprehensive efforts to systematize what was known about organizing—the tradition of work from Fayol, through Barnard and Selznick, and then Drucker,[8] as well as others. The basic thrusts of the dominant principles can fairly be characterized as:

- emphasizing application, as "practical" rather than "theoretical";
- being prescriptive, and sometimes so obscurely yet firmly value-laden that its adherents not only failed to recognize its normative bases but also saw it as the "one best way" (and of course the principles *were* the one

best way, but only for approaching the specific value set that more or less consciously underlay the approach!);
- emphasizing structural features—coordination, line/staff, and so on;
- having a broad socioeconomic focus, which could be reflected self-consciously in consideration of markets or environments, or even could be reflected carelessly in assumptions about "economic man";
- having a strong rational and deductive quality.

The approach was definitely hardy, in large part because it was inbred and in that sense self-reinforcing. Massie noted about "most writers on management" through 1955:[9]

[They] elaborated on earlier classical principles. . . . There were few challenges from those within the classical school of thought; therefore, significant innovations in thought on management developed only outside. . . .

Despite the overall domination of the bureaucratic principles in OA & T, suggestive evidence even in early work implied two defects. First, the quality of bureaucratic ideation had been suspect for a long time, even if only in what clearly constituted minority opinions.[10] Second, empirical observations—although limited to small populations and guided only by a general map of significant variables—began enlarging the suspicion that the bureaucratic principles had a broad range of unanticipated and undercutting effects.[11] These two converging suspicions often derived momentum from work solidly within the OA & T tradition, and over time limited the senses in which the principles were thought of as the glory road to organizational efficiency and effectiveness.

2. *Organization Behavior, or OB.* These growing suspicions motivated what developed into the voluminous literature usually designated organization behavior, or OB. Basically, early OB sought to test the growing suspicions about the bureaucratic principles by a basic methodological reorientation. In sum, OB verified and enlarged those suspicions by sharpening its analytical foci. Replication and validation became the watchwords, and they often required substituting a microscope for the systemic ambitions of OA & T. The Hawthorne studies, for example, in multiple senses characterized the essential early OB.[12] The focus on such targets as the Bank Wiring Test Room reflects that specificity and manageability had become leitmotifs. There is no free lunch, of course. So the effort to see more detail typically had the cost of narrowing the field of what was seen. Witness the focus on leadership or management styles, patterns of interaction in small groups, and so on. Witness also the meager attention given macrofactors, e.g., a roaring depression in the Hawthorne studies. More broadly, OB:

- was descriptive, often showing how bureaucratic assumptions either did not exist in organizations or that, when they did, efficiency was not the only or even the most probable outcome;

- was determinedly "scientific," which often meant that it was presented as "value-free" and sometimes as "universal";
- was microfocused and psychological, as in the emphases on behavior and needs, leadership styles, and so on;
- had a strong affective orientation, as in stressing the relevance of relationships and feelings at work—"morale," "employee satisfaction," and the like;
- focused on concerns "internal" to the organization, as on interaction patterns and communication processes.

In sum, OB and OA & T contrasted at a number of significant points. Thus, OA & T at its best had strong "relational" or "external" thrusts, as in variously articulating the interfaces of an organization with its environment. Moreover, OA & T's focus was broadly economic or sociological and macrofocused, while OB can be more reasonably described as psychological or sociopsychological and microfocused.

3. *Organization Development, or OD.* The last of our trio of approaches at once sought to amalgamate major aspects of its two predecessors, as well as to transcend their limitations. An oft-cited definition helps develop the complex point:[13]

... organization development is a long-range effort to improve an organization's problem-solving and renewal processes, particularly through a more effective and collaborative management or organization culture—with special emphasis on the culture of formal work teams—with the assistance of a change agent, or catalyst, and the use of the theory or technology of applied behavioral science, including action research.

Let us do some reading-between-the-lines of this contemporary definition. Organization development, or OD, is a tradition of work having a history of three decades or so, and has multiple contrasts/assimilations with organization behavior as well as with organization analysis and theory. For example, OD sought a strong base in rigorous empirical observation and theory, like OB and unlike most of OA & T. In addition, OD had a strong prescriptive base which distanced it from OB in that particular; and OD shared a prescriptive predisposition with OA & T even as it rejected the specific values underlying much work in that tradition. Finally, OD stressed application *and* research, which made it both unlike and like OA & T and OB in different particulars.

Even these brief characterizations imply that OD's synergistic intentions had to be approached over *terra incognita,* if not actual minefields. Paramountly, perhaps, OD's multiple agendas were formidable, and implied issues of identity for both the "area" and its adherents. What is OD? Where is its home base? Such questions give continuing concern to ODers.[14] Easy answers are not possible, given the cross-cutting of traditional approaches, as well as the innovation of novel approaches, necessary to encompass the research and applications implied by any robust statement of OD mission-and-roles.

No doubt the most apt characterization of OD is that it has shown continuing developmental progress. Major problems clearly remain in OD's future,[15] including philosophical and empirical ramifications of major proportions. Also, much present speculation focuses on whether or not presently conceived OD will remain a robust area for identification, inquiry, and application, or whether we now see only a passing fascination that will soon become the caboose rather than the engine in some more comprehensive approach to organizational phenomena.

Opinions clearly do differ, then, but OD has at least proved to have a growing reach and grasp. So far, so good, in short. Consider the "laboratory stem" of OD, for example, which emphasizes "learning about learning" via specific modes of interaction that facilitate feedback and disclosure, learning associated early on and almost exclusively with T-Groups or sensitivity training.[16] This technology-*cum*-values constituted a comfortable base for most of those associated with early OD; indeed, some rank the approach among the major achievements of the 20th century.[17] Basically, the laboratory stem assumes a "tender" model rather than a "tough" one. It emphasizes what might be called love/truth, as contrasted with power/advantage. As Schmuck and Miles explain:[18]

Such a "tender" model states that shared expectations involving trust, warmth, and supportiveness are formed as the members of a working team gain confidence and skill in communicating clearly and openly. These norms and skills, in turn, support collaborative problem-solving and the rational use of information in making decisions. This model assumes [that] work . . . is carried on through interpersonal interactions and that heightening abilities for problem-solving must commence with new norms for interpersonal openness and helpfulness.

Although the laboratory stem constitutes *a* basic central focus for those identifying with OD, however, it soon became obvious to growing numbers that the stem could hardly serve as *the* exclusive focus. To be sure,[19] direct implementations in organizations have been made of the love/truth approach, but ample evidence reflects that this constitutes too great a leap for those in many organizations, tactically if not strategically. Many liked the tender model, and perhaps more still saw it as necessary in complex organizations. But they also saw a huge gap between "here" and "there"—between common practices in many organizations and OD values; between small learning collectivities like T-Groups and large organizations; between interpersonal openness *cum* helpfulness and the always-substantive and often-political collective life in large organizations; as well as between the essentially unstructured and agenda-free T-Group and the patterned if not regimented "real world."

How to facilitate movement from "here" to "there"? Three basic approaches have come over time to complement the laboratory stem of OD:

● attention shifted from T-Groups to interaction-centered learning designs that engage feedback and disclosure processes in organizations while variously bounding those processes, as in

—team-building[20] with intact formal work groups, which emphasized an analysis of interaction processes as well as of technical and substantive issues so central in organizational life;

—various limited-purpose and short-cycle designs which sought to energize T-Group-like processes for specific needs—for conflict resolution,[21] for confrontation to clear the air as a prelude to action,[22] and so on;

• major emphasis was accorded the "survey stem" of OD, which used opinion polling techniques to help induce feedback and disclosure processes in large aggregations of people, often as a prelude to action-planning in small groups[23] to improve the worksite in more or less specific ways;

• growing attention has been directed at a broad range of designs dealing with organizational structures and policies/procedures,[24] which are consistent with OD values but which do not derive from—although they may rest on—the extended preparatory socioemotional work envisioned by the tender model of the laboratory stem.

Hence OD became more of a blend: the long-run goal of a comprehensive social contract remained; but, that view was supplemented by various designs consistent with what can be called limited-purpose contracts consistent with OD values but only moving toward the ideal social order and culture.

The ideal synthesis for OD is still incomplete and conceivably out of reach, although well begun. That synthesis involves blending the several approaches sketched above while preserving a sense of identification with common values. The tensions are very real[25] and, to hazard a too-facile contrast, can engage common polarities—populism *versus* elitism, observant and committed participation *versus* detached and objective observation, comprehensive *versus* incremental approaches, and so on. The laboratory stem seeks problem solving *via* interaction and agreement, as it were, while emphasizing participation, involvement, and commitment within a trusting environment. The survey stem of OD and the various approaches relating to structure or policies/procedures provide a substantial but not complete contrast. They emphasize problem solving *via* the accumulation of knowledge through research leading to theory building.

The core issue should be clear. How to exploit the potency of research/theory without jeopardizing the participation, involvement, and commitment of specific individuals at particular application sites? Put otherwise, the challenge involves resisting polarization while seeking to exploit the potential in the dynamic interplay of the polarities.

4. *Organization Research/Application as Venn Diagrams.* The brief discussion above suggests that life did not come in three distinct varieties, and we

need to be a good deal more specific on this central point. In general, an interactive model suggests the subtle blendings and shadings of the three basic approaches to organization research and application:

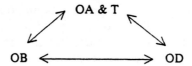

More specifically, three cases illustrate the complex forms in which our three basic approaches manifest themselves. Venn diagrams will be used to describe these three cases, if but crudely.

Case I. Serious and Open Conflict

In Venn terms, the three approaches to organizing often amount to nonintersecting sets, even hostile and rejecting sets. Graphically, then, Case I takes this form:

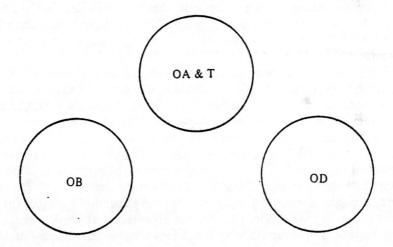

The convention implies major distance and differences between the three approaches, with proponents being engaged in serious and open conflict.

Whence derives such conflict? Consider only two mutually heightening sources—one practical and the other normative. First, normative contention between proponents of the three approaches often has been spirited—indeed, sometimes bitter. Thus, OD aficionados have disparagingly contrasted their need-serving and freedom-enhancing values with the "surplus repression" said to characterize bureaucratic variants of OA & T;[26] or ODers can contrast their value-guided "action research" with the normatively deadening and dead-end assumptions of the rationalist assumptions underlying much of OA & T.[27] This hardly settles matters, of course. Much of the OB literature rejects both approaches to values. Indeed, OB proponents often reflect a value-free scientific posture. Given that this position has been softened and variously modified over the years, it can still become manifest in vital ways. For example, the OB posture about values contrasts with the easy assumptions about values often made by work in the OA & T tradition, a contrast which this writer sees as useful, on balance. But the same posture has encouraged the position that OD's use of data in "action research" contaminates results, or at best creates only ephemeral "Hawthorne effects,"[28] a view which this writer sees as less useful, overall. Such diverse manifestations of the value-free posture come to at least one common bottom line, moreover, which adds to the contentiousness. Those identifying with OA & T and OD can aspire only to a status very inferior to that of OB scientists, given such an OB perspective.

Second, practical considerations exacerbate such normative contentiousness. Somewhat loosely, OB had been the "top-dog" for several decades through the 1960s or so, having unceremoniously unseated OA & T as *the* locus where the major things were happening in the study of organizations. For many practical purposes, this shifted the prime locus of work from sociology to psychology.[29] Beginning with the late 1960s and early 1970s, however, OD came on very strong—in part building on the empirical contributions of OB research, and yet essentially trumpeting the inadequacy of OB's contributions.

These OB inadequacies were both methodological and substantive. Methodologically, OB was limited by its basic descriptive bias, as well as by the lack of a "theory of action" for application. This left OB vulnerable to OD, in part only because the latter's proponents—many in OB and even some in OD would say—set lower standards for a theory of action acceptable to them. Substantively, also, OB was vulnerable because of its common microfocus on psychological variables. The basic points got made in countless (and often unfair) ways by both those with OA & T and OD perspectives. Witness the anti-OB (and, sometimes, anti-OD) argument that "organization" is more than a congeries of small groups. Or, consider the argument that employees do respond to variations in supervisory style, but very broad determinants—basically, economic and political determinants for those in OA & T,[30] and cultural determinants for those in OD[31]—often will dominate in influencing reactions to the worksite.

These details sketch a battlefield. Several factors encouraged challenges to OB's "top-dog" status, no doubt for a range of motives. Moreover, OB's defense to the challenges had roots not only in its proponents' sense of intellectual integrity, but also in such mundane matters as where students would major, where jobs for them could be found, and where educational budgets would flow.

Case I rests on a classic source of contention, in sum. Basic differences in values got energized by special interests in conflict.

Case II. Complementary Perspectives and Developments

At other times and in other areas, Venn diagrams show a different pattern. To wit:

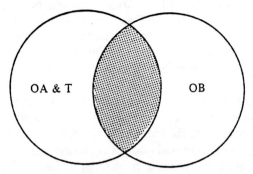

A number of illustrations falling in the shaded area above could be offered, but here consider only the interplay between "organization" and "environment." A substantial line of OA & T research had emphasized the O ↔ E interaction, as in Woodward's research with some macrocorrelates of broadly differentiated technologies,[32] or in Chandler's insightful demonstration that various strategies for growth would be best served by different structures for organizing work.[33] In its several more popular forms,[34] such work basically led to an important modification of the notion of a one-best structure that had characterized much of OA & T. At base, such work continued to argue that the bureaucratic structure was best adapted to steady-state organizational missions. The modification? For various high-technology organizations, as well as for innovative or change-oriented areas in many or all organizations, an alternative structure was more appropriate. Such an O ↔ E notion led others to conclude that there should be a macro-OB to complement the usual micro-OB, with the former taking into account the broad range of environmental differences that would affect the choice of an appropriate structure—market share, economic concentration, among many possible differences.[35]

A corresponding line of research also developed among those observers with definite OB identifications. Their initial focus was on the interaction of different products/markets with aspects of managerial performance or style; and, more generally, the same view has been expressed in "contingency theory." With greater or less precision, the contingency view proposes in connection with the choice of an organization's structure "that it all depends" on a broad range of factors, emphasizing but not restricted to psychological variables.[36]

This intersection of OB and OA & T suggests that the two sets in some particulars came out in more or less the same place, but they went their own way in others.

The situation is somewhat more complicated for OD, which has not fully bought into the O ↔ E formulation. Normative concerns, for example, have inhibited the basic O ↔ E interpretation that any structural arrangement "fit" different "environments" with varying degrees of precision that got reflected in variable organization performance. Argyris, among others, was not happy with the facile association or "fit" of E variations with specific O features. All organization structures and policies imply models of learning as well as supporting attitudes and skills, he noted. Even a high degree of O ↔ E fit should not finesse the evaluation of those models of learning, Argyris implied.[37] Moreover, convenience no doubt also influenced OD's small if growing emphasis on "environmental textures." For example, cross-cultural OD has just fairly begun. And those in OD have hardly devoted final attention to a broad range of ethical and practical issues related to the environmental settings of applications: e.g., what would/should constrain OD in Nazi Germany?; or what OD designs, if any, seem appropriate in various political settings, in "closed societies" or under coercive regimes?

Case III. Convergent Perspectives and Developments

In a small but growing number of cases, our three approaches constitute intersecting sets, as depicted by the shaded area below. An example? Well, job enrichment will do for illustrative purposes. Over a period of two decades or so, the word got around in ways more or less convincing to all three traditions of work. Thus Drucker—best classified as within OA & T—quite early and effectively demonstrated that the bureaucratic principles forfeited many opportunities for enhanced output and satisfaction,[38] at least during a war which no doubt generated enough patriotism to overcome the generally realistic suspicion that a "speed-up" would follow any increases in productivity. Increased output would only result in pay cuts, went this aspect of the common wisdom, so that more effort would be required to earn a constant wage.

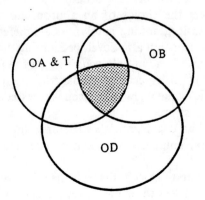

The base of support for job enrichment was broad, if qualified. Job enrichment got added impetus from those who accepted some "growth psychology," as did practically everyone associated with OD and (perhaps less dominantly) those identifying with OB. Job enrichment met individual needs and thus permitted heightened employee satisfaction and productivity. The common wisdom generally accepted this crucial point, usually *via* Maslow's "pyramid of needs" or McGregor's Theory Y *versus* X. OB research reinforced the point, albeit with suitable cautions. Thus, individual motivation seemed more contingent and complicated than implied by common interpretations of the models of individual needs generated by Maslow, Argyris, Herzberg, and others. Applications took on greater specificity in at least two senses. Useful attention was given to specific properties, as in distinguishing "enlargement" from "enrichment." Moreover, conditions more or less suitable for applications of the technique were specified."

A Specific Locus:
The Three Approaches in Public Administration

Our focus now shifts from the generic to the specific—to how the three approaches sketched above can provide some guidance for first reviewing the literature of public administration, and then for introducing a handful of selections from 40 volumes of the *Public Administration Review*. Three steps will be required. In turn, this section will:

● comment on the incidence of the three approaches in the literature of public administration;
● sketch the search process for selecting representative articles from the *Public Administration Review;*
● outline a way of presenting these representative articles to the reader.

1. *Charting Incidence of Three Approaches in PA.* The history of the development of organization studies in public administration roughly reflects the impact of the three approaches sketched above, for good or ill, with some interesting wrinkles here and there. We give attention below both to the broad sweep of the PA literature, as well as to its specific character and quality in *PAR.*

Organization Analysis and Theory in Public Administration

Until after World War II, the public administration literature reigned as the primary exponent of the administrative arts and sciences. Most of the historic strength of the PA literature clearly lies in its OA & T aspect, that is, as organization analysis and theory. Both early and late, in contributions widely cited and in those that got less attention than they deserved, public administration at its best was characterized by work in the OA & T tradition. The central

Papers of Gulick and Urwick[40] rightly enough represent the high water mark for this phase in the development of public administration.

Organization Behavior in Public Administration

A fast fall from grace quickly followed. Why? A full answer would be complicated, but a good part of the general explanation seems direct enough. Organization study began to emphasize OB far more than OA & T in the years bracketing World War II. Major advances in OB were made, in fact, but public administrationists were but poorly represented in that flurry of research and application. As but one sign of the point, note that OB textbooks flourished for decades in business circles while the appearance of such teaching aids for the public sector has been both late and in small numbers.

Again, *that* question: Why was OB lacking in contributions from public administrationists? Let a short list of probable causes suffice.

- The macroemphases in public administration—on the nation-state, the presidency, and so on—were so powerful as to inhibit public administrationists in numbers from taking the sub-systemic route implied by OB. And those few public administrationists who did so could be accused of avoiding the "real issues."
- Early OB often came in value-free guise, which most public administrationists found hard to accept, especially given the vigorous rejection of the politics/administration dichotomy that characterized so much of PA in the post-World War II period.
- Public administrationists—due to training and interests—tended to be consumers of OB, at best, not creators.
- Even when public administrationists contributed to the OB literature, moreover, that tended to occur in sources with low visibility to their fellow specialists.

Organization Development in Public Administration

More recently, OD has had an easier acceptance in public administration, for at least four probable reasons. First, the past three decades or so of work in OB have substantially sifted the wheat of solid theory and results from the chaff of exuberant value-free postures. This has served to create a better understanding of the role behavioral analysis can plan in organization study and application.

Second, OD has a strong applied orientation, as well as a relatively clear sense of the specific and determinedly anti-bureaucratic values that should guide applications. Both features no doubt encouraged OD's acceptance by public administrationists, a point that may not be obvious but which can be credibly argued. From one perspective, OD avoided the primary barbs directed at OB, which was often represented as determinedly value-free and pure science. Neither emphasis resonated positively with many public administrationists, who were themselves then just shaking off similar conceptual shackles of the "principles" approach to administration as a universal science. Viewed positively, OD gained impetus from the new public administration, in at least two senses. The core values of OD and NPA were substantially congruent,[41] which eased OD's general acceptance by many. Moreover, OD provided a technology with supporting research relevant to approaching those shared core values. The new public administration did not excel in either of these particulars. Writing in that tradition implied but did not provide a technology for change; moreover, the NPA generated little empirical research to support its core values that were attractive to many.

Third, OD implies a systemic emphasis which conceptually makes it easier to accept for many public administrationists than the sub-systemic bias that so definitely characterized early OB. There have been variable flurries of interest in political science and public administration which focused on interpersonal dynamics and the small group,[42] of course. But the basic concern remains with systems—large aggregations peaking in nation-states and the ties between them.

Fourth, some contributors to the OD literature had a degree of acceptance in public administration, which no doubt encouraged an early and fair hearing. In contrast, OB had often been seen as suspect by public administrationists for that literature's general failure to notice contributions by students associated with political science or public administration, with the exception of people like Herbert Simon and James March whose identifications with PS or PA many saw as tenuous. Witness Waldo's 1961 judgment in reviewing six books, reflecting basic emphases on organization behavior as well as organization analysis and theory:[43]

Conspicuously absent are writers identified (at least presently and prominently) with public administration, political science, or history. This surely is no accident, but a judgment . . . that whatever the usefulness of these disciplines they have nothing at present to contribute to sophisticated organization theory or research.

Noting that OD had an easier acceptance in public administration than OB certainly does not mean that this acceptance was uneventful, or unqualified, or even general. Early concern about OD among public administrationists led some to conclude that the public sector provided different and perhaps more difficult targets,[44] while a few even concluded that the targets represented impossibilities or something close to that.[45] Much of that concern focused on the perceived mismatch between OD's "tender" or integrative model, so exclusively prominent in OD's early days, and the "tough" or distributive character of politics. Love/truth, in short, would not stand a chance when confronted with power/advantage. Relatedly, others saw public sector management as far more complicated and less articulated than in business or industry. In the latter sphere, for example, one might speak with some real if limited confidence of a "management structure" or a "chain of command," especially beyond the first level of supervision where union membership typically ceased. The public sector was deliberately organized to encourage less tidiness, and especially at the highest levels—as in the separation of powers overlayed by checks and balances, or in the significant interface between short-term political appointees and longer-term career employees, and so on.[46]

Hence, the common conclusion about the public sector, especially in earlier days: OD doesn't work here, or at least it doesn't work nearly as well as in business.

More lately, this conclusion has been softened and qualified even by many of the more zealous critics, although holdouts certainly have not disappeared. I can bear personal witness to that point. I cite only the reviewer of one of my tomes. He opined that "OD" to him meant "over-dosed" with verbiage that he identified as "psycho-babble."

But rolling readjustment there seems to have been, for at least three motivating reasons. First, OD designs have found at least some room for truth/love in politics. Consider LeBaron's conclusion about local political office holders:[47]

. . . [they] live within a dichotomy of power and trust; but they are more familiar with—and therefore more capable of handling—power than trust. . . . Politics is the struggle for power [but] is dependent upon its recognition, and [upon] it being given to someone from someone.

Various interaction-centered designs can enhance sensitivities and skills related to the trust aspects of the dichotomy within which these officials exist, LeBaron also reports.

Second, the applicability of OD efforts has been widened appreciably over the last decade or so. Interaction-centered efforts have tended to move toward team-building variants or various short-cycle confrontation designs, as contrasted with the earlier reliance on T-Groups or sensitivity training. Both technically and tactically, this expands OD's applicability. In addition, various designs utilizing survey/feedback have increased OD's flexibility in dealing with large systems, with an emphasis on policies and procedures as well as on interaction.[48] Moreover, OD applications also have given some telling attention to structural change in public agencies,[49] with multiple enhancement of OD's potency. Changes in interaction may fade out if they are not suitably reinforced by organization structures and policies, clearly. Structural change provides an alternative venue for initiating OD efforts—in environments not culturally prepared for interaction-oriented efforts, as well as at low levels of organization where structure largely determines employee behavior and reaction to the worksite.

Third, accumulating evidence does not support major elements of the folk wisdom about OD applications. Specifically, data about success rates require major modifications of these three opinions about OD:[50]

1. OD's batting average in business is adequate, perhaps, but not high enough to imply a solid theoretical base;
2. public-sector OD efforts are rare, the constraints there being more exotic and formidable than in the private sector;
3. public-sector OD has lower success rates than does business OD, in addition to being less frequent.

These three opinions about OD seem to be off-base—not flat wrong, necessarily, but definitely not serviceable guides for informed opinion. Let's examine the three common opinions in order.

On any reasonable grounds, the first opinion about OD's efficacy is at least not generous. Consider six sources of data, using different indicators and relating to various OD interventions which cannot be distinguished here:

- 8 percent of Morrison's 26 cases deal with "failures"[51]
- in Dunn and Swierczek's 67 cases, 65-70 percent were considered "effective"[52]
- in Porras' 35 cases selected for high degrees of methodological rigor, variables changed in the predicted directions in about 50 percent of the cases[53]
- Margulies and his associates rated 73 percent of 30 applications as "positive," with 10 percent "mixed," 24 percent "no change," and 3 percent as "negative"[54]
- in Proehl's batch of 574 applications each scored for every relevant variable in a panel of 308 variables, over 70 percent of the scores showed "positive reported change"[55]
- in the same batch of 574 cases, 86.9 percent were rated as having effects that were "highly positive and intended" or "definite balance of positive and intended effects," with the other categories being "no appreciable effects" and negative effects"[56]

No absolute interpretation of such results seems appropriate. Thus, one might argue that "successes" are more likely to be written up, which may have been true early in the game, but the reporting of "failures" now has a growing legitimacy.[57] Moreover, research designs do vary substantially. But even Porras' rigorous criteria generate a 50 percent success rate; and Morrison's data imply similar effects in all classes of study designs she distinguished.

Not much doubt about the inadequacy of general opinion in the second case —not even a few small scholarly ifs, ands, or buts. Over 45 percent of the cases in Proehl's comprehensive inventory of OD efforts come from the public sector. "Rare" applied neither to 270 cases, nor to nearly 50 percent of all OD applications discovered by a systematic search.

At the very least, to conclude, the common opinion about OD's batting average in the public sector does not provide reasonable guidance. Multiple comparisons show no marked differences in success rates between applications in the public and business sectors:[58]

	304 Private-Sector Cases	270 Public-Sector Cases	138 Public-Sector Cases
Highly positive and intended effects	40%	41%	50%
Definite balance of positive and intended effects	49	43	41
No appreciable effects	5	7	9
Negative effects	6	9	0
Total	100%	100%	100%

The data above do not imply that public sector OD is any easier or more difficult than, similar to, or different from, that which occurs in business organizations. Rather, the data imply that—whatever the specific and complex characteristics of individuals sites for applications—the kind of OD intervenors who write up their experiences have two qualities, overall. They can diagnose individual sites; and they can select from the growing inventory of OD approaches and techniques those that are appropriate for moving toward OD values. This may seem a cute conclusion, but it is critical.

2. *Selecting Representative Articles from PAR.* Illustrating how these three approaches to organization phenomena became manifest in the *Public Administration Review* involved a complex process of choice. The basic search was quite simple. This author read all 40 *PAR* volumes, and that first cut generated about 125 articles that dealt with organization/reorganization. In addition, approximately 50 public administrationists were asked to nominate candidates. In most cases, these nominations were already included in the batch of 125. Where that was not the case, the nominations were directly added to the working pool, swelling it to about 150 possible articles.

Since only about 15 articles would be selected finally, the choice process required early and explicit guidance. *The* key decision was an easy one—"executive reorganization or reform" was seen as constituting an agenda item for some other volume in the *PAR Classics.* This literature is both large and complex, and could not be done any reasonable justice here. Indeed, only a lick-and-a-promise would be possible. On the theory that anything worth doing should be done completely and well, or not at all, a large number of notable selections were not considered further. These excluded selections dealt with the federal level, in substantial part, and included: Dimock's essay on basic objectives;[59] the Report of the President's Advisory Committee on Management;[60] Mansfield's overview of 30 years of experience with reorganization;[61] and Thayer's astringent critique of President Carter's administrative reforms.[62] Also affected were selections dealing with other governmental levels, such as Kneier's useful book review concerning state reorganization[63] and Zimmerman's survey of metropolitan reform.[64]

Within the context of this major policy decision, six other criteria for selection also became central. Introducing them will not only reflect the choice process but also will sample many of the fine selections which the present volume could not encompass.

First, the batch of 150 was reduced by eliminating articles that related to areas that will (or at least should) have separate volumes in this series devoted to them. For example, comparative and development administration were so judged, which eliminated a number of quality articles—among them selections by Presthus,[65] Riggs,[66] Loveman,[67] and Boyer.[68]

Similarly, ethical and philosophical issues related to public administration seem to require full-fledged treatment. This accounts for the omission of numerous excellent sources: Fox on the signal contributions of Mary Parker Follett;[69] Denhardt on the critical relation of citizenship in organizations and personal freedom;[70] Kaplan's critique of organizational humanism;[71] and Hart's theoretical treatment of citizen participation and decentralization;[72] as well as Harmon on social equity,[73] among others.

And finally on this first criterion for eliminating selections likely to have separate volumes of *PAR Classics* devoted to them, the presidency and the chief executive officer certainly deserve explicit attention. This urged excluding a large number of meritorious selections: Sayre on the general manager idea;[74] Carey on presidential staffing;[75] Appleby on organizing around heads of large departments;[76] and so on. Sad to note, for me personally, this criterion also led to the exclusion of the one *PAR* piece which has given me most pleasure over the years, even if the article's form has a too-fulsome quality—Stephen K. Bailey's "A Structured Interaction Pattern for Harpsichord and Kazoo,"[77] which engagingly embroiders (I take it) on the selective experiences of one chief executive.

Second, some articles were nested in complex and dated institutional and policy contexts, even as they dealt with significant organizational issues. Scarce space mitigated against reproducing such selections, which eliminated a number of fine studies (for example) of the controversy surrounding the unification of American armed services. These selections include contributions by Huzar;[78] Henry, Masland, and Radway;[79] and Mosher,[80] as well as others.

Third, the emphasis got placed on selections that performed multiple duties, all other things being more or less equal. Hence, the excellent contributions of Landau on redundancy[81] and Wildavsky on organizational self-evaluation[82] are not reprinted below because their well-developed themes get treated by several included pieces, if less fully so.

Fourth, a definite bias was accorded to selections that had a specific applied thrust. Hence, Levine's piece appears below, even as his central point could have been expressed by a number of selections—as by Wildavsky on self-evaluation.[83] Hence, also, the inclusion of the piece by Golembiewski and Kiepper on an application of planned change in mass urban transit when several other selections could have well represented aspects of their presentation—Argyris on the limits of rational theory,[54] Culbert and Reisel on the general dimensions of OD,[55] Eddy and Saunders on applications of the behavioral sciences in urban governance,[56] Gardner on non-hierarchical organizations,[57] and so on.

Fifth, preference went to selections that had summary and integrative emphases, when several equally meritorious selections were available. This explains the exclusion—despite the rarity of its genre in *PAR*—of Peabody's empirical work on authority,[58] and of Palumbo's research on roles and power.[59] And this choice-guide likewise explains the inclusion of the piece by Marcus and Cafagna summarizing a large number of studies about control in organizations.

Sixth, in many cases, a choice had to be made between selections that had similar thrusts and treatment. Here choice was particularly difficult, as in the cases of a substantial number of articles dealing with decentralization. Selections by Benson[90] and others could have well represented the costs/benefits of various ways of structuring patterns of delegated authority.

3. *Presenting Representative Articles from PAR.* As might be expected from the introductory materials on the three approaches to organization study, most of the pieces selected can be classified under OA & T, or organization analysis and theory. OB and OD get less robust representation. A few pieces also seek consciously to build bridges between the three approaches. In sum, the eventual selections can be classified as in Figure 1.

Perhaps consistency urges a follow-through in the future structuring of this volume in terms of the three approaches, even given the variable number of selections classified under each. If so, consistency loses in this case. The selections from *PAR* will be arrayed again in three parts, but those parts emphasize, in turn:

- four perspectives on viewing the act of organizing;
- five foci for guiding the design of organizations;
- seven ways of utilizing experience to guide the development of organizations.

This provides users with a way of structuring the selections that differs from Figure 1, and adds perspective on how the final 16 *PAR* selections may be interpreted and categorized. At various points, the introductions below also will refer to the three basic approaches to organization analysis and application just discussed.

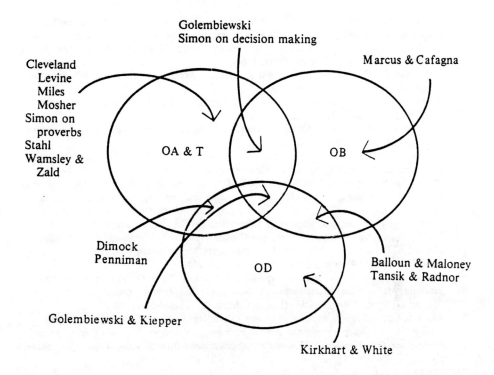

Golembiewski
Simon on decision making

Cleveland
Levine
Miles
Mosher
Simon on
proverbs
Stahl
Wamsley &
Zald

Marcus & Cafagna

OA & T

OB

Dimock
Penniman

OD

Balloun & Maloney
Tansik & Radnor

Golembiewski & Kiepper

Kirkhart & White

FIGURE 1
A Rough Depiction of the Approaches to Organization Analysis in 16 *PAR* Articles

Notes

1. Harold Koontz introduced this metaphor in "The Management Theory Jungle," *Academy of Management Journal,* Vol. 4 (December, 1961), pp. 174-188.
2. Dwight Waldo, "Organization Theory: An Elephantine Problem," *Public Administration Review,* Vol. 21 (Autumn, 1961), pp. 210-225.
3. Henry Fayol, *Administrative Industrielle et Général* (Paris: Dunod, 1925).
4. For example, see Philip Selznick, *TVA and the Grass Roots* (Berkeley: University of California Press, 1949); and Herbert Kaufman, *The Forest Ranger* (Baltimore: Johns Hopkins Press, 1960).
5. Chester I. Barnard, *The Functions of the Executive* (Cambridge: Harvard University Press, 1938).
6. James D. Thompson, *Organizations in Action* (New York: McGraw-Hill, 1967).
7. See, especially, Frederick W. Taylor, *The Principles of Scientific Management* (New York: Harper, 1911).
8. As in Peter F. Drucker, *The Practice of Management* (New York: Harper, 1954).
9. Joseph L. Massie, "Management Theory," p. 403, in James G. March, editor, *Handbook of Organizations* (Chicago: Rand McNally, 1965).
10. E.g., *ibid.,* pp. 405-408.

11. Dating events can be misleading, but these concerns began surfacing at least as early as the British Munitions Board studies around the time of World War I. In more recent times, Crozier's work had a similar thrust. See Michael Crozier, *The Bureaucratic Phenomenon* (Chicago: University of Chicago Press, 1964).
12. Fritz Jules Roethlisberger and William J. Dickson, *Management and the Worker* (Cambridge: Harvard University Press, 1939).
13. Wendell L. French and Cecil H. Bell, Jr., *Organization Development* (Englewood Cliffs, N.J.: Prentice-Hall, 1973), p. 15.
14. E.g., Frank Friedlander, "OD Approaches Adolescence," *Journal of Applied Behavioral Science,* Vol. 12 (January, 1976), pp. 7-21.
15. See, for example, Larry Kirkhart and Orion F. White, Jr., "The Future of Organization Development," *Public Administration Review,* Vol. 34 (April, 1974), pp. 129-140.
16. On the "laboratory stem," see French and Bell, *op. cit.,* pp. 21-25. Robert T. Golembiewski and Arthur Blumberg, editors, *Sensitivity Training and the Laboratory Approach* (Itasca, Ill.: F. E. Peacock, 1970), provide wide-ranging detail on that "stem"—its development, several component designs, underlying values, and developmental lacunae.
17. Carl R. Rogers, *Carl Rogers on Encounter Groups* (New York: Harper and Row, 1970), p. 1.
18. Richard A. Schmuck and Matthew B. Miles, editors, *Organization Development in Schools* (Palo Alto, Calif.: National Press Books, 1971), p. 234.
19. The prototype for large applications is Alfred J. Marrow, David G. Bowers, and Stanley E. Seashore, *Management by Participation* (New York: Harper and Row, 1967).
20. William G. Dyer, *Team Building* (Reading, Mass.: Addison-Wesley, 1977).
21. Richard Walton, *Interpersonal Peacemaking* (Reading, Mass.: Addison-Wesley, 1969).
22. E.g., Robert T. Golembiewski and Arthur Blumberg, "Confrontation as a Learning Design in Complex Organizations," *Journal of Applied Behavioral Science,* Vol. 3 (December, 1967), pp. 529-536.
23. French and Bell, *op. cit.,* pp. 25-29.
24. See Robert T. Golembiewski, *Approaches to Planned Change* (New York: Marcel Dekker, 1979), Part 2.
25. The tensions between truth-seeking *via* interaction or consensus versus theory or research are generic. For a development of the issues, see Charles E. Lindblom and David K. Cohen, *Usable Knowledge* (New Haven, Conn.: Yale University Press, 1979).
26. This was a dominant theme of the organizational humanist, for example. See Eugene P. Dvorin and Robert H. Simmons, *From Amoral to Humane Bureaucracy* (San Francisco: Canfield Press, 1972).
27. Chris Argyris, "Some Limits of Rational Man Organizational Theory," *Public Administration Review,* Vol. 33 (May, 1973), pp. 253-267.
28. E.g., Selwyn Becker, "The Parable of the Pill," *Administrative Science Quarterly,* Vol. 15 (March, 1970), pp. 94-96.
29. This point was made emphatically by the sociologist Perrow, who also expressed pleasure that in the 1970s the pendulum had started to swing back. See Charles Perrow, *Organizational Analysis* (Belmont, Calif.: Wadsworth Publishing, 1970).
30. As in Robert H. Miles, *Macro Organizational Behavior* (Santa Monica, Calif.: Goodyear, 1980).
31. OD calls for creating appropriate social structures and cultures at work, for example.
32. Joan Woodward, *Industrial Organization* (London: Oxford University Press, 1965).
33. Alfred D. Chandler, Jr., *Strategy and Structure* (Cambridge: MIT Press, 1962).
34. E.g., Perrow, *op. cit.*
35. Miles, *op. cit.*
36. E.g., see Jay W. Lorsch and John J. Morse, *Organizations and Their Members: A Contingency Approach* (New York: Harper & Row, 1974).
37. Chris Argyris, *The Applicability of Organizational Sociology* (Cambridge, Eng.: Cambridge University Press, 1972) pp. viii-ix, and numerous other places, questions the general point. A

specific contrast of models of learning appears in Argyris and Donald A. Schön, *Theory in Practice* (San Francisco: Jossey-Bass, 1974), and in their *Organizational Learning* (Reading, Mass.: Addison-Wesley, 1978).

38. Drucker, *op. cit.*

39. Linda L. Frank and J. Richard Hackman, "A Failure of Job Enrichment," *Journal of Applied Behavioral Science,* Vol. 11 (October, 1976), pp. 413-436.

40. Luther Gulick and Lyndall Urwick, editors, *Papers on the Science of Administration* (New York: Institute of Public Administration, 1937).

41. See, for example, Orion F. White, Jr., "Social Change and Administrative Adaptation," pp. 59-83, in Frank Marini, editor, *Toward a New Public Administration* (Scranton, Pa.: Chandler, 1971).

42. Robert T. Golembiewski, *The Small Group in Political Science* (Athens, Ga.: University of Georgia Press, 1978).

43. Waldo, "Organization Theory: An Elephantine Problem," p. 211.

44. Robert T. Golembiewski, "Organization Development in Public Agencies," *Public Administration Review,* Vol. 29 (July, 1969), pp. 367-377.

45. Edward J. Giblin, "Organization Development: Public Sector Theory and Practice," *Public Personnel Management,* Vol. 5 (March, 1976), p. 108.

46. For some extended treatments of the differences, see Leonard D. Goodstein, *Consulting with Human Service Systems* (Reading, Mass.: Addison-Wesley, 1978); and Paul R. Mico, "Doman Theory," *Journal of Applied Behavioral Science,* Vol. 15 (December, 1979), pp. 449-469.

47. Melvin LeBaron, "New Perspectives Toward More Effective Local Elected Councils and Boards," p. 237, in Robert T. Golembiewski and William Eddy, editors, *Organization Development in Public Administration* (New York: Marcel Dekker, 1978), Part 2.

48. E.g., David A. Nadler, *Feedback and Organization Development* (Reading, Mass.: Addison-Wesley, 1977); and Robert T. Golembiewski and Richard Hilles, *Toward the Responsive Organization* (Salt Lake City: Brighton Publishing, 1979).

49. E.g., Donald K. Carew, *et al.,* "New York State Division for Youth: A Collaborative Approach to the Implementation of Social Change in a Public Bureaucracy," *Journal of Applied Behavioral Science,* Vol. 13 (July, 1977), pp. 327-339.

50. See Robert T. Golembiewski, "Organization Development in the Public Sector: Major Movement Toward an Applied Behavioral Science," *ASPA Newsletter,* Vol. 1 (June, 1981), pp. 2 and 4. See also Golembiewski, Carl W. Proehl, Jr., and David Sink, "Success of OD Applications in the Public Sector: Toting Up the Score for a Decade, More or Less," *Public Administration Review* (forthcoming).

51. Peggy Morrison, "Evaluation in OD," *Group and Organization Studies,* Vol. 3 (March, 1978), pp. 42-70.

52. William N. Dunn and Frederic W. Swierczek, "Planned Organizational Change," *Journal of Applied Behavioral Science,* Vol. 13 (April, 1977), pp. 135-158.

53. Jerry Porras, "The Comparative Impact of Different OD Techniques and Intervention Intensities," *Journal of Applied Behavioral Science,* Vol. 15 (April, 1979), pp. 156-178.

54. Newton Margulies, Penny L. Wright, and Richard W. Scholl, "Organization Development Techniques: Their Impact on Change," *Group and Organization Studies,* Vol. 2 (December, 1977), pp. 449-460.

55. Carl W. Proehl, Jr., *Planned Organizational Change.* Unpublished doctoral dissertation, University of Georgia, 1980.

56. *Idem.*

57. Philip H. Mirvis and David N. Berg, editors, *Failures in Organization Development and Change* (New York: Wiley, 1977).

58. Data in the first two columns come from Proehl, *op. cit.* Data in the third column derive from Gerald Miller's earlier research, *The Laboratory Approach to Planned Change in the Public Sector.* Unpublished doctoral dissertation, University of Georgia, 1979.

59. Marshall E. Dimock, "The Objectives of Governmental Reorganization," *Public Administration Review,* Vol. 11 (Autumn, 1951), pp. 233-241.
60. President's Advisory Committee on Management, "Improvement of Management in the Federal Government," *Public Administration Review,* Vol. 13 (Winter, 1953), pp. 38-49.
61. Harvey C. Mansfield, "Federal Executive Reorganization: Thirty Years of Experience," *Public Administration Review,* Vol. 29 (July, 1978), pp. 309-314.
62. Frederick C. Thayer, "The President's Management 'Reforms': Theory X Triumphant," *Public Administration Review,* Vol. 38 (July, 1978), pp. 309-314.
63. Charles M. Kneier, "Reorganization: How It Works," *Public Administration Review,* Vol. 2 (No. 3, 1942), pp. 255-259.
64. Joseph F. Zimmerman, "Metropolitan Reform in the U.S.: An Overview," *Public Administration Review,* Vol. 30 (September, 1970), pp. 531-543.
65. Robert V. Presthus, "Behavior and Bureaucracy in Many Cultures," *Public Administration Review,* Vol. 19 (Winter, 1959), pp. 25-35.
66. Fred W. Riggs, "The Ecology and Context of Public Administration: A Comparative Perspective," *Public Administration Review,* Vol. 40 (March, 1980), pp. 107-115.
67. Brian Loveman, "The Comparative Administration Group, Development Administration, and Antidevelopment," *Public Administration Review,* Vol. 36 (December, 1976), pp. 616-621.
68. William C. Beyer, "The Civil Service of the Ancient World," *Public Administration Review,* Vol. 19 (Autumn, 1959), pp. 243-249.
69. Eliott M. Fox, "Mary Parker Follett: The Enduring Contribution," *Public Administration Review,* Vol. 28 (November, 1968), pp. 520-529.
70. Robert B. Denhardt, "Organizational Citizenship and Personal Freedom," *Public Administration Review,* Vol. 28 (January, 1968), pp. 47-54.
71. H.. Roy Kaplan, "Humanism in Organizations: A Critical Appraisal," *Public Administration Review,* Vol. 37 (March, 1977), pp. 171-180.
72. David K. Hart, "Theories of Government Related to Centralization and Citizen Participation," *Public Administration Review,* Vol. 32 (October, 1972), pp. 603-621.
73. Michael M. Harmon, "Social Equity and Organizational Democracy," *Public Administration Review,* Vol. 34 (January, 1974), pp. 11-18.
74. Wallace S. Sayre, "The General Manager Idea for Large Cities," *Public Administration Review,* Vol. 14 (Autumn, 1954), pp. 253-258.
75. William D. Carey, "Presidential Staffing in the Sixties and Seventies," *Public Administration Review,* Vol. 29 (September, 1969), pp. 450-458.
76. Paul H. Appleby, "Organizing Around the Head of a Large Federal Department," *Public Administration Review,* Vol. 6 (Summer, 1946), pp. 205-212.
77. Stephen K. Bailey, "A Structured Interaction Pattern for Harpsichord and Kazoo," *Public Administration Review,* Vol. 14 (Summer, 1954), pp. 202-204.
78. Elias Huzar, "Notes on the Unification Controversy," *Public Administration Review,* Vol. 6 (Autumn, 1946), pp. 297-311.
79. Andrew F. Henry, John W. Masland, and Lawrence I. Radway, "Armed Forces Unification and the Pentagon Officer," *Public Administration Review,* Vol. 15 (Summer, 1955), pp. 173-180.
80. Frederick C. Mosher, "Decision-Making in Defense," *Public Administration Review,* Vol. 18 (Summer, 1958), pp. 169-175.
81. Martin Landau, "Redundancy, Rationality, and the Problem of Duplication," *Public Administration Review,* Vol. 29 (July, 1969), pp. 346-358.
82. Aaron Wildavsky, "The Self-Evaluating Organization," *Public Administration Review,* Vol. 32 (September, 1972), pp. 509-520.
83. *Idem.*
84. Argyris, "Some Limits of Rational Man Organizational Theory."
85. Samuel Culbert and Jerome Reisel, "Organization Development: An Applied Philosophy for

Managers of Public Enterprise," *Public Administration Review*, Vol. 31 (March, 1971), pp. 159-169.

86. Wiliam Eddy and Robert J. Saunders, "Applied Behavioral Science in Urban/Administrative Political Systems," *Public Administration Review*, Vol. 32 (January, 1972), pp. 11-17.
87. Neely Gardner, "The Non-Hierarchical Organization of the Future," *Public Administration Review*, Vol. 36 (September, 1976), pp. 591-598.
88. Robert L. Peabody, "Authority Relations in Three Organizations," *Public Administration Review*, Vol. 23 (June, 1963), pp. 87-92.
89. Dennis Palumbo, "Power and Role Specificity in Organization Theory," *Public Administration Review*, Vol. 29 (July, 1969), pp. 237-248.
90. George C. Benson, "A Plea for Administrative Decentralization," *Public Administration Review*, Vol. 7 (Summer, 1947), pp. 170-178.

Perspectives on the Act of Organizing: Four Views—From Inside-Out and Outside-In

1. Herbert A. Simon, "Decision-Making and Administrative Organization"
2. Gary L. Wamsley and Mayer N. Zald, "The Political Economy of Public Organizations"
3. Robert T. Golembiewski, "Organization as a Moral Problem"
4. Charles H. Levine, "Organizational Decline and Cutback Management

PART I rests on a basic premise: where you sit determines what you see. This common wisdom[1] urges multiple perches for serious observers of organizations, lest they miss too much of the essence they view from vantage points that remain inadequate because they are too few and too selective. For now is not the time, if ever it will come, that a comprehensive theory of organizations exists. Multiple perspectives help guard against overselectivity and unspecificity.

This section not only preaches, but seeks to follow its own advice. Specifically, four perspectives on the act of organizing will be introduced, four general vantage points from which to triangulate on always-significant but sometimes-subtle collective phenomena. The four perspectives have both internal and external foci, as it were. They focus on the processes that go on inside an organization; and the perspectives also apply external standards against which those internal processes must be judged.

Herbert A. Simon leads off with his "Decision-Making and

Administrative Organization." In a piece published in 1944, our recent Nobel laureate theoretically frames his approach to organization in contemporary terms. He emphasizes multiple influence processes that seek to raise the probability that employees will make appropriate decisions. In ways generally compatible with the flood of organization behavior (or OB) research that followed World War II, Simon develops the multiple ways in which employees can be influenced: by authority, identification, the criterion of efficiency, advice and information, and training. These elements can be variously congruent and reinforce one another, or they can negate one another.

Simon's approach is wide-reaching, and clearly presages the ways in which organization analysis must become interdisciplinary lest it remain limited and limiting. In this sense, Simon transcends the boundaries of much of the work classified above as organization analysis and theory, or OA & T. Better put, perhaps, Simon sought to save the bulk of that literature from itself, even as he wrote at a time before the development of much of the empirical research necessary to provide the details required by his general approach.

"The Political Economy of Public Organizations," by Gary L. Wamsley and Mayer N. Zald, brings us forward in time three decades beyond the publication of Simon's contribution and also extends his perspective. Basically, Wamsley and Zald propose that viewing an organization "internally"—as Simon tends to do in "Decision-Making and Administrative Organization"—is necessary but far from sufficient. They add a variegated "external" perspective, and also argue for its causal precedence. In their words: "political-economic variables are the major determinants of structure and change."

In effect, Wamsley and Zald propose that sophisticated research and praxis must rest on an interactive model—Environment ↔ Organization, or E ↔ O in shorthand. The authors provide anecdotal materials supporting that model, and also seek to formalize an approach based on that core insight. In so doing, they parallel in the public sector the research—depicted in the introductory essay of this volume as an intersection of the OA & T and OB approaches to organization—which was triggered by Lawrence and Lorsch[2] as well as Woodward[3] in business organizations. In this basic sense, Wamsley and Zald's approach is generic even as they urge on the reader the several significant distinguishing features of the public arena. These features include the symbolic significance of public organizations, differences in funding, a limited sense of "ownership" or rights and privileges, resulting resource constraints, and the relationships of public agencies to public policy. Such features do multiple duty. They respect the authors' advice that E ↔ O interactions must be taken into account in organization research and practice; and they also isolate a distinct area of inquiry and practice for *public* administration.

A similar extension-*cum*-integration is attempted by Robert T. Golembiewski in his "Organization as a Moral Problem." He emphasizes another sense in which organizations must be viewed from an external reference—this time, from a normative or value perspective. This reflects a common theme in much of the OA & T literature, which has long emphasized the organizational relevancies of differences in environmental "textures"—of social, cultural, and historical forces and characteristics. Golembiewski seeks to reorient that OA & T emphasis in a significant particular, by illustrating one way in which OB research can be put to use. That is, values from the Judaeo-Christian tradition are shown to conflict with a number of standard approaches and practices based on traditional organization theory. This message has been heard before, of course, but Golembiewski also goes on to summarize the thrust of numerous empirical OD studies which have a proactive quality. He isolates a small catalog of specific organizational approaches and practices consistent with Judaeo-Christian values that tend to generate high employee satisfaction and output. He consequently urges that organization theory and practice could profit from a closer fit with traditional moral values, in practical as well as normative senses.

Charles H. Levine adds detail on another and crucial sense in which public organizations must be externally oriented. His "Organizational Decline and Cutback Management" emphasizes a truism that has been neglected for most of the past several decades. The funding of public enterprises can vary, despite our just-passed history of budgetary increase upon increase. This elemental fact apparently must be rediscovered every now and then, often painfully so. However learned, it has profound implications for public management. As Levine articulates that bottom line: "Government organizations are neither immortal nor unshrinkable."

The basic point overwhelms even though it has been underappreciated in the three approaches to organization outlined above—OA & T, or Organization Analysis and Theory; OB, or Organization Behavior; and OD, or Organization Development.

All three approaches have tended to emphasize growth and expansion,[4] as Levine notes.

In this basic sense, in effect, Levine enlarges the field of vision of the three basic approaches to organization. He devotes useful detail to charting the profound implications of organizational cutback or decline for administrative theory, for example, as well as for the strategic and tactical choices that are suited to the other side of growth and expansion. These adaptations will be tricky as well as momentous, Levine warns. For example, one scenario appears likely. Thus, some sectors may be shrinking, even as others are experiencing frenzied growth and expansion. Our management and organization theories will have to be subtle and comprehensive to guide the required fine-tuning, patently.

Notes

1. Originally phrased as, "Where you stand depends on where you sit," by Rufus E. Miles, Jr. See his "The Origin and Meaning of Miles' Law," *Public Administration Review*, Vol. 38 (September, 1978), pp. 399-403.
2. Paul R. Lawrence and Jay W. Lorsch, *Organization and Environment* (Boston: Harvard Graduate School of Business Administration, 1967).
3. Joan Woodward, *Industrial Organization* (London: Oxford University Press, 1965).
4. Emphases are shifting, however. In OD, for example, once-neglected organizational themes—separation, decline, and "smaller is better"—now get increasing attention. See Robert T. Golembiewski, *Approaches to Planned Change* (New York: Marcel Dekker, 1979), Part 2, pp. 185-214.

HERBERT A. SIMON

Decision Making and
Administrative Organization

It is clear that the actual physical task of carrying out an organization's objectives falls to the persons at the lowest level of the administrative hierarchy. The automobile, as a physical object, is built not by the engineer or the executive, but by the mechanic on the assembly line. The fire is extinguished, not by the fire chief or the captain, but by the team of firemen who play a hose on the blaze.

It is equally clear that the persons above this lowest or operative level in the administrative hierarchy are not mere surplus baggage, and that they too must have an essential role to play in the accomplishment of the agency's objectives. Even though, as far as physical cause and effect are concerned, it is the machine-gunner, and not the major, who fights battles, the major will likely have a greater influence upon the outcome of a battle than will any single machine-gunner.

How, then, do the administrative and supervisory staff of an organization affect that organization's work? The nonoperative staff of an administrative organization participate in the accomplishment of the objectives of that organization to the extent that they influence the decisions of the operatives— the persons at the lowest level of the administrative hierarchy. The major can influence the battle to the extent that his head is able to direct the machine-gunner's hand. By deploying his forces in the battle area and assigning specific tasks to subordinate units, he determines for the machine-gunner where he will take his stand and what his objective will be. In very small organizations the influence of all supervisory employees upon the operative employees may be direct, but in units of any size there are interposed between the top supervisors and the operative employees several levels of intermediate supervisors who are themselves subject to influences from above and who transmit, elaborate, and modify these influences before they reach the operatives.

If this is a correct description of the administrative process, then the construction of an efficient administrative organization is a problem in social psychology. It is a task of setting up an operative staff and superimposing on that staff a supervisory staff capable of influencing the operative group toward a pattern of coordinated and effective behavior. I have deliberately

28

used the term "influencing" rather than "directing," for direction—that is, the use of administrative authority—is only one of several ways in which the administrative staff may affect the decisions of the operative staff; and, consequently, the construction of an administrative organization involves more than a mere assignment of functions and allocation of authority.

It is the operative employee who must be at the focus of attention in studying an organization, for the success of the structure will be judged by the way in which he performs within it. In this paper administrative theory will be approached from this standpoint: by analyzing the manner in which the decisions and behavior of operative employees are influenced by the organization.

Necessity for "Vertical" Specialization

Most analyses of organization have emphasized "horizontal" specialization —the division of work—as the basic characteristic of organized activity. Luther Gulick, for example, in his "Notes on the Theory of Organization," says: "Work division is the foundation of organization; indeed, the reason for organization."[1]

In this paper we shall be primarily concerned with "vertical" specialization —the division of decision-making duties between operative and supervisory personnel. Our first inquiry will be into the reasons why the operative employees are deprived of a portion of their autonomy in the making of decisions and subjected to the authority and influence of supervisors.

There would seem to be at least three reasons for vertical specialization in organization. First, if there is any horizontal specialization, vertical specialization is absolutely essential to achieve coordination among the operative employees. Second, just as horizontal specialization permits greater skill and expertise to be developed by the operative group in the performance of their tasks, so vertical specialization permits greater expertise in the making of decisions. Third, vertical specialization permits the operative personnel to be held accountable for their decisions: to the board of directors in the case of a business organization; to the legislative body in the case of a public agency.

Coordination. Group behavior requires not only the adoption of *correct* decisions, but also the adoption by all members of the group of the *same* decisions. Suppose ten persons decide to cooperate in building a boat. If each has his own plan, and they don't bother to communicate their plans, the resulting craft is not apt to be very seaworthy; they would probably have met with better success if they had adopted even a very mediocre design, and if then all had followed this same design.

By the exercise of authority or other forms of influence, it is possible to centralize the function of deciding so that a general plan of operations will govern the activities of all members of the organization. This coordination may be either procedural or substantive in nature: by procedural coordination is meant the specification of the organization itself—that is, the generalized description of the behaviors and relationships of the members of the organization. Procedural coordination establishes the lines of authority and outlines the spheres of activity of each organization member, while substantive coordination specifies the content of his work. In an automobile factory, an organization chart is an aspect of procedural coordination; blueprints for the engine-block of the car being manufactured are an aspect of substantive coordination.

Expertise. To gain the advantages of specialized skill at the operative level, the work of an organization must be so subdivided that all processes requiring a particular skill can be performed by persons possessing that skill. Likewise, to gain the advantages of expertise in decision making, the responsibility for decisions must be so allocated that all decisions requiring a particular skill can be made by persons possessing that skill.

To subdivide decisions is rather more complicated than to subdivide performance; for while it is not usually possible to combine the sharp eye of one workman with the steady hand of another to secure greater precision in a particular operation, it *is* often possible to add the knowledge of a lawyer to that of an engineer in order to improve the quality of a particular decision.

Frederick Taylor's theories of shop organization were primarily concerned with this aspect of the decision-making process. The purpose of his scheme of functional foremanship was to make certain that the decisions respecting every aspect of the workman's job would be reached by a highly specialized and expert technician.

Responsibility. Writers on the political and legal aspects of authority have emphasized that a primary function of organization is to enforce the conformity of the individual to norms laid down by the group, or by its authority-wielding members. The discretion of subordinate personnel is limited by policies determined near the top of the administrative hierarchy. When the maintenance of responsibility is a central concern, the purpose of vertical specialization is to assure legislative control over the administrator, leaving to the administrative staff adequate discretion to deal with technical matters which a legislative body composed of laymen would not be competent to decide.

In designing an organization all three factors—expertise, coordination, and responsibility—must be given weight. Taylor's theory, for example, has been deservedly criticized for ignoring the factors of coordination and responsibility, while some of his critics can perhaps be accused of undervaluing the importance of expertise in decision making. The real question is one of how much each of these aims is to be sacrificed to the others, and our present knowledge of administrative theory does not permit us to give any *a priori* answer to this question.

The Range of Discretion

The term "influence" covers a wide range, both in the degree to which one person affects the behavior of another and in the method whereby that influence is exercised. Without an analysis of these differences of degree and kind no realistic picture can be drawn of an administrative organization. It is because of its failure to account for variations in influence that the usual organization chart, with its oversimplified representation of the "lines of authority," fails to record the complexity of actual organizations. The organization chart does not reveal the fact that the actual exercise of authority may, and often does, cut across formal organizational lines, and that forms of influence other than authority—information, training, identification—may be far more important than the former in securing coordination throughout the organization.

Influence is exercised in its most complete form when a decision promulgated by one person governs every aspect of the behavior of another. On the parade ground, the marching soldier is permitted no discretion whatsoever. His every step, his bearing, the length of his pace are all governed by authority. Frederick the Great is reported to have found the parade-ground deportment of his Guards perfect—with one flaw. "They breathe," he complained. Few examples could be cited, however, from any other realm of practical affairs where influence is exercised in such complete and unlimited form.

Most often, organizational influences place only partial limits upon the exercise of discretion. A subordinate may be told what to do, but given considerable leeway as to how he will carry out the task. The "what" is, of course, a matter of degree also and may be specified within narrower or broader limits. The commands of a captain at the scene of a fire place much narrower limits on the discretion of the firemen than those placed on a fire chief by the city charter which states in general terms the function of the fire department.

Since influence can be exercised with all degrees of specificity, in order to determine the scope of influence or authority which is exercised in any concrete case, it is necessary to dissect the decisions of the subordinate into their component parts and then determine which of these parts are controlled by the superior and which are left to the subordinate's discretion.

Influence over Value and Fact. Any rational decision may be viewed as a conclusion reached from certain premises. These premises are of two different kinds: value premises and factual premises—roughly equivalent to ends and means, respectively. Given a complete set of value and factual premises, there remains only one unique decision which is consistent with rationality. That is, with a given system of values and a specified set of possible alternatives, there is one alternative of the set which is preferable to the others.

The behavior of a rational person can be controlled, therefore, if the value and factual premises upon which he bases his decisions are specified for him. This control can be complete or partial—all the premises can be specified, or some can be left to his discretion. The scope of influence and conversely the scope of discretion, are determined by the number and importance of the premises which are specified and the number and importance of those which are left unspecified.

There is one important difference between permitting a subordinate discretion over value premises and permitting him discretion over factual premises. The latter can always be evaluated as correct or incorrect in an objective, empirical sense (of course, we do not always have the evidence we would need to decide whether a premise is correct or incorrect, but at least the terms "correct" and "incorrect" are applicable to a factual premise). To a value premise, on the other hand, the terms "correct" and "incorrect" do not apply. To say that a means is correct is to say that it is appropriate to its end; but to say that an end is correct is meaningless unless we redefine the end as a means to some more final end—in which case its correctness as means ceases to be a value question and becomes a factual question.

Hence, if only factual premises are left to the subordinate's discretion, there is, under the given circumstances, only one decision which he can correctly reach. On the other hand, if value premises are left to the subordinate's discretion, the "correctness" of his decision will depend upon the value premises he selects, and there is no universally accepted criterion of right or wrong which can be applied to his selection.[2]

This distinction between factual and value premises has an obvious bearing on the question of how discretion is to be reconciled with responsibility and accountability, and what the line of division is to be between "policy" and "administration." To pursue this subject further would take us beyond the bounds of the present analysis, and we leave it with a reference to two recent contributions to the problem.[3]

Implications for Unity of Command. When it is admitted that influence need extend to only a few of the premises of decision, it follows that more than one order can govern a given decision, provided that no two orders extend to the same premise. An analysis of almost any decision of a member of a formal organization would reveal that the decision was responsive to a very complex structure of influences.

Military organization affords an excellent illustration of this. In ancient warfare, the battlefield was not unlike the parade ground. An entire army was often commanded by a single man, and his authority extended in a very complete and direct form to the lowest man in the ranks. This was possible because the entire battlefield was within range of a man's voice and vision and because tactics were for the most part executed by the entire army in unison.

The modern battlefield presents a very different picture. Authority is exercised through a complex hierarchy of command. Each level of the hierarchy leaves an extensive area of discretion to the level below, and even the private soldier, under combat conditions, exercises a considerable measure of discretion.

Under these circumstances, how does the authority of the commander extend to the soldiers in the ranks? How does he limit and guide their behavior? He does this by specifying the general mission and objective of each unit on the next level below and by determining such elements of time and place as will assure a proper coordination among the units. The colonel assigns to each battalion in his regiment its task; the lieutenant colonel to each company; the captain to each platoon. Beyond this the officer ordinarily does not go. The internal deployment of each unit is left to the officer in command of that unit. The United States Army Field Service Regulations specify that "an order should not trespass upon the province of a subordinate. It should contain everything that the subordinate must know to carry out his mission, but nothing more."[4]

So far as field orders go, then, the discretion of a subordinate officer is limited only by the specification of the objective of his unit and its general schedule. He proceeds to narrow further the discretion of his own subordinates so far as is necessary to specify what part each sub-unit is to play in accomplishing the task of the whole.

Does this mean that the decision of the officer is limited only by his objective or mission? Not at all. To be sure, the field order does not go beyond this point, for it specifies only the "what" of his action. But the officer is also governed by the tactical doctrine and general orders of the army which specify in some detail the "how." When the captain receives field orders to deploy his company for an attack, he is expected to carry out the deployment in accordance with the accepted tactical principles in the army. In leading his unit, he will be held accountable for the "how" as well as the "what."

The same kind of analysis could be carried out for the man who actually does the army's "work"—the private soldier; and we would see that the mass of influences that bear upon his decisions include both direct commands and tactical training and indoctrination.

We find, then, that to understand the process of decision in an organization it is necessary to go far beyond the on-the-spot orders which are given by superior to subordinate. It is necessary to discover how the subordinate is influenced by standing orders, by training, and by review of his actions. It is necessary to study the channels of communication in the organization in order to determine what information reaches him which may be relevant to his decisions. The broader the sphere of discretion left to the subordinate by the orders given him, the more important become those types of influence which do not depend upon the exercise of formal authority.

Once this complex network of decisional influences comes into view it becomes difficult to defend either the sufficiency or the necessity of the doctrine of "unity of command." Its sufficiency must be questioned on the same grounds that the sufficiency of the organization chart is questioned: at best it tells only a half-truth, for formal authority is only one aspect—and that probably not the most important—of organizational structure.

The necessity of "unity of command" must be questioned because there do not appear to be any *a priori* grounds why a decision should not be subject to several organizational influences. Indeed, a number of serious students of administration have advocated this very thing—we have already mentioned Taylor's theory of functional supervision—and their arguments cannot be waved aside with the biblical quotation that "no man can serve two masters."[5] It remains to be demonstrated that "unity of command" rather than "plurality of command" either is, or should be, the prevalent form of administrative structure.

Organizational Influences on the Subordinate

Thus far we have been talking about the extent of the organization's influence over its employees. Next we must consider the ways in which this influence is exerted. The subordinate is influenced not only by command but also by his organizational loyalties, by his strivings toward "efficient" courses of action, by the information and advice which is transmitted to him through the organization's lines of communication, and by his training. Each of these items deserves brief discussion.

Authority. The concept of authority has been analyzed at length by students of administration. We shall employ here a definition substantially equivalent to that put forth by C. I. Barnard.[6] A subordinate is said to accept authority whenever he permits his behavior to be guided by a decision reached by another, without independently examining the merits of that decision. When exercising authority, the superior does not seek to convince the subordinate, but only to obtain his acquiescence. In actual practice, of course, authority is usually liberally admixed with suggestion and persuasion.

An important function of authority is to permit a decision to be made and carried out even when agreement cannot be reached, but perhaps this arbitrary aspect of authority has been overemphasized. In any event, if it is attempted to carry authority beyond a certain point, which may be described as the subordinate's "zone of acquiescence," disobedience will follow.[7] The magnitude of the zone of acquiescence depends upon the sanctions which authority has available to enforce its commands. The term "sanctions" must be interpreted broadly in this connection, for positive and neutral stimuli—such as community of purpose, habit, and leadership—are at least as important in securing acceptance of authority as are the threat of physical or economic punishment.

It follows that authority, in the sense here defined, can operate "upward" and "sidewise" as well as "downward" in the organization. If an executive delegates to his secretary a decision about file cabinets and accepts her recommendation without reexamination of its merits, he is accepting her authority. The "lines of authority" represented on organization charts do have a special significance, however, for they are commonly resorted to in order to terminate debate when it proves impossible to reach a consensus on a particular decision. Since this appellate use of authority generally requires sanctions to be effective, the structure of formal authority in an organization usually is related to the appointment, disciplining, and dismissal of personnel. These formal lines of authority are commonly supplemented by informal authority relations in the day-to-day work of the organization, while the formal hierarchy is largely reserved for the settlement of disputes.

Organizational Loyalties. It is a prevalent characteristic of human behavior that members of an organized group tend to identify with that group. In making decisions their organizational loyalty leads them to evaluate alternative courses of action in terms of the consequences of their action for the group. When a person prefers a particular course of action because it is "good for America," he identifies with Americans; when he prefers it because it will "boost business in Berkeley," he identifies with Berkeleyans. National and class loyalties are examples of identifications which are of fundamental importance in the structure of modern society.

The loyalties which are of particular interest in the study of administration are those which attach to administrative organizations or segments of such organizations. The regimental battle-flag is the traditional symbol of this identification in military administration; in civil administration, a frequently encountered evidence of identification is the cry: "Our Bureau needs more funds!"

The psychological bases of identification are obscure, but seem to involve at least three elements. First, personal success often depends upon organizational success—the administrator who can build up his unit expects (with good reason) promotion and salary increases. Second, loyalty seems based partly on a transfer to the field of public management of the spirit of competition which is characteristic of private enterprise. Third, the human mind is limited in the number of diverse considerations which can occupy the area of attention at one time, and there is a consequent tendency to overemphasize the importance of those elements which happen to be within that area. To the fireman, fires are the most serious human problem; to the health officer, disease, and so forth.

This phenomenon of identification, or institutional loyalty, performs one very important function in administration. If an administrator, each time he is faced with a decision, must perforce evaluate that decision in terms of the whole range of human values, rationality in administration is impossible. If he need consider the decision only in the light of limited organizational aims, his task is more nearly within the range of human powers. The fireman can concentrate on the problem of fires, the health officer on problems of disease, without irrelevant considerations entering in.

Furthermore, this concentration on a limited range of values is almost essential if the administrator is to be held accountable for his decisions. When the organization's objectives are specified by some higher authority, the major value-premise of the administrator's decisions is thereby given him, leaving to him only the implementation of these objectives. If the fire chief were permitted to roam over the whole field of human values—to decide that parks were more important than fire trucks, and consequently to remake his fire department into a recreation department—chaos would displace organization, and responsibility would disappear.

Organizational loyalties lead also, however, to certain difficulties which should not be underestimated. The principal undesirable effect of identification is that it prevents the institutionalized individual from making correct decisions in cases where the restricted area of values with which he identifies must be weighed against other values outside that area. This is a principal cause of the interbureau competition and wrangling which characterizes any large administrative organization. The organization members, identifying with the bureau instead of with the over-all organization, believe the bureau's welfare more important than the general welfare when the two conflict. This problem is frequently evident in the case of "housekeeping" agencies, where the facilitative and auxiliary nature of the agency is lost sight of in the effort to force the line agencies to follow standard procedures.

Institutional loyalties also result in incapacitating almost any department head for the task of balancing the financial needs of his department against the financial needs of other departments—whence the need for a centrally located budget agency which is free from these psychological biases. The higher we go in the administrative hierarchy, the broader becomes the range of social values which must come within the administrator's purview, the more harmful is the effect of valuational bias, and the more important is it that the administrator be freed from his narrower identifications.

The Criterion of Efficiency. We have seen that the exercise of authority and the development of organizational identifications are two principal means whereby the individual's value premises are influenced by the organization. What about the issues of fact which underlie his decisions? These are largely determined by a principle which underlies all rational behavior: the criterion of efficiency. In its broadest sense, to be efficient simply means to take the shortest path, the cheapest means, toward the attainment of the desired goals. The efficiency criterion is completely neutral as to what goals are to be attained.

The concept of efficiency has been discussed at length by economists and writers on administration, and there is little that can be added to that discussion within the scope of the present paper. Suffice it to say that the commandment: "Be efficient!" is a major organizational influence over the decisions of the members of any administrative agency; and a determination whether this commandment has been obeyed is a major function of the review process.[8]

Advice and Information. Many of the influences the organization exercises over its members are of a less formal nature than those we have been discussing. These influences are perhaps most realistically viewed as a form of internal public relations, for there is nothing to guarantee that advice produced at one point in an organization will have any effect at another point in the organization unless the lines of communication are adequate to its transmission and unless it is transmitted in such form as to be persuasive. It is a prevalent misconception in headquarters offices that the internal advisory function consists in preparing precisely worded explanatory bulletins and making certain that the proper number of these are prepared and that they are placed in the proper compartment of the "router." No plague has produced a rate of mortality higher than the rate which customarily afflicts central-office communications between the time they leave the issuing office and the moment when they are assumed to be effected in the revised practice of the operative employees.

These difficulties of communication apply, of course, to commands as well as to advice and information. As a matter of fact, the administrator who is serving in an advisory capacity is apt to be at some advantage in solving problems of communication, because he is likely to be conscious of the necessity of transmitting and "selling" his ideas, while the administrator who possesses authority may be oblivious of his public-relations function.

Information and advice flow in all directions through the organization—not merely from the top downward. Many of the facts which are relevant to decision are of a rapidly changing nature, ascertainable only at the moment of decision, and often ascertainable only by operative employees. For instance, in military operations knowledge of the disposition of the enemy's forces is of crucial importance, and military organization has developed elaborate procedures for transmitting to a person who is to make a decision all relevant facts which he is not in a position to ascertain personally.

Information and advice may be used as alternatives to the actual exercise of authority, and vice versa. Where promptness and discipline are not primary considerations, the former have several very impressive advantages. Chief among these is that they preserve morale and initiative on the part of the subordinate—qualities which may disappear if excessively harassed by authority. Again, when the influences are advisory in nature, the formal organization structure loses its unique position as the sole channel of influence. The relation between the adviser and the person advised is essentially no different when they are members of the same organization than when the adviser is outside the organization. The extent of the influence of the adviser will depend on the desire of the decision maker for advice and on the persuasiveness with which it is offered.

Training. Like institutional loyalties, and unlike the other modes of influence we have been discussing, training influences decisions "from the inside out." That is, training prepares the organization member to reach satisfactory decisions himself, without the need for the constant exercise of authority or advice. In this sense, training procedures are alternatives to the exercise of authority or advice as means of control over the subordinate's decisions.

Training may be of an in-service or a pre-service nature. When persons with particular educational qualifications are recruited for certain jobs, the organization is depending upon this pre-training as a principal means of assuring correct decisions in their work. The mutual relation between training and the range of discretion which may be permitted an employee is an important factor to be taken into consideration in designing the administrative organization. That is, it may often be possible to minimize, or even dispense with, certain review processes by giving the subordinates training which enables them to perform their work with less supervision. Similarly, in drafting the qualifications required of applicants for particular positions, the possibility should be considered of lowering personnel costs by drafting semi-skilled employees and training them for particular jobs.

Training is applicable to the process of decision whenever the same elements are involved in a large number of decisions. Training may supply the trainee with the facts necessary in dealing with these decisions, it may provide him a frame of reference for his thinking, it may teach him "approved" solutions, or it may indoctrinate him with the values in terms of which his decisions are to be made.

Training, as a mode of influence upon decisions, has its greatest value in those situations where the exercise of formal authority through commands proves difficult. The difficulty may lie in the need for prompt action, in the spatial dispersion of the organization, or in the complexity of the subject matter of decision which defies summarization in rules and regulations. Training permits a higher degree of decentralization of the decision-making process by bringing the necessary competence into the very lowest levels of the organizational hierarchy.

Implications for Organization. It can be seen that there are at least five distinct ways in which the decisions of operative employees may be influenced: authority, identification, the efficiency criterion, advice, and training. It is the fundamental problem of organization to determine the extent and the manner in which each of these forms of influence is to be employed. To a very great extent, these various forms are interchangeable—a fact which is far more often appreciated in small than in large organizations.

The simplest example of this is the gradual increase in discretion which can be permitted an employee as he becomes familiar with his job. A secretary learns to draft routine correspondence; a statistical clerk learns to lay out his own calculations. In each case, training has taken the place of authority in guiding the employee's decisions.

Another illustration is the process of functional supervision whereby technical experts are given advisory, but not usually authoritative, relations with subordinate employees. This substitution of advice for authority may prove necessary in many situations in order to prevent conflicts of authority between line officers, organized on a geographical basis, and functional experts, organized along subject-matter lines. To the extent that these forms of influence supplement, or are substituted for, authority, the problem of influence becomes one of education and public relations, as has already been explained.

Administrators have increasingly recognized in recent years that authority, unless buttressed by other forms of influence, is relatively impotent to control decision in any but a negative way. The elements entering into all but the most routine decisions are so numerous and so complex that it is impossible to control positively more than a few. Unless the subordinate is himself able to supply most of the premises of decision, and to synthesize them adequately, the task of supervision becomes hopelessly burdensome. To cite an extreme illustration: no amount of supervision or direction, and no quantity of orders, directives, or commands, would be sufficient to enable a completely untrained person to prepare a legal brief for a law suit. In such a case, the problem is definitely not one of direction, but one of education or training.

Viewed from this standpoint, the problem of organization becomes inextricably interwoven with the problem of recruitment. For the system of influence which can effectively be used in the organization will depend directly upon the training and competence of employees at the various levels of the hierarchy. If a welfare agency can secure trained social workers as interviewers and case workers, broad discretion can be permitted them in determining eligibility, subject only to a sampling review and a review of particularly difficult cases. If trained workers can be obtained only for supervisory positions, then the supervisors will need to exercise a much more complete supervision over their subordinates, perhaps reviewing each decision and issuing frequent instruction. The supervisory problem will be correspondingly more burdensome than in the first example, and the effective span of control of supervisors correspondingly narrower.

Likewise, when an organization unit is large enough so that it can retain within its own boundaries the specialized expertise that is required for some of its decisions, the need for functional supervision from other portions of the organization becomes correspondingly less. When a department can secure its own legal, medical, or other expert assistance, the problems of functional organization become correspondingly simpler, and the lines of direct authority over the department need less supplementation by advisory and informational services.

Hence, problems of organization cannot be considered apart from the specifications and actual qualifications of the employees who are to fill the positions established by the organization. The whole subject of job classification must be brought into close coordination with the theory of organization. The optimum organizational structure is a variable, depending for its form upon the staffing of the agency. Conversely, the classification of a position is a variable, depending upon the degree of centralization or decentralization which is desired or anticipated in the operation of the organizational form.

The Communication of Influence

It has already been pointed out that if it is wished to bring orders or advice to bear on the decisions of a subordinate, the orders or advice must be communicated to the subordinate; and that this communication is not merely a matter of physical transmission, but a process of actually inducing changes in the subordinate's behavior. The costs of the communication process are comparable to, and as real as, a manufacturer's advertising costs.

A manufacturer determines his advertising budget by the amount by which additional advertising will increase sales. When the additional receipts he expects are no longer sufficient to cover the additional advertising and manufacturing costs, he stops the expansion of his advertising program. An approach of a very similar kind needs to be introduced in the designing of administrative organizations. The cost of "producing" decisions in the supervisory staff and the cost of communicating these decisions to the operating personnel must be weighed against the expected increase in effectiveness of the latter.

The different forms of organizational influence must be balanced against each other in the same way. A training program involves a large initial investment in each operative employee, but low "maintenance" costs; orders and commands require no initial investment, but high and continuous costs of "production" and communication; if pre-trained employees are recruited, salaries may be higher, but a less elaborate supervisory structure will be required; and so forth. Again, we have reached a question of *how much,* and theory, without data, cannot give us an answer.

Administrative Processes for Ensuring Correct Decisions

Having analyzed the various kinds of influence which condition the decisions of members of administrative organizations, we turn next to some concrete administrative processes to see how they fit into our scheme of analysis. The first of these is planning—the process whereby a whole scheme is worked out in advance before any part of it is carried out through specific decisions. The second of these is review—the process whereby subordinates are held to an accounting for the quality of their decisions and of the premises from which these decisions were reached.

Planning. Plans and schedules are ordinarily carried into effect by the exercise of authority, but of greater importance than this final act of approving or authorizing a plan are the decisional processes which go into the making of the plan. Planning is an extremely important decision-making process because of the vast amount of detail that can be embodied in the plan for a complex project and because of the broad participation that can be secured, when desirable, in its formulation.

As a good illustration of this we may summarize the procedure a navy department goes through in designing a battleship, as described by Sir Oswyn A. R. Murray. First, the general objectives are set out—the speed, radius of action, armor, and armament it is desired to attain in the finished design. Next, several provisional designs are developed by a staff of "generalists" who are familiar with all aspects of battleship design. On the basis of these alternative provisional designs, a final decision is reached on the general lines of the new ship. At this point the specialists are brought in to make recommendations for the detailed plan. Their recommendations will often require modification of the original design, and they will often recommend mutually conflicting requirements. To continue with Sir Oswyn's description:

> In this way the scheme goes on growing in a tentative manner, its progress always being dependent upon the cooperation of numbers of separate departments, all intent upon ensuring the efficiency of different parts, until ultimately a more or less complete whole is arrived at in the shape of drawings and specifications provisionally embodying all the agreements. This really is the most difficult and interesting stage, for generally it becomes apparent at this point that requirements overlap, and that the best possible cannot be achieved in regard to numbers of points within the limits set to the contractors. These difficulties are cleared up by discussion at round-table conferences, where the compromises which will least impair the value of the ship are agreed upon, and the completed design is then finally submitted for the Board's approval. Some fourteen departments are concerned in the settlement of the final detailed arrangements.'

The point which is so clearly illustrated here is that the planning procedure permits expertise of every kind to be drawn into the decision without any difficulties being imposed by the lines of authority in the organization. The final design undoubtedly received authoritative approval, but, during the entire process of formulation, suggestions and recommendations flowed freely from all parts of the organization without raising the problem of "unity of command." It follows from this that to the extent to which planning procedures are used in reaching decisions, the formal organization has relevance only in the final stages of the whole process. So long as the appropriate experts are consulted, their exact location in the hierarchy of authority need not much affect the decision.

This statement must be qualified by one important reservation. Organizational factors are apt to take on considerable importance if the decision requires a compromise among a number of competing values which are somewhat incompatible with each other. In such a case, the focus of attention and the identifications of the person who actually makes the decision are apt to affect the degree to which advice offered him by persons elsewhere in the organization actually influences him.

Our illustration of the warship throws into relief the other aspect of the planning process which was mentioned above: that the plan may control, down to minute detail, a whole complex pattern of behavior—in this case, the construction of the battleship down to the last rivet. The task of the construction crew is minutely specified by this design.

Review. Review enables those who are in a position of authority in the administrative hierarchy to determine what actually is being done by their subordinates.

Review may extend to the results of the subordinate's activities measured in terms of their objectives; to the tangible products, if there are such, of his activities; or to the method of their performance.

When authority is exercised through the specification of the objective of the organizational unit, then a primary method of review is to ascertain the degree to which the organizational objective is attained—the results of the activity. A city manager, for instance, may evaluate the fire department in terms of fire losses, the police department in terms of crime and accident rates, the public works department in terms of the condition of streets and the frequency of refuse collection.

A second very important method of review is one which examines each piece of completed work to see whether it meets set requirements of quantity and quality. This method assumes that the reviewing officer is able to judge the quality and quantity of the completed work with a certain degree of competence. Thus, a superior may review all outgoing letters written by his subordinates, or the work of typists may be checked by a chief clerk, or the work of a street repair crew may be examined by a superintendent.

It has not often enough been recognized that in many cases the review of work can just as well be confined to a randomly selected sample of the work as extended to all that is produced. A highly developed example of such a sampling procedure is found in the personnel administration of the Farm Credit Administration. This organization carries out its personnel functions on an almost completely decentralized basis, except for a small central staff which lays down standards and procedures. As a means of assuring that local practices follow these standards, field supervisors inspect the work of the local agencies and, in the case of certain personnel procedures such as classification, the setting of compensation scales, and the development of testing materials, assure themselves of the quality of the work by an actual inspection of a sample of it.

The third, and perhaps simplest method of review is to watch the employee at work, either to see that he puts in the required number of hours, or to see that he is engaging in certain movements which if continued will result in the completion of the work. In this case, the review extends to procedures and techniques, rather than to the product or results. It is the prevalent form of review at the foremanship level.

To determine what kind of a review method should be employed in any concrete administrative situation, it is necessary to be quite clear as to what this particular review process is to accomplish. There are at least four different functions which a review process may perform: diagnosis of the quality of decisions being made by subordinates, modification through influence on subsequent decisions, the correction of incorrect decisions which have already been made, the enforcement of sanctions against subordinates so that they will accept authority in making their decisions.[10]

In the first place, review is the means whereby the administrative hierarchy learns whether decisions are being made correctly or incorrectly, whether work is being done well or badly at the lower levels of the hierarchy. It is a fundamental source of information upon which the higher levels of the hierarchy must rely heavily for their own decisions. With the help of this information, improvements can be introduced into the decision-making process.

This leads to the second function of review—to influence subsequent decisions. This is achieved in a variety of ways. Orders may be issued covering particular points on which incorrect decisions have been made or laying down new policies to govern decisions; employees may be given training or retraining with regard to those aspects of their work which review has proved faulty; information may be supplied them, the lack of which has led to incorrect decisions. In brief, change may be brought about in any of the several ways in which decisions can be influenced.

Third, review may perform an appellate function. If the individual decision has grave consequences, it may be reviewed by a higher authority, to make certain that it is correct. This review may be a matter of course, or it may occur only on appeal by a party at interest. The justification of such a process of review is that (1) it permits the decision to be weighed twice, and (2) the appellate review requires less time per decision than the original decision, and hence conserves the time of better-trained personnel for the more difficult decisions. The appellate review may, to use the language of administrative law, consist in a consideration *de novo,* or may merely review the original decision for substantial conformity to important rules of policy.

Fourth, review is often essential to the effective exercise of authority. Authority depends to a certain extent on the availability of sanctions to give it force. Sanctions can be applied only if there is some means of ascertaining when authority has been respected, and when it has been disobeyed. Review supplies the person in authority with this information.

Decision making is said to be centralized when only a very narrow range of discretion is left to subordinates; decentralized when a very broad range of discretion is left. Decision making can be centralized either by using general rules to limit the discretion of the subordinate or by taking out of the hands of the subordinate the actual decision-making function. Both of these processes fit our definition of centralization because their result is to take out of the hands of the subordinate the actual weighing of competing considerations and to require that he accept the conclusions reached by other members of the organization.

There is a very close relationship between the manner in which the function of review is exercised and the degree of centralization or decentralization. Review influences decisions by evaluating them and thereby subjecting the subordinate to discipline and control. Review is sometimes conceived as a means of detecting wrong decisions and correcting them. This concept may be very useful as applied to those very important decisions where an appellate procedure is necessary to conserve individual rights or democratic responsibility; but, under ordinary circumstances, the function of correcting the decisional processes of the subordinate which lead to wrong decisions is more important than the function of correcting wrong decisions.

Hence, review can have three consequences: (1) if it is used to correct individual decisions, it leads to centralization and an actual transfer of the decision-making functions; (2) if it is used to discover where the subordinate needs additional guidance, it leads to centralization through the promulgation of more and more complete rules and regulations limiting the subordinate's discretion; (3) if it is used to discover where the subordinate's own resources need to be strengthened, it leads to decentralization. All three elements can be, and usually are, combined in varying proportions in any review process.

Summary

We may now briefly retrace the path we have traveled in the preceding pages. We have seen that a decision is analogous to a conclusion drawn from a number of premises—some of them factual and some ethical. Organization involves a "horizontal" specialization of work and a "vertical" specialization in decision making—the function of the latter being to secure coordination of the operative employees, expertness in decision making, and responsibility to policy-making agencies.

The influence of an organization, and its supervisory employees, upon the decisions of the operative employees can be studied by noting how the organization determines for the operative employee the premises—factual and ethical—of his decisions. The organization's influence is a matter of degree. As we travel from top to bottom of the administrative hierarchy, we note a progressive particularization of influence. Toward the top, discretion is limited by the assignment of broad objectives and the specification of very general methods; lower in the hierarchy, more specific objectives are set, and procedures are determined in greater detail.

Within the limits fixed by his superiors, each member of the organization retains a certain sphere of discretion, a sphere within which he is responsible for the selection of premises for decision. For the most part, this sphere of discretion lies within the factual area of the decisional process rather than within the area of values; but the individual's decision is not "free" even within the area of discretion, in the sense that his superiors are indifferent what decision he will make. On the contrary, he will be held for the correctness of his decision even within that area.

There are at least five ways in which influence is exerted over the individual: (1) authority, (2) identification, (3) the criterion of efficiency, (4) advice and information, and (5) training. To a large extent, these are interchangeable, and a major task of administration is to determine to what extent each will be employed. The structure of influence in an organization and the lines of communication are far more complex than the structure of authority. In designing an organization, it is not enough to establish lines of authority; it is equally important to determine the ways in which all forms of influence are to be exercised.

Two organizational processes are of particular importance to decision making: planning and review. Planning permits the control of decisions in very great detail and permits all the available expertise to be brought to bear on a particular decision, with little concern for the lines of formal authority. Review is a source of information to the administrative hierarchy, a means of influencing subsequent decisions of subordinates, a means for correcting decisions on important individual matters, and a means for enforcing authority by determining when sanctions need to be applied. Depending upon the way in which they are employed, review processes may lead either to the centralization or to the decentralization of decision making.

Notes

1. Luther Gulick and L. Urwick (eds.), *Papers on the Science of Administration,* p. 3.
2. In a sense, the discretion over factual questions which is left the operative is illusory, for he will be held accountable for reaching correct conclusions even with respect to those premises which are not specified in his orders. But it is a question of salient importance for the organization whether the subordinate is guided by orders *in making his decision* or whether he makes it on his own responsibility, subject to subsequent review. Hence, by "discretion" we mean only that standing orders and "on-the-spot" orders do not completely determine the decision.
3. Wayne A. R. Leys, "Ethics and Administrative Discretion," 3 *Public Administration Review* 10-23 (Winter, 1943); and Herman Finer, "Administrative Responsibility in Democratic Government," 1 *Public Administration Review* 335-50 (Summer, 1941).
4. *U.S. Army Field Service Regulations* (1941), p. 31.
5. For a recent advocacy of plural supervision, see Macmahon, Millet, and Ogden, *The Administration of Federal Work Relief* (Chicago: Public Administration Service, 1941), pp. 265-68.
6. Chester I. Barnard, *The Functions of the Executive* (Cambridge: Harvard University Press, 1940), pp. 163ff.
7. Barnard calls this the "zone of indifference" (*op. cit.,* p. 169), but I prefer the term "acquiescence."
8. For further discussion of the efficiency concept, see Clarence E. Ridley and Herbert A. Simon, *Measuring Municipal Activities* (Chicago: International City Managers' Association, 1943).
9. "The Administration of a Fighting Service," 1 *Journal of Public Administration* 216-17 (July, 1923).
10. A somewhat similar, but not identical, analysis of the function of review can be found in Sir H. N. Bunbury's paper, "Efficiency as an Alternative to Control," 6 *Public Administration* 97-98 (April, 1928).

GARY L. WAMSLEY
MAYER N. ZALD

The Political Economy of
Public Organizations

The search for a theory of public administration often takes on aspects of a quest for the Holy Grail or a hunt for the mythical unicorn. Public administration theory has meant variously: a search for "scientific principles"; broad ruminations on what phenomena are included within "the field"; and general orientations of students of the subject, both professional and academic.[1]

Seldom has theory referred to systematic, empirically based explanations of a phenomenon; a system of related and proven propositions that answer the question "Why?" Though this article cannot begin to present such a theory, hopefully, it does more than issue another pious call for one. It is intended to set forth a framework with roots in organizational analysis that is simple but has enough heuristic power to make its application appealing to a wide range of students of public administration; that can pose questions for those areas still in need of exploration, and conceptually link them with those areas already well defined. A framework that can perform such an integrative role would represent a major step toward explanations of why individuals, groups, or organizations behave as they do in that part of the political system we have analytically abstracted and labeled public administration; and it would tell us something about how that behavior affects public policy. If we can better answer the "why" questions, we can also answer better the "how to do it," or the "what should be done" questions that have been so important to the field in the past.

Needless to say, we feel no such framework currently exists. A consensus approach to theory building is needed that can integrate knowledge not only within the field, but from different disciplines; one that focuses on the study of *public* rather than general administration, and therefore has organic links to political science and policy analysis, as well as to organizational sociology.

The Prior Question: Is There "Public" Administration?

After decades of debate, public administration theory is still mired down in debate over whether a meaningful distinction can be made between public and private administration. While granting that to understand the political system, it is necessary to understand public agencies, some argue that for those interested in administration-*qua*-administration, the distinction is counterproductive since it obscures important similarities. Others contend that even if the aim is to understand the political system, it is still possible to assume all administration is the same, and merely "plug in" variables and concepts borrowed from the study of private management.

Our position is that public organizations have distinctive characteristics which make it useful to study them in a separable but interrelated discipline. If we seek to understand public agencies and treat some aspect of them as dependent variables, we find that they are subject to a different set of constraints and pressures than private ones. Specific variables take on different weights in the public sector. If one treats public policies and the agencies that shape and execute them as *independent variables* affecting political effectiveness and legitimacy, he will need an understanding of public organizations quite different from that necessary to understand the effectiveness and legitimacy of private organizations.

A government is a system of rule, distinctive from nongovernmental institutions in that: (1) it ultimately rests upon coercion and a monopoly of force, and (2), if legitimate, it symbolically speaks for the society as a whole, or purports to do so. From these fundamental features flow definitions of membership, rights, expectations, and obligations in relation to the state and its agencies. Citizens and ruling elites both feel they have different "rights" and "expectations" with regard to the FBI than they have with General Motors.

The public organization is more dependent upon funds influenced by political processes or agents. The recipient of services is usually not the immediate funder;[2] and the taxpayer finds it hard to discern linkage between his taxes and any benefits accruing from organizational output. The price-utility relationship is lost, and political considerations not found in the marketplace result. When, for example, the British National Health Service decided to charge for prescriptions, the issue was raised in the House of Commons.

Public administration is also distinctive in the crucial role played by public organizations in shaping and executing public policy, of visibly rewarding and depriving the name of society. Some organizations and their processes contribute to certain policy outcomes, and others facilitate different outcomes. Current concern over policy analysis calls for a theory of public rather than general administration; a theory that can be focused on the consequence of organizational structure and process for policy development and implementation. The abilities, problems, and limits of agencies in developing and carrying out policies are part of the process by which allegiances and regime support are shaped and effected.

These distinctive aspects of public organizations—symbolic significance, differences in funding, perceptions of "ownership" or rights and privileges, and resulting resource constraints—and the relationship of public organizations to public policy point to a potential unity and intellectual coherence in the field of public administration that will be useful for both analytical and normative purposes.

The Political Economy Approach

Granted that the phenomenon called public administration evokes some relatively distinctive concerns, can the previous approaches to the subject which have come from a variety of sources and disciplines be unified and integrated? Elsewhere we have reviewed and criticized such approaches.[3] The political economy approach draws strongly upon the literature of "organizational analysis" or "complex organizations" (as contrasted with scientific management, bureaucratic analysis, or human relations approaches).

Organizational analysis has been most useful to us because it treats organizations as social systems—dynamic, adapting, and internally differentiated—eschews the search for a "one best" model of organization, and has been non-normative, or at least accompanied prescriptions for effectiveness, with contingency statements.[4]

Since it is a structural-functional approach, organizational analysis has tended to treat the full range of social system processes—recruitment and socialization, authority and control patterns, conflict and tension resolution, role conflict, goal adaptation, management processes, technology of task accomplishment, and adaptation to environment—as ongoing processes of an integrated social system. This breadth of approach, however, is also one of its limitations. Analysts alternately claim the greatest heuristic and analytic leverage lies in goals, communications, raw materials and technology, socialization, etc. There has been little agreement about what are the most important variables accounting for structure and change. The political economy framework, however, tries to overcome this weakness by focusing attention on precisely such key variables.

The phrase "political economy" has a long history and several different meanings. It once meant that relationship of government to the economy which promoted a competitive marketplace and thus produced efficient allocation of resources and production. Modern welfare economics uses the phrase in a normative sense to refer to the quest for that policy alternative benefiting most people at least cost. The late 1960s saw the development of a variety of techniques for analyzing policy options. We use the phrase descriptively as the interrelationship between structure of rule (polity) and a system for producing and exchanging goods and services (economy).

We suggest that just as nation-states vary in their political economies—their structure of rule authority, succession to high office, power and authority distribution, division of labor, incentive systems and modes of allocation of resources—so, too, do organizations. And political-economic variables are the major determinants of structure and change.

Throughout this article the term "political" will refer to matters of legitimacy and distribution of power as they affect the propriety of an agency's existence, its functional niche (in society, political system or policy subsystem),[5] its collective institutional goals, the goals of the dominant elite faction (if they vary from institutionalized goals), major parameters of economy, and in some instances the means of task accomplishment (if the task is vague enough to raise value questions or if values change sufficiently to bring established means into question).[6]

"Economic" refers to the arrangement of the division of labor and allocation of resources for task accomplishment and maximization of efficiency; and the combination of factors affecting the cost of producing and delivering a given level of services or output.[7] If goals are well-established and means routinized, an organization becomes largely an administered device, an economy.

An organization's political economy can be analytically divided into internal and external aspects.[8] Analysis of the external political economy focuses on the interaction of the organization and its environment.

External Political Environment: Structure and Interaction

Traditional and neo-classical writings in public administration have tended to treat both external political and economic factors as given, beyond the scope of public administration theory. For us they are central concerns in efforts to develop dynamic analyses because so many of the pressures for change occur in the external environment.

Public organizations exist in an immediate environment of users and suppliers, of interested and disinterested "others." Together, the organization and its relevant others make up a policy subsystem; an arena of individuals, groups, and organizations affected by and interested in influencing, a policy for which the organization has prime responsibility and concern. These relevant others include a variety of actors in and out of government: interest groups, competing public organizations, legislative committees, control agencies. They may be competitive, hostile, overseeing, etc.; regardless, a policy subsystem shapes the conditions of existence for an agency.

An external political structure represents the distribution of sentiment and power resources among an agency's relevant others, i.e., opposition or support to the agency, its goals and programs. The distribution of sentiment and power is a reflection of: the dramaturgy or emotive element in the public organization's operations; its perceived expertise; the degree to which its impact is felt; the breadth (number of groups and individuals affected or interested) of its relevant others; the intensity of their interest; the resources they can bring to bear in exerting influence, and their ability and willingness to use resources.[9]

Sentiment distribution alone offers only a partial description of an agency's political environment. The power resources of actors, their willingness or ability to use them, and their skill in building coalitions also represent an important part of the equation. Some actors have intense interest but are relatively powerless, e.g., prisoners *vis-à-vis* the U.S. Bureau of Prisons; others have power resources but fail to use them because of political costs or internal conflicts over which action to take. Thus, sentiment patterns are weighted by the power resources and capabilities of relevant others.

Nor do public organizations merely accept the existing sentiment and power distribution; they also manipulate it with varying degrees of success. Administrators try to routinize the controversial by obtaining an equilibrium of interests, by benignly institutionalizing their environments.[10] The task is never complete, for the equilibrium can be upset by administrative error, changes in influence patterns and technology, or the suddenly negative attention of a latently powerful actor, e.g., the U.S. Tea Tasting Board's "discovery" and proposed abolition in 1970, or the CIA in the aftermath of the Bay of Pigs fiasco.

External political structures tend toward rigidity. Change does not come easily in a public organization or its policy subsystem either by dint of its manipulation *or* impingements of the environment. Goals and procedures may be frozen by conditional patterns of support and hostility. A press for change mobilizes opposition. The incentive system of public organizations seldom works for change. A change agent must generate issues, mobilize a coalition of forces, and gain the support of key proximal others in a policy subsystem. Though difficult, change does occur through interaction and political exchange. Political exchanges result from conscious efforts of: (1) external actors to affect a public organization's niche and related goals; or (2) an agency to manipulate its relevant others in order to alter its legitimacy and the order of magnitude of resources, and thus its overall goals and direction. The effects can thus alter niche, the general functional goals related to it, internal political patterns, processes of task accomplishment (if they involve legitimacy), and even survival.

When we think of the external political interactions of an organization and its environment, most of us think of the obvious, such as the Nixon administration's efforts to subtly shift the goals of the Civil Rights Division of Justice and the Office of Civil Rights for HEW from zealous pursuit of desegregation in the South to a diverse nationwide approach of lower intensity, less inimicable to the growth of Republicanism in the South.[11] But this is the obvious. The more subtle and ongoing source of interactions are the efforts by the executive cadres of organizations to alter their own domain or that of their neighbors, and thus alleviate uncertainty. Domain may include claims on future functional-level goals and the requisite resources to achieve them as well as those presently held.[12] In this ongoing political interaction over niche or domain, agencies vary along several dimensions in their sensitivity to political impingements and capacity to manipulate.

Goals, Ambiguity and Clarity. Where goals are clearly defined and subject to surveillance, an agency like the Social Security Administration may be left little room for choice or maneuver in goals, program objectives, and perhaps even means of task accomplishment. But if goals are ambiguous or multiple, an organization's elite may press for one definition or another and, within the bounds of political feasibility, allocate resources internally in pursuit of this choice (correctional institutions: treatment or custody).

Surveillance. Some agencies effectively avoid scrutiny by superiors and other external actors. The CIA with its budget hidden in other departments' appropriations, is the most notable example. But ambiguity of goals, hidden missions, or simply overwhelming complexity of programs and accounting information also hinder effective surveillance and diminish sensitivity.

Centrality of Values. If a public organization is perceived to fulfill a central value of the political culture, its autonomy is enhanced as long as it does not drastically alter niche goals. If the agency loses effectiveness, surveillance increases and autonomy declines. A state fire marshal's office charged with ensuring fire safety in schools, institutions, and public buildings may hardly be reviewed until a tragic fire occurs.

Personnel and Funding Allocation. Not all agencies are equally subject to influence by external and superior actors in the matter of funds and personnel. Special, strategically placed allies like a chairman of an appropriations subcommittee can help or hurt them in terms of financial support. Or those operating on users fees, trust funds, or special funds may enjoy greater freedom from surveillance by superiors than those operating from general funds, though they are subject to special scrutiny from the clientele from which the revenues derive.

Public organizations have a relative lack of control over executive appointments. Central budget and personnel offices often have "position control" over personnel. But the nature and extent of this control varies. Some terms of appointment are long, and in the case of many boards they are staggered. Other agencies at the state level are headed by elected officials, which gives them a strong base of autonomy.

The Structure of Support and an Established Feed-Back Loop. Autonomy increases if an organization offers a well-received product to efficacious clientele who are able to influence key, proximal others. They, in turn, enlarge the organization's share of resources and legitimacy. This requires the right balance of numbers, geographic dispersion, and of efficacy. Sometimes this means the establishment of advisory committees, propaganda aimed at relevant others, news media, and mass public, or even the actual organization of interest groups by the agency.

Political interactions and exchanges take place between an agency and relevant others at its boundary. Transactions involve such outputs as strategically timed withholding or providing of products or services, "leaks" to news media, providing of information to allies; and such inputs as interest group demands, demands of a chief executive, influence of an appropriation subcommittee chairman. Inputs or outputs are political rather than economic if they are of sufficient magnitude to alter niche, overall goals and direction, the order of magnitude of resources, or major economic parameters.

Economic Environments and Exchanges

An examination of a public organization's economic environment requires an analysis of costs and behavior necessary in obtaining factors of production and exchange of output at organizational boundaries. It means emphasizing what in the private sector would be called "industry structure," markets, and the elasticity of supply and demand. Special attention must be given to the degree of "industry concentration," the relationships among competitors, distinctive aspects of technology, supply of raw materials and labor, and "markets" or factors affecting the distribution network for outputs.

The industry structure of public organizations is generally ignored on the assumption that they have monopolistic or oligopolistic status. But many have competitors among other agencies and in the private sector as well. In addition, the supply and prices of the factors of production for public organizations are directly affected by events in the economy at large.

However, many phenomena which might be treated as economic in the private sector must be treated as political-economic in the public sector. Demands are aggregated, filtered, and channeled through the budget process and an agency's policy subsystem, as questions about the legitimacy of spending public funds for certain purposes are raised and as its resource needs are thrown into competition with others. The process is pronounced in the United States with its strong separation of executive and legislative functions and its weak party system, but is also found elsewhere.

The lack of market controls for a public organization and the corresponding lack of efficiency incentives have led to elaborate accounting and budgeting controls in an effort to simulate market functions. Contract clearance, position control, independent audits, control of category transfers, competitive bidding, apportionments, cost-benefit analysis, and performance budgeting are devices for controlling cost and registering preferences. Often these are purely instrumental and economic in nature, but the analyst must be aware of their political ramifications as well.[13]

The cost curves of producing and delivering a public organization's product vary considerably and can become political in nature. The steep costs of putting in a new weapons system for deterrence or damage limitation may trigger a national debate over national priorities, the risks of attacks, etc. In contrast, political crises over school costs are slower to develop because they rise incrementally rather than in "lumps" that might mobilize opposition.

What, then, is treated as strictly an external economic exchange for a public organization? Economic exchanges are neither intended to nor do they actually affect niche, functional goals, order of magnitude of resources, or major economic parameters; rather they are designed merely to implement established goals and tasks, and are seen as legitimate by both the dominant coalition of an organization, its opposition, and by relevant others. Government agencies, for example, bargain over price and quality of certain elements of production, but do so without conscious effort to manipulate their environment politically.

Often economic considerations are ignored in the literature of public administration because of a failure to conceptualize public organizations as obtaining raw materials from an economic environment and processing or converting them into products offered to consumers.[14] Even public organizations which we assume have highly charged political environments have established some niche and carry on some "production" that no longer raises questions of legitimacy. For example, the Joint Chiefs of Staff produce "products" like advice to the Joint Staff, translation of policy into strategic orders, decisions on weapon systems and force level priorities that we normally fail to recognize as products. Many of the JCS's products resemble those of a private consulting firm. They are produced by collating information and beliefs (the raw materials) through "technologies" of debate, compromise, defined disagreement, suppression of the source of raw materials, delay in processing, ambiguous decisions, agreement not to disagree, and technical loyalty to the administration but covert disloyalty. Some products like decisions on weapon systems have definite political effects, but many of them, like advice to the Joint Staff, no longer raise questions of legitimacy and are most meaningfully seen as economic[15] because they are relatively routine. If public organizations are viewed as procurers and processors of raw materials, and offerers of products at their boundaries, then their external economic exchange (and internal economic structures) become more readily apparent.

General economic and manpower pictures can also affect a public organization. Full employment and inflationary economy make it more difficult for public organizations to recruit personnel because of their lower status and lag in pay scales. The costs of public organizations are closely tied to labor rates because they produce services rather than manufactured goods, and it is difficult for them to substitute machines for labor. As wages rise, public costs spiral. Workloads also respond to economic and manpower outlooks. Some workloads rise as the economy declines, e.g., welfare and unemployment insurance agencies; while that of others, like Selective Service, decline as unemployed men volunteer and lower draft calls result.

Broad and diffuse changes in demand are also economic and are so perceived by agencies, e.g., the increase in camping that has vastly changed the National Park Service. Similarly, technological changes are usually perceived as economic, though they may drastically alter an agency and its exchanges with its environment—Internal Revenue Service and computers; the Army and helicopters.

Public organizations seek to manipulate their economic as well as political environments. Competitive bidding and mass central purchasing are obvious examples; but cost-plus-fixed-fee contracts, grants, loans, and leasing out of capital assets are all methods used to overcome hesitancy of contractors and suppliers.

Public agencies exist in a web of political and economic exchange structures that shape long-run functions and directions of change, as well as short-run interactions and concerns. Changes in societal values and the values of relevant others can alter an agency's functional goals and legitimacy, while cost factors and the pattern of "industry structure" affect its ability to accomplish tasks. Public administration must be able to analyze agencies' environments in order to predict change, and an understanding of public policy and changes in it calls for a political economy analysis of the organizations that are prime actors and relevant others in a policy subsystem.

Internal Political Structure and Process

The internal policy refers to the structure of authority and power and the dominant values, goals, and ethos institutionalized in that structure. The executive cadres of agencies may have their range of domain options more limited by statute and oversight than is true of private organizations. But because statutes are vague and extraordinarily complex, and because oversight is imperfect, there remains room for interpretation that marks the political function. Executive cadres also come to identify with the agency, its ethos and goals, and its long-range survival, growth, and status in a way that is more than merely utilitarian. Because public organizations are involved in pursuing commonwealth values, cadres are likely to see their agencies as embodying high purpose. This infusion of an instrumental structure with values that give it purpose other than task accomplishment (maintenance, survival, aggrandizement) provides another fundamental basis for political functions.[16]

Four major political functions of the executive cadre can be identified: (1) developing and defining agency mission, ethos, and priorities; (2) developing boundary-spanning units and positions to sense and adapt to environmental pressures and changes; (3) ensuring recruitment and socialization of agency elite to maintain coherence and pursuit of goals; (4) overseeing the internal economy, harmonizing it with shifts in niche or goal proprieties.

The four polity functions are initiated and carried out by executive cadres to ensure survival, growth, and adaptation. Sometimes they are less than successful: goal consensus among cadres is seldom perfect; adequate boundary-spanning units are often not established; elites are improperly socialized; and internal economies are sometimes poorly monitored. To some extent the manner in which cadres perform these functions is dependent upon the shape of the internal political structure as it varies along several dimensions: (1) constitutions, (2) degree of goal consensus, (3) unity of authority, (4) patterns of subunit power, demand aggregation-articulation, and conflict resolution, and (5) patterns of leadership succession and cadre maintenance.

Constitutions. The constitution (written or unwritten) of any social group consists of the basic norms involving the ends and means of power—conceptions of legitimate purposes and of legitimate ways of wielding authority in pursuit of them.[17] They determine the types of incentive exchanges existing or possible for an organization, i.e., time, energy, and commitment it can expect from different members and what rewards they expect. If norms of exchange are weak or non-binding, an organization's polity tends to be fragile. For example, if its exchange system is solidly utilitarian, it will find it difficult to survive a crisis requiring near total commitment of its cadre, unless utilitarian rewards can be made extraordinarily high.

Constitutional norms also indicate the range of discretion and decision responsibilities for organizational elite and mass. For example, the keystone of Selective Service's constitution historically was "local board autonomy." This established roles in hierarchical interaction over cases. Quiet but intense daily struggles occurred in operationalizing the norms, but always within constitutional parameters. Such norms also set parameters for the relationships between an organization and its relevant others. To whom is it responsible or responsive, and under what conditions? Is the Corps of Engineers more responsive to presidential policy guidelines on ecology or congressional demands for pork barrel projects?[18]

Constitutions specify the political foci of collective actions, i.e., the matters within or without its area of concern—domain, clientele groups. Often they prevent adaption of a new assigned function because of inability to give the proper attention.

Goal Consensus. Few public organizations have total cadre unity over purpose and general direction; moreover, they are often vulnerable to divisiveness from external political influences. But usually there is a prevailing coalition (perhaps supported by outside actors) with its own *Weltanschauung*. Factionalism crises arise from sources like empire building by units, ambiguity of statutory mandate, influences of external actors, lack of cadre homogeneity, operations that must span wide areas, and tasks that are complex, vague, or diverse.[19]

Unity of Authority. Some organizations have goal consensus but a splintered authority structure; not all have a singular head and a unitary chain of command. Most obviously, boards and commissions are structures fostering factionalism, coalition patterns, and pursuit of multiple goals. Other organizations represent a conglomeration of functions thrown together by fate and congressional whimsy. A federated authority pattern often results.

Patterns of Sub-Unit Power, Demand Aggregation-Articulation, and Conflict Resolution. Because they are usually responsible for different goals or phases of task accomplishment, sub-units develop differing interests, and their power capabilities differ because of: their essentiality to accomplishment of overall goals, or epitomization of organizational mission; their access to and influence over information and communications (internal and external); or the support they marshal from the general public or powerful in-contact others.

Internal polities differ in the way demands of sub-units, lower-level membership, or elite factions are patterned. Many of the demands themselves are of an instrumental or economic nature, but the particular *patterns* followed are a reflection of internal polity, for they shape direction, goals, and functional niche. The patterns determine responsiveness to change, vulnerability to pressures, indeed survival capacity. Patterns are shaped by sub-group identity and cohesion, perceived grievances, and the costs and benefits of expressing them. Some public organizations are unionized and face strike threats, others have elaborate employee associations that lobby, a few have lower-level members that are so dispersed and fractionated in their interests that scarcely any demand pattern emerges, and in still others the costs of expressing demands or grievances are so great as to militate against pattern emergence. The inability of an organization to handle demands and resolve conflict at lower levels vitally affects its direction and existence.[20]

Leadership Succession, Cadre Recruitment, and Socialization. The formal structure of the executive cadre, appointment power and criteria for dismissal, promotion, and transfer are often set for an agency by external political forces. Still, some discretion remains. What appears to be the external imposition of a procurator is often an established pattern that also reflects internal forces. Appointments of political executives must satisfy expectations of organizational elite as well as those of relevant others (unless outside powers are trying to bring about drastic change). Succession patterns may take several forms: a "crown prince" system with an anointed successor; a "stand-off" or consensus successor wearily agreed upon by intensely conflicting factions; a "new majority" and clandestine coups; or a discontented sovereign outside the organization may send a procurator.

Public organizations do not merely tap into civil service pools for cadre. Cadre recruitment and socialization follow definite patterns in each organization. The State Department cadre is drawn heavily from "prestige" universities and socialized into a "gentlemen's club," while the Department of Agriculture draws upon land-grant colleges, and the military intensely socialize in academies. Organizations find ways of being selective about cadre either in recruitment or socialization.[21]

Public administration has not yet begun to provide the concepts and schemas for analyzing the rich variations in internal polities of organizations—the widely varying ways in which the authority relating to overall goals and directions of an agency is organized.

Internal Economy

At the heart of every organization is a "sub-organization whose 'problems' are focused upon effective performance of the technical function." The main concern of persons filling the cluster of roles in the internal economy are: the "exigencies imposed by the nature of the technical task";[22] problems growing out of the nature of the raw materials to be processed; the division of work and responsibilities so that the cooperation required for task accomplishment is forthcoming; and allocating resources and maintaining an incentive system to efficiently accomplish tasks. Public organizations, like private, must coordinate behavior and allocate resources in order to produce an output which satisfies relevant others.

It is the internal economy in which the broader technological aspects of the organization are concentrated, where instrumental and efficiency norms take precedence over legitimacy. In this realm, role incumbents are likely to see problems of overall direction and survival as "someone else's business."

Buffering and Nourishing the Technological Core. Organizational polities seek to protect and insulate the technological core from external contingencies that would disrupt task accomplishment. They do so because they are established to accomplish tasks, and efficiency concerns are thrust upon them by scarcity, goal achievement drives, budget constraints, or output evaluations. Efficiency efforts can bring about major changes, a possibility that links internal economy to both internal/and external political concerns. The quest for efficiency leads to efforts to buffer out disruptions of constant and routine affairs by smoothing input and output flows, or by forecasting fluctuations and scheduling adjustments.

Buffering can be done in some organizations by "stockpiling," preventive maintenance, or an extension of organizational jurisdiction and operations to encompass crucial contingencies. An example of the latter is public organizations like narcotic rehabilitation centers which seek to change people. Often they seek to induct the raw material so as to better monitor it, control it, or cope with contingencies.

One means of nourishing the internal economy is to expand clientele. An agency that applies standard techniques to large populations may have considerable slack resulting from putting in new technology or equipment, e.g., automation of a records system is done with machinery designed for existing load *plus* future growth. The resulting slack may be a temptation to enemies or an embarrassment to the organization that motivates client expansion. Sometimes slack is handled by diversification of functions to avoid charges of waste.

Not all agencies can protect their technological core. To the extent they cannot, they lose economies of scale, lose advantages of specialization, incur high coordination costs, and run risks of collecting bad accounting information.

Task Structures. Structure within the internal economy refers to the patterned interaction of sub-units and roles in accomplishment of organizational tasks. Classical public administration theorists like Gulick and Urwick sought to discuss how work should be organized (purpose, process, clientele, or area). Neo-classicists like Simon convincingly showed that their predecessors had no firm answers, but their work too was more directed at "how" to organize to obtain "correct" decisions than it was at explaining "why" task structures follow the patterns they do.

To the extent that norms of efficient task accomplishment prevail (a matter to be settled empirically in each case), the basic dimensions of hierarchy and coordination in an agency's internal economy are laid down primarily by raw materials, technologies, and task dimensions.[23]

Within the basic dimensions, however, task structure is further elaborated by: (1) the variety of "products" offered by the organization (the Department of Commerce offers everything from commercial statistics to weather forecasts); (2) the scope of operations necessary to deliver a product (in order to develop the Tennessee River and its tributaries, TVA must do everything from build dams to produce fertilizer); (3) the degree of geographic dispersion (TVA and the Corps of Engineers have similar scopes of operations and products to deliver, but the Corps is much more geographically dispersed); and (4) by the particular nature of role interdependencies requiring role clustering at different hierarchical levels in order to reduce coordination costs.

The internal economy is thus an arrangement of authority and power, but on the level of instrumentality and efficiency rather than on the level of legitimacy and survival—the economic aspects of authority rather than the political. One affects the other and the two power structures may be one and the same, with role incumbents merely acting out different facets of their multidimensional roles. But they *do* make the distinction and it is observable in their behavior. Nor is it a distinction confined to certain types of political systems. Both parliamentary and revolutionary regimes, for example, may recognize the distinction between political and technical functions, e.g., the Red Army.

Resource Allocation and Incentive Systems. Budgets and accounting systems are means of allocating resources within the internal economy. They are vital mechanisms for maintaining the level of activity and types of cooperation necessary for efficient task accomplishment.[24] Accounting systems record variable data which communicate trends in efficiency, effectiveness, inter-unit comparison, etc., to organization elite concerned with internal economy.[25] For example, a new division assigned a crucial function for the first time may incur unexpectedly heavy costs, indicating a need for change in task structure or drastic upward revision of appropriation requests. Resource allocation needs to be looked at as a key part of internal economy: a compounded function of traditional rules, intergroup bargains, mechanics for deciding economy conflicts, and elite perception of new areas for opportunity.

Within the internal economy, incentives are allocated to motivate performance. They may be symbolic, monetary, or nonmonetary (status, interpersonal), and vary not only in the "needs" they fulfill but in their delivery rate, tangibility, divisibility, and pervasiveness. Organizations have different stocks of incentives to draw on: the Peace Corps uses psychic incentives; the Post Office, monetary and security; and Selective Service uses symbolic and psychic incentives. A major organizational change often entails a change in the incentive system.

In the rush to study "politics" of bureaucracy, political scientists have left analysis of internal economy to business administration, organization analysts studying the private sector, or Bureaus of Public Administration (viewed by universities as community service agencies). But the subject requires more serious attention in broader perspectives. Alterations in internal economy can be a major source of change, setting off an internal polity struggle or fundamentally altering an organization's relation to its environment.

Is the Approach Useful?

The political economy approach can only become a true paradigm for empirical theory building if it can (1) help unify the fractionated fields that are related to public administration, (2) contribute to traditional and emerging concerns of scholars in those fields, and (3) at the same time merge the strengths and move beyond the weaknesses of each. In conclusion, let us briefly indicate how our framework might contribute to these goals.

Each of the traditional concerns of public administration dealt with a key aspect of organizational political economies, but in a piecemeal and normative fashion and without conscious conceptual distinction between political and economic matters. Scientific management was, and a substantial part of the field today remains, concerned with structuring the task environment for efficiency—a matter of internal economy. Students of budgeting from the Taft Commission of 1912 to the PPBS of today have placed most of their emphasis on budgeting as a surrogate market mechanism. Only recently have the political aspects of the subject been acknowledged or effort made to sort out whether "reforms" are having political or economic effects. Similarly, personnel administration has gone through one trend after another from the great civil service reform to the more recent "decentralization" moves. Always students of public administration played more of a participant role than one of analytical observer, and seldom did they differentiate between political and economic matters. What has been most lacking is a focus on an empirical entity—the public organization as a key actor in a policy subsystem.

Even if the American students of public administration become less reform-minded and interventionist, this seems unlikely to hold for persons studying "developing administrative systems." Many of these persons are taking up these concerns with fresh zeal. But it would be unfortunate if the same pitfalls experienced by the field in America were to be repeated. To avoid past mistakes these subjects must be approached in a broader and less normative way. The concerns of "interventionist-practitioners" are spotlighted by our framework as internal economy matters. An effort by them to apply the framework objectively can result in dividends. Their work will be better informed of the interaction between political and economic variables, and assuming the framework aids theory development, and advances toward answers to "why" questions, there will also be better answers to the "how to" questions. The unintended consequences of the many reforms or counter-reforms, and the political-economic costs and benefits that ensue would be made clearer.[26]

The framework could also be useful in a new concern bordering the field of public administration—policy analysis. Recent efforts have focused on systemic inputs; but this focus has left the field considerably short of explaining why certain policies take the particular patterns they do. This "input" approach of Dye and others has tended to show high correlations between economic development variables and policy outputs in certain areas; but low correlations between the outputs and so-called political variables.[27] The results are provocative but explain little, for the research has defined politics too narrowly (voter participation, party competition, degree of malapportionment). The entire realm of interplay in policy making between public organizations and their relevant others has remained untapped. Policy is made at the nexus of politics (particularly micro-politics) and economics. Economic development merely provides the resource backdrop for such policy making. A more thorough analysis must penetrate the organizational and policy context in which policy is made, and the political economy framework could prove useful.

The framework may also make a contribution in political analysis of regimes. Such analysis has sought to find out who is behind certain policy and government action. The answer in more cases than has heretofore been acknowledged is not necessarily a power elite, voters, or a consensual outcome of plural elite struggle, but an organization and its particular political economy needs; or an individual actor playing a role defined by his organizational membership, his organization's processes, or its place in a policy subsystem. Policy then, is as much, or more a product of the political economy of conversion structures within the interstices of the system's "black box"—as it is of pressures or inputs from outside.

Analysis has seen actions of government as a chess game with pieces moved by "outside forces," i.e., "the people," "the power elite," or a squabbling team of plural elites. But perhaps we need to think of them moving as a result of "internal forces," as though each piece has a set of wheels, internal motor, sensory devices, miniature computer and guidance system. That is to say, it may be moved by outside forces or players, but it also moves in response to its own environment reading and its own internal dynamics. Imagine also that each piece's ability to "read" environment responsively, and its repertory of responses, are limited and conditioned by political and economic factors.[28]

To carry things further, picture all of the above conditions plus the fact that as observers we can see only one game board, but that each piece is playing in several other unseen games; and further that the game boards overlap in a variety of ways. Accordingly, the visible self-directed piece, unbeknownst to us, is moving in several games at once, playing out strategies dictated by differing locations on each game board. A particular organizational move may be a function of simultaneous calculations in several different games.[29] The visible move may or may not be a conscious, coordinated synthesis of the different game strategies. Thus, public organizations are not merely important actors in a policy process; often their goals, myths, processes, procedures, or domain consciousness in effect "make" policy.

Utilization of the political economy framework could be not only a serious step toward developing a systematic empirical theory of public administration, but could also contribute to development of important areas of study in both political science and sociology. It would be a useful enterprise, however, if it contributed to any one of these goals.

Notes

1. Martin Landau, "Sociology and the Study of Formal Organization," in CAG Special Series No. 8, Washington, D.C., 1966. His description of a preparadigmatic field should be uncomfortably familiar to students of public administration. See p. 38.
2. Some public organizations such as the Post Office are funded by customers, but there are still differential costs and benefits, and rates are subject to political constraints.
3. Wamsley and Zald, *The Political Economy of Public Organizations: A Critique and Approach to the Study of Public Administration* (Lexington, Mass.: D.C. Heath, 1973). Previous work on our framework can be found in Mayer N. Zald, *Organizational Change: The Political Economy of the YMCA* (Chicago: University of Chicago Press, 1970), and in his essay "Political Economy: A Framework for Comparative Analysis," in Mayer N. Zald (ed.), *Power in Organizations* (Nashville: Vanderbilt University Press, 1970), pp. 221-261.
4. Prominent among the contributors to the literature of organization analysis are the works of Philip Selznick and his students upon whom we draw heavily. Representative of other "strands" are the works of Alvin Gouldner and Peter Blau and their students.
5. The concept of niche is borrowed from studies of biotic communities in which each organism has a niche in an interdependent and symbiotic relationship. Similar and used interchangeably is the concept of "domain." See Sol Levine and Paul White, "Exchange as a Conceptual Framework for the Study of Interorganizational Relationships," *Administrative Science Quarterly,* Vol. V (March 1957), pp. 444-463.
6. Even tasks performed by lower functionaries can become political if values within and without the organization are affected by the discretion they wield. Performance of a vague task may define values, or a long-established pattern of task accomplishment may run afoul of changed environmental values.
7. More than a few economists will be unhappy with our definition. Modern analytic economics tend to focus on maximization and resource allocation. Our definition includes them, but focuses on the structure of the economy, the extent and limits of differentiation and coordination.
8. If our framework focused solely on *internal* political economy the phrase "political-administration" or "political-managerial" might suffice, but it is also important to describe the structure of the *external* economic environment.
9. Rourke, *Bureaucracy, Politics and Public Policy* (Boston: Little Brown, 1969), chapters 2, 3, and 4.
10. For example, see Gary L. Wamsley, *Selective Service and a Changing America* (Columbus, Ohio: Chas. E. Merrill, 1969), chapter 7.
11. See L. E. Panetta and P. Gall, *Bring Us Together: The Nixon Team and Civil Rights Retreat* (New York: Lippincott, 1971).
12. Levine and White, *op. cit.*

13. Aaron Wildavsky, "The Political Economy of Efficiency, Cost Benefit Analysis, Systems Analysis, and Program Budgeting," *Public Administration Review,* Vol. XXVI (1966). For examples of accounting becoming "political," see Thomas J. Anton, *The Politics of State Expenditure in Illinois* (Urbana: University of Illinois Press, 1966), pp. 46-47, 69-70, 203-204.

14. See Charles Perrow, "A Framework for the Comparative Analysis of Organizations," *American Sociological Review,* Vol. XXVI (1961).

15. The JCS operate in a highly competitive milieu. Their legitimacy depends on an occasional product acceptance. They not only act as a "consulting firm" but a "coalition of normally competing firms." Each member (except the chairman) plays a role as representative of his service as well as a collegial role. Example based on analysis as of early 1960s.

16. Selznick, *Leadership in Administration* (New York: Harper & Row, 1957).

17. In public organizations, constitutional analysis begins with statutes, promulgated regulations, and various memoranda. Also revealing are: documents describing the organization to outsiders or new members; histories written by members; or situations in which there has been a violation of a constitutional norm, conflict, or withdrawal of resources.

18. Arthur Maas, *Muddy Waters: The Army Engineers and the Nation's Rivers* (Cambridge: Harvard University Press, 1951), p. 63.

19. See Anthony Downs, *Inside Bureaucracy* (Boston: Little Brown, 1967), pp. 224-226.

20. Public administration theory lacks a typology of conflict resolving mechanisms within agencies paralleling knowledge of those in the society and legislative arenas. A good beginning, though not applied directly to public organizations, is found in James D. Thompson, "Organizational Management of Conflict," *Administrative Science Quarterly,* Vol. 4, No. 4 (1960), pp. 389-402.

21. See Harold Seidman, *Politics, Position and Power* (New York: Oxford University Press, 1970), pp. 113-114.

22. James D. Thompson, *Organizations in Action* (New York: McGraw-Hill, 1967), p. 10. This section draws on Thompson and Charles Perrow, *op. cit.*

23. For a discussion of the types of technologies see Thompson, *op. cit.*

24. They may also be used in polity struggles to reward and punish and bring about change. Here we single out their economic importance.

25. They also transmit information that may be used politically to cadre factions and other actors in the policy subsystem.

26. But caution is needed in applying organizational analysis to societies with quasi-organizations or in which organizations are "fronts" for other social groups. See Fred W. Riggs, "Organization Theory and International Development" (Bloomington, Ind.: Carnegie Seminar on Political and Administration Development, 1969).

27. Thomas R. Dye, *Politics, Economics and Public-Policy Outcome in the American States* (Chicago: Rand-McNally, 1966).

28. Graham T. Allison, "Conceptual Models and the Cuban Missile Crisis," *American Political Science Review,* Vol. LXII (September 1969), pp. 689-718.

29. Norton E. Long, "Local Community as an Ecology of Games," *American Journal of Sociology,* Vol. 64, pp. 251-261.

ROBERT T. GOLEMBIEWSKI

Organization as a Moral Problem

The act of organizing often has been considered a technical problem, and a low level technical problem at that. Hence, the uncomplicated, Tinker-Toy-like terms in which the study of organization commonly is formulated. To Lepawsky, for example, organization is to administration as skeletology is to medicine. "An organization," he noted, "can be sketched and charted just as the human body can be physically depicted." The graphics are not of over-powering difficulty. Indeed, organization is "mainly a matter of structure" and, Lepawsky concluded, organization is the "most elementary aspect of ad-ministration."[1]

Such analysis has tended to paralyze thought about organization. The analogy of the healthy body, or the well-oiled machine, is not far below the surface of much of the work on organization. The mirage of a "healthy" organization, of an optimum and invariant arrangement of parts, has guided many students and practitioners. The early work in "scientific management" illustrates the point. This early work assumed that "the system emerges from and is immanent in the 'facts' of existence and emerges from them when they are recorded and manipulated"[2] in much the same way as observation reveals the proper relation of the bones of a body or the parts of a machine. Time has not eliminated this bias. Recent observers still stress the search for *the* organization theory.[3]

This view of organization may be challenged from many points of ap-proach. One of these approaches will be taken here—that the emphasis upon one single organization theory forecloses a moral evaluation of organization.

The Complex Problem of Organization

The neglect of organization as a moral problem cannot be condoned. For the man-to-man relations implied in patterns of organization have more than a technical aspect. Organization, in this sense, is more akin to psychiatry than to skeletology. The concept of "healthy" in skeletology can be determined (for general purposes) by observing many specimens. Observing individuals or organizations, in contrast, merely describes. Observation does not determine "moral health."

Organization theorists, then, have tended to neglect an important distinction between types of theories. The complex problem of organization derives from the two types of questions which must be treated: What is related to what in organizations? and, What relations are desirable and how are they to be achieved in organizations? The first question implies an empirical theory. Considerable progress has been made of late toward such a theory. The second question requires a moral, or value, orientation. Values guide the prescription of how various sets of desired states may be achieved, given a knowledge of the important relations which exist under the full range of conditions encountered in organizations. These prescriptions, or guides for action, may be called goal-based, empirical theories. Their development has been conspicuously lacking in organization theory.

The development of goal-based, empirical theories complicates the study of organization substantially. This is the case in a number of senses. First, patently, there can be many goal-based, empirical theories of organization. Gone, therefore, is the solace of *an* organization theory. In contrast, there will be *one* general empirical theory of organization. Of course, this theory will change substantially over time, as it is extended to more and more phenomena. Empirical theory in the physical sciences, for example, has followed this course while working toward a single network of propositions which uniquely and convincingly describe reality.

Moreover, not every goal-based, empirical theory is "right" in a moral sense. For example, such a theory could be developed around the goal of increasing friendly social contact on the job. Similarly, a goal-based, empirical theory could be developed—relying heavily on the experience with SS officers during World War II—to guide selection and training consistent with the goal of a smoothly run extermination program. These theories are generically similar. But, it is hoped, they would be evaluated as more and less desirable, respectively.

These considerations suggest the burden of the following approach. First, a set of values which should guide the act of organizing will be hazarded. These values—J-C, for convenience—derive from the Judaeo-Christian tradition. Second, some behavioral findings relevant to organization will be reviewed with the purpose of determining whether they support the values implied in traditional organization theory or the J-C values. These findings support this important point; it is realistic to approach the Judaeo-Christian values in organizing.

Man in Organization

If organizations were a complex of gears and driveshafts, the development of theories of organization would not be onerous. It would be enough to deal with empirical properties in achieving desired states. That is, if a design were decided upon (a value choice), only factors like gear speed, the nature of materials, and so on, would require attention. Such part-to-part relations are relatively uncomplicated.

But man is a prime component of organizations. These man-to-man relations add important dimensions to the difficulty of developing goal-based, empirical theories of organization. Thus, it is necessary to know that such-and-such a leadership style will have such-and-such consequences for behavior which will accomplish the required job. In addition, however, the moral desirability of those behavioral consequences must be determined.

There is an even more confusing aspect of the problem, finally. The choice of a leadership style, for example, might be based upon a value-preference that authoritarian supervision is desirable. The use of this style, in turn, might have the self-fulfilling effect of causing employees to act as if such a style were certainly necessary to restrain them. The employees, then, might be expressing their dissatisfaction with the style of leadership by various forms of behavior management considers undesirable (which the research literature tells us often happens). Such behavior easily could be interpreted as proof that an authoritarian style is not only desirable but is necessary as well. This visible reinforcement of a value by an apparent necessity often makes it difficult to raise the question of values, for it can be argued that realistically no choice exists.

The task of raising value questions is further obstructed because we have not developed a full set of values to guide such man-to-man relations. Also, we are less than perfect in consistently respecting the partial set of guidelines which have been developed. But the Judaeo-Christian tradition implies a set of values applicable to man-to-man relations in organizations. Consider this possible set of values, although it is offered without pretense of completeness:

1. work must be psychologically acceptable to the individual, that is, its performance cannot generally threaten the individual;
2. work must allow man to develop his faculties;
3. the work task must allow the individual considerable room for self-determination;
4. the worker must have the possibility of controlling, in a meaningful way, the environment within which the task is to be performed; and
5. the organization should not be the sole and final arbiter of behavior; both the organization and the individual must be subject to an external moral order.

These five value guidelines are goals toward which the act of organizing should point. Any organization-in-being, then, will fall somewhere along a continuum (for example, from 0 to 100 percent compliance) for each of the five values. The question is: Where?

This may seem a formidable WHERE? Traditional organization theory, however, provides a convenient reference for this analysis. The theory has been an important guide in planning many organizations. Therefore, traditional organization theory is not an analytical straw man. But it does outline a more extreme set of conditions than often exists in practice. Evaluating traditional organization theory in terms of the J-C values is meaningful, then, even if some modifications are necessary to fit particular organizing efforts.

Man in Traditional Organization Theory

Traditional organization theory—despite its limitations for present purposes—has an immense advantage as a frame of reference for this analysis. One need not search for it. Indeed, one cannot avoid it. Almost any textbook on organization or administration is a very probable source. Nor is there great disagreement about the properties of this theory. For present purposes, four properties of this traditional organization theory may be emphasized. They are:

1. authority should be "one-way"; it should flow in a single stream from organization superiors to subordinates;
2. supervision should be detailed and the span of control should be narrow;
3. the organization of work should respect only the physiological properties of the individual, who is considered as a social isolate; and
4. work should be routinized.

Traditional organization theory patently has little sensitivity for the set of J-C values outlined above. Indeed, the two lists negate one another. Thus the traditional theory of organization calls for a routinized job, whose performance is monitored closely by a supervisor with a narrow span of control, in an organization in which authority is a one-way relation. The contrast could not be more pointed.

The disregard of man-as-an-end in traditional organization theory has many reflections in practice. The "boon of stupidity," for example, has been cited by a testing expert as the most desirable quality of workers on some routinized operations. More to the point, the dehumanization of work has gone so far that morons and (believe it or not) pigeons have replaced "normal" human beings on some operations with marked success. These, of course, are extreme cases. Much work—both in industrial operations and in the so-called "administration of paper"—also leans in the same direction, if not so markedly.

Man-Centered Organization: Some Hardheaded Support

Let us begin with a conclusion. There seem to be substantial limits on the degree to which work, especially in our "developed" economy, can violate the values derived from the Judaeo-Christian tradition without paying a heavy price.

This position contradicts commonly held views. For example, the Marxian analysis, which assumes an inevitable conflict between the "forces of production" (roughly, the technology) and the "relations of production" (roughly the values which give meaning to man's life). Traditional organization theory seems to support this analysis. That is, the closer the approach to the traditional theory, the greater the tension between the technology and the J-C values which have given meaning to western man's "relations of production."

This conflict, however, does not seem to be inevitable. Indeed, the "forces of production" and the "relations of production" can (and perhaps must) complement one another under certain conditions. Consider only two such conditions. First, there is the growing inapplicability of the mass-production model which is at the heart of the traditional theory of organization and of the Marxian analysis as well. Technicians characterize the new economy, not unskilled operatives; and services increasingly displace manufacturing as employers of men. This improves the chances of approaching the J-C values.

Second, the development of a particular "force of production," the technology of behavioral science, also makes it possible (and reasonable) to approach more closely the J-C values. Some main elements of this behavioral research will be summarized later. However, the new behavioral science technology forces this point: the more closely work approximates the set of J-C values outlined above, under imprecisely known but general conditions, the more effective performance will be.

This general analysis is given body in a summary way in Table 1. The table presents two types of information: (a) the values which should underlie man-to-man relations, and (b) the conditions isolated by behavioral research which approach this set of values and which are associated with high output. Table 1, of course, summarizes large aggregates of data from behavioral research. The findings do not always apply to individual cases.[4] The behavioral findings are presented in the sense of central tendencies, of more or less dominant relations which have been isolated in the study of man in organization.

Evidence for each of the conditions in the right-hand column of Table 1 could be cited. Only the asterisked conditions—one for each of the five values —will be supported here, however, and those only briefly.

Psychological Acceptability of Work

Consider, to begin, the psychological acceptability of work. Testing, of course, is not novel. Indeed, tremendous sums are expended for the purpose each year. And substantial progress in the area cannot be denied. But, if we can look forward to the future payoffs of testing, available dimensions of personality leave much to be desired.[5] In the testing of intelligence, which is quite advanced, intelligence scores have substantial limits in the prediction of per-

TABLE 1
Behavioral Conditions Associated with High Output Consistent with Judaeo-Christian Values which Should Guide Man-to-Man Relations in Organizations

Values Guiding Man-to-Man Relations	Conditions Associated with High Output
1. work must be psychologically acceptable, generally non-threatening	1. congruence of personality and job requirements 1a. compatibility of personalities of work-unit members*
2. work must allow man to develop his faculties	2. job enlargement 2a. job rotation* 2b. training, on and off the job 2c. decentralization
3. the task must allow the individual room for self-determination	3. job enlargement 3a. general supervision* 3b. wide span of control
4. the worker must influence the environment within which he works	4. group decision making* 4a. peer representation in promotion 4b. self-choice of work-unit members 4c. decentralization
5. the formal organization must not be the sole and final arbiter of behavior	5. decentralization* 5a. group decision making

formance in organizations. There are many sluggards who perform well and other personality characteristics must be known to increase the accuracy of predictions.

Recent work has attempted with some success to isolate and measure additional major personality characteristics, what may be called "general predispositions to action." This work has great promise. William Schutz, for example, experimented with three major behavioral predispositions of individuals. They were:[6]

1. a *power orientation,* referring to the predisposition of an individual to become a power figure or to be subject to a power figure;
2. A *personalness-counterpersonalness orientation,* referring to an individual's predisposition to seek close personal relations; and
3. an *assertiveness orientation,* referring to an individual's predisposition to make his views known in a group.

Based upon these basic predispositions, Schutz constructed experimental groups which were "compatible" and "incompatible." An "incompatible" group, for example, included individuals with extremely different scores on the personalness-counterpersonalness orientation.

Schutz's manipulations proved their point. "Compatible" groups were more effective on a number of tasks. Output, satisfaction, group "togetherness," and so on, were among the measures employed.

While most measures of such basic personality characteristics have been crudely defined, testing for such personality characteristics has enormous potential for assuring that work is psychologically acceptable to employees. This is the case despite the cries of critics, such as William H. Whyte, Jr., for whom testing means only a violation of the privacy of individuals. There are risks in the use of testing, to be sure, and quackeries aplenty in its practice. But the payoffs—for individuals and for the organization—seem well worth the risks and the humbug.

Development of Individual Faculties

Next, the literature seems quite definite on the point that techniques which allow the individual to develop his faculties generally are associated with high output. Job enlargement, therefore, has gained quite a reputation. Humbler techniques, such as the simple rotation between routine jobs, often have a similar impact. Effective assembly lines, for example, have been found to practice (quite secretly) job rotation. The experience at the Endicott, New York, plant of IBM seems typical. There, while the boss was away, the employees began to rotate jobs informally to break the monotony. Rotation was a tonic:[7]

By the time the switch was discovered, the men were all doing so much better that the boss decided to rotate jobs in his department . . . as a matter of policy. That was a year ago. Since then manufacturing costs in the department have dropped about 19 percent.

Approaching the value of allowing the individual to develop his faculties, in short, is an attractive proposition from a cost, as well as from a moral, standpoint. This relation seems to hold for all organization levels, which makes it particularly noteworthy. Moreover, job enlargement often will have the effects of reducing supervisory costs and of freeing supervisors to perform functions of management other than close supervision.

Room for Self-Determination

Tasks which allow the individual room for self-determination, the third condition, also have a double-barreled effect which is attractive from a cost standpoint. They approach one of the values which should guide man-to-man relations in organization, and they are associated with high output.

General supervision, for example, allows the individual room for self-determination on the task. A wide span of control has a similar effect. Output tends to respond favorably. This was the case, for example, for about three-quarters of the supervisors in one sample.[8] First-line supervisors who utilized general supervision—setting objectives and allowing the worker considerable leeway in reaching them—tended overwhelmingly to have work units with high productivity. Close supervision, in contrast, was associated very strongly with low output. Significantly, also, second-line supervisors who employed general supervision almost always had subordinate foremen who used the same style. Those employing close supervision also had subordinates who used the same style. The point, then, seems to hold for all organization levels.

Controlling the Environment

The fourth value, possibility of controlling the environment, which should guide man-to-man relations covers a broader field than allowing the individual room for self-determination on the task. It extends to the general environment within which the task is performed. Again, techniques which approach this value tend to be associated with high output.

Group decision making concerning changes in jobs or output levels—certainly among the more important aspects of the environment within which a task is performed—illustrates the point. The technique is a simple, if revolutionary, one. A typical application would involve the setting by management of general goals, for example, to meet increasingly sharp competition. Work units in the concern, cognizant of these general goals, would determine and enforce a level of output. Traditional organization theory, of course, countenances no such falderal. An order would suffice, in its terms.

Group decision making generally leads to increased output, although what precisely makes for success (or failure) is not known. This may seem surprising, but the explanation is plausible. Group decision making implies a low degree of threat, as opposed to exhortation by management. Consequently, less resistance results (for example, to high levels of output). Moreover, the group is free to develop and enforce a norm. This norm, in turn, often serves as a very potent guide for the behavior of members, even when the supervisor is away. The group, then, makes strong medicine and it is often far stronger than management can brew under present economic and cultural conditions.

Despite the fuzziness surrounding the concept, group decision making seems to encourage participation and, therefore, increases the probability of involvement in decisions by those who must carry them out. One experiment strikingly makes the point. Three degrees of participation in a minor change in a job were studied: *total participation*, or group decision making by a formal work unit; *representative participation*, in which members of a work unit chose representatives to participate in the decision making; and *no participation*, in which the workers were simply told that a change was necessary and that it would be made.

The degree of participation made a substantial difference. Originally, the work units had comparable output levels which clustered around 60 units per hour. *Total participation* led to the highest output after the change, substantially above the levels reached before the change. *No participation* resulted in the lowest output. Indeed, the *no-participation* unit fell far below its previous output and did not recover during a 32-day period of observation. The data in Table 2 summarize these results.'

Curiously, the principle of group decision making has had few full-fledged applications. Various bastardized "participation plans" do exist, of course. Often they attempt to get without giving and must take their place in the store-house of gimmicks that might (or might not) work in the short run and are likely to fail in the longer run. The Scanlon Plan, in contrast, attempts to ex-ploit the possibilities of participation *and* distributes the benefits among all. It does not pussyfoot. The heart of the plan is a Production Committee, com-posed of equal numbers of management personnel and hourly employees who are elected periodically. The Committee considers the spectrum of manage-ment problems and serves an important role in communicating decisions.

The available evidence, none of it very complete, suggests that such full-scale participative efforts as the Scanlon Plan have much to offer employees and management. Co-determination (as practiced in Yugoslavia, for example) can have similar effects.

Whatever its scope, however, the possibility of the worker influencing the productive environment tends to pay off in increased output and heightened satisfaction. Again, approaching this fourth value governing man-to-man rela-tions has practical, as well as moral, support.

Management, indeed, has only a limited choice in such areas as group deci-sion making. For denying the worker such "legitimate" means of influencing the environment does not close the matter. The environment often will be con-trolled informally in ways unfavorable to management. For example, informal groups will develop which control the behavior of employees in the matter of output. This is a substantial way of controlling the work environment, and the informal group has a relatively clear field. It controls the rewards of status, ef-fect, and emotional support which can be provided to members in the group

TABLE 2
Degree of Participation in Decisions on
Introducing Minor Changes and Its Effect on Output

Condition	Production (in units per hour) at Five-Day Intervals After the Change in the Job					
	5	10	15	20	25	30
Total Participation	64	63	75	71	71	72
Representative Participation	50	53	60	68	64	66
No Participation	45	53	55	51	49	55

context. Management, in contrast, does not (and cannot) provide such satisfactions directly and continuously for most employees.

At best, then, management can choose between attempting to mesh the norms of the informal group with the goals of the formal organization and thrusting its head into the proverbial sand by neglecting the need for participation.

Recent history, of course, suggests that the unreasonable choice often has been made. The massive effort, through unionization and government action, to gain influence over the work situation suggests the mass demand for such influence and the not-quite-equally-successful general attempt to thwart that demand.

This recent history also implies a lesson for the future. Speculation of whether things had to be this way is futile. But, at the very least, techniques for giving the employee the opportunity to exert meaningful influence over the job environment can be conceived which do not run the risk of frustrating the individual by confronting him (or management) with a union or government bureaucracy which the employee (or management) cannot influence. Group decision making, for example, would provide such an opportunity at all levels of an organization. These opportunities, it is safe to guess, would take much of the steam out of extreme efforts by large organized units to influence the work situation.

Subject to an External Moral Order

The fifth value which should govern man-to-man relations, finally, is in many senses the linchpin of the J-C values. For, if the organization is the ultimate measure of man, the first four values could hardly be attained in great measure. The importance of the point about control of organization by an external moral order was stressed in the war trials following World War II, for example. The military organizations of many western countries, in addition, often have emphasized that an immoral order need not be obeyed.

The favorable consequences of approaching this fifth value cannot be presented with as much confidence as was possible with the previous examples. But a convincing case can be developed for the position that consciousness of this fifth value has useful consequences for administration. Thus, creativity would be more likely in organizations in which the "true believer" was rare. This might seem to apply with most force to upper levels of the organization. But, fortunate is the organization which can tap the enormous pool of creativity among its lower-level operatives.

In addition, the person who accepts the formal organization as the sole and final arbiter is a caricature of a man who might find it difficult to supply the most miniscule adaptations required by his work until they were programmed.

Moreover, communication in such an organization would have an Alice-in-Wonderland quality. The German experience in World War II is instructive on this score. Intelligence percolating up to Hitler told him what he wanted to hear rather than what he should have heard. For the head of the German government had made it very clear—sometimes by executions—that he had already predicted what would happen and that intelligence ought not contradict the predictions. Consequently, some of the most incredible decisions imaginable were made; for example, emasculating a jet-aircraft program which was far ahead of similar Allied programs. Too much obedience to the organization, clearly, prejudiced its chances for survival. If Hitler's techniques were extreme, the lesson of the example has many applications.

In these terms, Whyte's conclusion that the successful executive typically has a somewhat jaundiced view of "the organization" rings true. The successful executive seems to support the organization only so long as it generally supports his needs and values. Is it reasonable to expect any employee to sacrifice his personality without exacting a high payoff for so doing? And, can you really trust someone who would do anything to keep his job, even if it means sacrificing his needs and values?

Decentralization seems the major high-level technique which approaches the value that the formal organization is not the sole and final arbiter of behavior. Indeed, a decentralized system requires precisely the kind of manager who has the strength of character and ability to make his decisions and let others make theirs. The very act of decentralization—of setting an individual loose within general boundaries—is optimistic.[10] Decentralization also implies that there is much to be gained in terms of increasing the chances for adaptation, training, and involvement at lower levels. This is accomplished by cultivating the attitude that the formal organization above an officer's level is not the sole and final arbiter of behavior.

With some reservations, then, the fifth value which should guide man-to-man relations seems to contribute to organization effectiveness. This is the case despite the patent difficulty of saying "when" to attempts at decentralization, of training personnel, and of developing suitable controls.

Indeed, the position here may be overcautious. The experience of firms like Sears, Roebuck supports the usefulness of decentralization. Its middle-sized stores, for example, which developed internal decentralized structures had higher sales and developed more promotable executives than stores with centralized patterns.[11] The returns of a 1935-39 decentralization at Westinghouse, similarly, appear to have been very substantial.[12] And, the comparison of a sample of centralized and decentralized firms favored the latter on such significant measures as turnover of the work force, absenteeism, and accident severity and frequency.[13]

Conclusion

There is considerable evidence, then, that in organizing it is advisable in practice to approach those values relevant to man-to-man relations which have been accepted in general at an intellectual level in western cultures.

The difficulty of approaching these values should not be underestimated. One must have acute ideological foresight indeed to envision the time when these values will be achieved in substantial measure. Even inch-by-inch advances will often come dearly. Major changes in attitudes and techniques will be required. Also, fundamental changes in traditional organization theory must be made. Job enlargement, for example, is not consistent with that theory, empirically or in a value sense.

Whether these changes are made or not, however, one point cannot be neglected: *organization is a moral problem*. Findings such as those cited above make it attractive to recognize the point, but a moral problem is a moral problem, whatever the research technology tells us. Conveniently, the research technology gives a generally clear go-ahead to efforts to face this moral problem in practice.

Notes

1. Albert Lepawsky (ed.), *Administration: The Art and Science of Organization and Management* (Knopf, 1952), p. 219.
2. Dwight Waldo, *The Administrative State* (Ronald, 1948), p. 178.
3. William G. Scott, "Organization Theory: An Overview and an Appraisal," 4 *Journal of the Academy of Management*, esp. pp. 22-26 (April 1961).
4. For some of the qualifications necessary for more precise prediction, see Robert T. Golembiewski, "The Small Group and Public Administration," 19 *Public Administration Review* 154-56 (Summer 1959).
5. Saul W. Gellerman, "A Hard Look at Testing," 38 *Personnel* 8-15 (May-June 1961).
6. William C. Schutz, "What Makes Groups Productive?" 8 *Human Relations* 429-66 (November 1955).
7. Chris Argyris, *Personality and Organization* (Harper, 1957), p. 276.
8. Robert L. Kahn and Daniel Katz, "Leadership Practices in Relation to Productivity and Morale," in Dorwin Cartwright and Alvin Zander (eds.), *Group Dynamics: Research and Theory* (Row, Peterson, 1953), p. 615.
9. Approximated from a graph in Lester Coch and John R. P. French, Jr., "Overcoming Resistance to Change," in Cartwright and Zander, *op. cit.*, p. 268.
10. Each General Manager of the 100 operating departments of General Electric is allowed to expend up to $500,000 for capital projects without specific authorization by headquarters, for example.
11. James C. Worthy, as cited in William F. Whyte, *Man and Organization* (Irwin, 1959), pp. 11-16.
12. Ernest Dale, "Some New Perspectives on Decentralization," 24 *Advanced Management* 17-20 (January 1959).
13. From a study reported in Ernest Dale, "Centralization Versus Decentralization," 21 *Advanced Management* 15 (June 1956).

CHARLES H. LEVINE

Organizational Decline and Cutback Management

Government organizations are neither immortal nor unshrinkable.[1] Like growth, organizational decline and death, by erosion or plan, is a form of organizational change; but all the problems of managing organizational change are compounded by a scarcity of slack resources.[2] This feature of declining organizations—the diminution of the cushion of spare resources necessary for coping with uncertainty, risking innovation, and rewarding loyalty and cooperation—presents for government a problem that simultaneously challenges the underlying premises and feasibility of both contemporary management systems and the institutions of pluralist liberal democracy.[3]

Growth and decline are issues of a grand scale usually tackled by only the most brave or foolhardy of macro social theorists. The division of scholarly labor between social theorists and students of management is now so complete that the link between the great questions of political economy and the more earthly problems of managing public organizations is rarely forged. This bifurcation is more understandable when one acknowledges that managers and organization analysts have for decades (at least since the Roosevelt administration and the wide acceptance of Keynesian economics) been able to subsume their concern for societal level instability under broad assumptions of abundance and continuous and unlimited economic growth.[4] Indeed, almost all of our public management strategies are predicated on assumptions of the continuing enlargement of public revenues and expenditures. These expansionist assumptions are particularly prevalent in public financial management systems that anticipate budgeting by incremental additions to a secure base.[5] Recent events and gloomy forecasts, however, have called into question the validity and generality of these assumptions, and have created a need to reopen inquiry into the effects of resource scarcity on public organizations and their management systems. These events and forecasts, ranging from taxpayer revolts like California's successful Proposition 13 campaign and financial crises like the near collapse into bankruptcy of New York City's government and the agonizing retrenchment of its bureaucracy, to the foreboding predictions of the "limits of growth" modelers, also relink issues of political economy of the most monumental significance to practices of public management.[6]

We know very little about the decline of public organizations and the management of cutbacks. This may be because even though some federal agencies like the Works Progress Administration, Economic Recovery Administration, Department of Defense, National Aeronautics and Space Administration, the Office of Economic Opportunity, and many state and local agencies have expanded and then contracted,[7] or even died, the public sector as a whole has expanded enormously over the last four decades. In this period of expansion and optimism among proponents of an active government, isolated incidents of zero growth and decline have been considered anomalous; and the difficulties faced by the management of declining agencies coping with retrenchment have been regarded as outside the mainstream of public management concerns. It is a sign of our times—labeled by Kenneth Boulding as the "Era of Slowdown"—that we are now reappraising cases of public organization decline and death as exemplars and forerunners in order to provide strategies for the design and management of *mainstream* public administration in a future dominated by resource scarcity.[8]

The decline and death of government organizations is a symptom, a problem, and a contingency. It is a symptom of resource scarcity at a societal, even global, level that is creating the necessity for governments to terminate some programs, lower the activity level of others, and confront trade-offs between new demands and old programs rather than to expand whenever a new public problem arises. It is a problem for managers who must maintain organizational capacity by devising new managerial arrangements within prevailing structures that were designed under assumptions of growth. It is a contingency for public employees and clients; employees who must sustain their morale and productivity in the face of increasing control from above and shrinking opportunities for creativity and promotion while clients must find alternative sources for the services governments may no longer be able to provide.

Organizational Decline and Administrative Theory

Growth is a common denominator that links contemporary management theory to its historical antecedents and management practices with public policy choices. William Scott has observed that ". . . organization growth creates organizational abundance, or surplus, which is used by management to buy off internal consensus from the potentially conflicting interest group segments that compete for resources in organizations."[9] As a common denominator, growth has provided a criterion to gauge the acceptability of government policies and has defined many of the problems to be solved by management action and organizational research. So great is our enthusiasm for growth that even when an organizational decline seems inevitable and irreversible, it is nearly impossible to get elected officials, public managers, citizens, or management theorists to confront cutback and decremental planning situations as anything more than temporary slowdowns. Nevertheless, the reality of zero growth and absolute decline, at least in some sectors, regions, communities, and organizations, means that management and public policy theory must be expanded to incorporate non-growth as an initial condition that applies in some cases. If Scott's assertions about the pervasiveness of a growth ideology in management are correct, our management and policy paradigms will have to be replaced or augmented by new frameworks to help to identify critical questions and strategies for action. Put squarely, without growth, how do we manage public organizations?

We have no ready or comprehensive answers to this question, only hunches and shards of evidence to serve as points of departure. Under conditions and assumptions of decline, the ponderables, puzzles, and paradoxes of organizational management take on new complexities. For example, organizations cannot be cut back by merely reversing the sequence of activity and resource allocation by which their parts were originally assembled. Organizations are organic social wholes with emergent qualities which allow their parts to recombine into intricately interwoven semi-lattices when they are brought together. In his study of NASA's growth and drawdown, Paul Schulman has observed that viable public programs must attain "capture points" of public goal and resource commitments, and these organizational thresholds or "critical masses" are characterized by their indivisibility.[10] Therefore, to attempt to disaggregate and cutback on one element of such an intricate and delicate political and organization arrangement may jeopardize the functioning and equilibrium of an entire organization.

Moreover, retrenchment compounds the choice of management strategies with paradoxes. When slack resources abound, money for the development of management planning, control, information systems, and the conduct of policy analysis is plentiful even though these systems are relatively irrelevant to decision making.[11] Under conditions of abundance, habit, intuition, snap judgments and other forms of informal analysis will suffice for most decisions because the costs of making mistakes can be easily absorbed without threatening the organization's survival.[12] However, in times of austerity, when these control and analytic tools are needed to help to minimize the risk of making mistakes, the money for their development and implementation is unavailable.

Similarly, without slack resources to produce "win-win" consensus-building solutions and to provide side payments to overcome resistance to change, organizations will have difficulty innovating and maintaining flexibility. Yet, these are precisely the activities needed to maintain capacity while contracting, especially when the overriding imperative is to minimize the perturbations of adjusting to new organizational equilibriums at successively lower levels of funding and activity.[13]

Lack of growth also creates a number of serious personnel problems. For example, the need to reward managers for directing organizational contraction and termination is a problem because without growth there are few promotions and rewards available to motivate and retain successful and loyal managers—particularly when compared to job opportunities for talented managers outside the declining organization.[14] Also, without expansion, public organizations that are constrained by merit and career tenure systems are unable to attract and accommodate new young talent. Without an inflow of younger employees, the average age of employees is forced up, and the organization's skill pool becomes frozen at the very time younger, more flexible, more mobile, less expensive and (some would argue) more creative employees are needed.[15]

Decline forces us to set some of our logic for rationally structuring organizations on end and upside down. For instance, under conditions of growth and abundance, one problem for managers and organizational designers is how to set up *exclusionary* mechanisms to prevent *"free riders"* (employees and clients who share in the consumption of the organization's collective benefits without sharing the burden that produced the benefit) from taking advantage of the enriched common pool of resources. In contrast, under conditions of decline and austerity, the problem for managers and organizational designers is how to set up *inclusionary* mechanisms to prevent organizational participants from avoiding the sharing of the *"public bads"* (increased burdens) that result from the depletion of the common pool of resources.[16] In other words, to maintain order and capacity when undergoing decline, organizations need mechanisms like long-term contracts with clauses that make pensions non-portable if broken at the employee's discretion. These mechanisms need to be carefully designed to penalize and constrain *"free exiters"* and cheap exits at the convenience of the employees while still allowing managers to cut and induce into retirement marginally performing and unneeded employees.

As a final example, inflation erodes steady states so that staying even actually requires extracting more resources from the organization's environment and effectuating greater internal economies. The irony of managing decline in the public sector is particularly compelling under conditions of recession or so called "stagflation." During these periods of economic hardship and uncertainty, pressure is put on the federal government to follow Keynesian dictates and spend more through deficit financing; at the same time, critical public opinion and legal mandates require some individual agencies (and many state and local governments) to balance their budgets, and in some instances to spend less.

These characteristics of declining public organizations are like pieces of a subtle jigsaw puzzle whose parameters can only be guessed at and whose abstruseness deepens with each new attempt to fit its edges together. To overcome our tendency to regard decline in public organizations as anomalous, we need to develop a catalogue of what we already know about declining public organizations. A typology of *causes* of public organizational decline and corresponding sets of *tactics* and *decision rules* available for managing cutbacks will serve as a beginning.

The Causes of Public Organization Decline

Cutting back any kind of organization is difficult, but a good deal of the problem of cutting back public organizations is compounded by their special status as authoritative, non-market extensions of the state.[17] Public organizations are used to deliver services that usually have no direct or easily measurable monetary value or when market arrangements fail to provide the necessary level of revenues to support the desired level or distribution of services. Since budgets depend on appropriations and not sales, the diminution or termination of public organizations and programs, or conversely their maintenance and survival, are political matters usually calling for the application of the most sophisticated attack or survival tactics in the arsenal of the skilled bureaucrat-politician.[18] These strategies are not universally propitious; they are conditioned by the causes for decline and the hoped-for results.

The causes of public organization decline can be categorized into a four-cell typology as shown in Figure 1. The causes are divided along two dimensions: (a) whether they are primarily the result of conditions located either internal or external to the organization, or (b) whether they are principally a product of political or economic/technical conditions.[19] This is admittedly a crude scheme for lumping instances of decline, but it does cover most cases and allows for some abstraction.

Of the four types, *problem depletion* is the most familiar. It covers government involvement in short-term crises like natural disasters such as floods and earthquakes, medium length governmental interventions like war mobilization and countercyclical employment programs, and longer-term public programs like polio research and treatment and space exploration—all of which involve development cycles. These cycles are characterized by a political definition of a problem followed by the extensive commitment of resources to attain critical masses and then contractions after the problem has been solved, alleviated, or has evolved into a less troublesome stage or politically popular issue.[20]

Problem depletion is largely a product of forces beyond the control of the affected organization. Three special forms of problem depletion involve

FIGURE 1
The Causes of Public Organization Decline

	Internal	External
Political	Political Vulnerability	Problem Depletion
Economic/Technical	Organizational Atrophy	Environmental Entropy

demographic shifts, problem redefinition, and policy termination. The impact of demographic shifts has been vividly demonstrated in the closing of schools in neighborhoods where the school age population has shrunk. While the cause for most school closings is usually neighborhood aging—a factor outside the control of the school system—the decision to close a school is largely political. The effect of problem redefinition on public organizations is most easily illustrated by movements to *de*institutionalize the mentally ill. In these cases, the core bureaucracies responsible for treating these populations in institutions has shrunk as the rising per patient cost of hospitalization has combined with pharmaceutical advances in anti-depressants and tranquilizers to cause public attitudes and professional doctrine to shift.[21]

Policy termination has both theoretical import and policy significance. Theoretically, it is the final phase of a public policy intervention cycle and can be defined as ". . . the deliberate conclusion or cessation of specific government functions, programs, policies, or organizations."[22] Its policy relevance is underscored by recent experiments and proposals for sunset legislation which would require some programs to undergo extensive evaluations after a period of usually five years and be reauthorized or be terminated rather than be continued indefinitely.[23]

Environmental entropy occurs when the capacity of the environment to support the public organization at prevailing levels of activity erodes.[24] This type of decline covers the now familiar phenomena of financially troubled cities and regions with declining economic bases. Included in this category are: market and technological shifts like the decline in demand for domestic textiles and steel and its effect on the economies and quality of life in places like New England textile towns and steel cities like Gary, Indiana, Bethlehem, Pennsylvania, and Youngstown, Ohio;[25] transportation changes that have turned major railroad hubs and riverports of earlier decades into stagnating and declining economies; mineral depletion which has crippled mining communities; and intrametropolitan shifts of economic activity from central cities to their suburbs.[26] In these cases, population declines often have paralleled general economic declines which erode tax bases and force cities to cut services. One of the tragic side effects of envirnmental entropy is that it most severely affects those who cannot move.[27] Caught in the declining city and region are the immobile and dependent: the old, the poor, and the unemployable. For these communities, the forced choice of cutting services to an ever more dependent and needy population is the cruel outcome of decline.[28]

Environmental entropy also has a political dimension. As Proposition 13 makes clear, the capacity of a government is as much a function of the willingness of taxpayers to be taxed as it is of the economic base of the taxing region. Since the demand for services and the supply of funds to support them are usually relatively independent in the public sector, taxpayer resistance can produce diminished revenues which force service reductions even though the demand and *need* for services remains high.

The *political vulnerability* of public organizations is an internal property indicating a high level of fragility and precariousness which limits their capacity to resist budget decrements and demands to contract from their environment. Of the factors which contribute to vulnerability, some seem to be more responsible for decline and death than others. Small size, internal conflict, and changes in leadership, for example, seem less telling than the lack of a base of expertise or the absence of a positive self-image and history of excellence. However, an organization's age may be the most accurate predictor of bureaucratic vulnerability. Contrary to biological reasoning, aged organizations are more flexible than young organizations and therefore rarely die or even shrink very much. Herbert Kaufman argues that one of the advantages of organizations over solitary individuals is that they do provide longer institutional memories than a human lifetime, and this means that older organizations ought to have a broader range of adaptive skills, more capacity for learning, more friends and allies, and be more innovative because they have less to fear from making a wrong decision than a younger organization.[29]

Organizational atrophy is a common phenomenon in all organizations but government organizations are particularly vulnerable because they usually lack market generated revenues to signal a malfunction and to pinpoint responsibility. Internal atrophy and declining performance which can lead to resource cutbacks or to a weakening of organizational capacity come from a host of system and management failures almost too numerous to identify. A partial list would include: inconsistent and perverse incentives, differentiation without integration, role confusion, decentralized authority with vague responsibility, too many inappropriate rules, weak oversight, stifled dissent and upward communication, rationalization of performance failure by "blaming the victim," lack of self-evaluating and self-correcting capacity, high turnover, continuous politicking for promotions and not for program resources, continuous reorganization, suspicion of outsiders, and obsolescence caused by routine adherence to past methods and technologies in the face of changing problems. No organization is immune from these problems and no organization is likely to be afflicted by them all at once, but a heavy dose of some of these breakdowns in combination can contribute to an organization's decline and even death.

Identifying and differentiating among these four types of decline situations provides a start toward cataloging and estimating the appropriateness of strategies for managing decline and cutbacks. This activity is useful because when undergoing decline, organizations face three decision tasks: first, management must decide whether it will adopt a strategy to resist decline or smooth it (i.e., reduce the impact of fluctuations in the environment that cause interruptions in the flow of work and poor performance); second, given this choice of maneuvering strategies it will have to decide what tactics are most appropriate;[30] and third, if necessary, it will have to make decisions about how and where cuts will occur. Of course, the cause of a decline will greatly affect these choices.

Strategic Choices

Public organizations behave in response to a mix of motives—some aimed at serving national (or state or local) purposes, some aimed at goals for the *organization as a whole,* and others directed toward the particularistic goals of organizational subunits. Under conditions of growth, requests for more resources by subunits usually can be easily concerted with the goals of the organization as a whole and its larger social purposes. Under decline, however, subunits usually respond to requests to make cuts in terms of their particular long-term survival needs (usually defended in terms of the injury which cutbacks would inflict on a program with lofty purposes or on a dependent clientele) irrespective of impacts on the performance of government or the organization as a whole.

The presence of powerful survival instincts in organizational subunits helps to explain why the political leadership of public organizations can be trying to respond to legislative or executive directives to cut back while at the same time the career and program leadership of subunits will be taking action to resist cuts.[31] It also helps to explain why growth can have the appearance of a rational administrative process complete with a hierarchy of objectives and broad consensus, while decline takes on the *appearance* of what James G. March has called a "garbage can problem"—arational, polycentric, fragmented, and dynamic.[32] Finally, it allows us to understand why the official rhetoric about cutbacks—whether it be to "cut the fat," "tighten our belts," "preserve future options," or "engage in a process of orderly and programmed termination"—is often at wide variance with the unofficial conduct of bureau chiefs who talk of "minimizing cutbacks to mitigate catastrophe," or "making token sacrifices until the heat's off."

Retrenchment politics dictate that organizations will respond to decrements with a mix of espoused and operative strategies that are not necessarily consistent.[33] When there is a wide divergence between the official pronouncements about the necessity for cuts and the actual occurrence of cuts, skepticism, cynicism, distrust, and noncompliance will dominate the retrenchment process and cutback management will be an adversarial process pitting top and middle management against one another. In most cases, however, conflict will not be rancorous, and strategies for dealing with decline will be a mixed bag of tactics intended either to *resist* or to *smooth* decline. The logic here is that no organization accedes to cuts with enthusiasm and will try to find a way to resist cuts; but resistance is risky. In addition to the possibility of being charged with nonfeasance, no responsible manager wants to be faced with the prospect of being unable to control where cuts will take place or confront quantum cuts with unpredictable consequences. Instead, managers will choose a less risky course and attempt to protect organizational capacity and procedures by smoothing decline and its effects on the organization.

An inventory of some of these cutback management tactics is presented in Figure 2. They are arrayed according to the type of decline problem which they can be employed to solve. This collection of tactics by no means exhausts the possible organizational responses to decline situations, nor are all the tactics exclusively directed toward meeting a single contingency. They are categorized in order to show that many familiar coping tactics correspond, even if only roughly, to an underlying logic. In this way a great deal of information about organizational responses to decline can be aggregated without explicating each tactic in great detail.[34]

The tactics intended to remove or alleviate the external political and economic causes of decline are reasonably straightforward means to revitalize eroded economic bases, reduce environmental uncertainty, protect niches, retain flexibility, or lessen dependence. The tactics for handling the internal causes of decline, however, tend to be more subtle means for strengthening organizations and managerial control. For instance, the management of decline *in the face of resistance* can be smoothed by changes in leadership. When hard unpopular decisions have to be made, new managers can be

FIGURE 2
Some Cutback Management Tactics

	Tactics to Resist Decline	Tactics to Smooth Decline
External Political	(Problem Depletion) 1. Diversify programs, clients and constituents 2. Improve legislative liaison 3. Educate the public about the agency's mission 4. Mobilize dependent clients 5. Become "captured" by a powerful interest group or legislator 6. Threaten to cut vital or popular programs 7. Cut a visible and widespread service a little to demonstrate client dependence	1. Make peace with competing agencies 2. Cut low prestige programs 3. Cut programs to politically weak clients 4. Sell and lend expertise to other agencies 5. Share problems with other agencies
Economic/ Technical	(Environmental Entropy) 1. Find a wider and richer revenue base (e.g., metropolitan reorganization) 2. Develop incentives to prevent disinvestment 3. Seek foundation support 4. Lure new public and private sector investment 5. Adopt user charges for services where possible	1. Improve targeting on problems 2. Plan with preservative objectives 3. Cut losses by distinguishing between capital investments and sunk costs 4. Yield concessions to taxpayers and employers to retain them

FIGURE 2 (continued)

	Tactics to Resist Decline	Tactics to Smooth Decline
Internal Political	(Political Vulnerability) 1. Issue symbolic responses like forming study commissions and task forces 2. "Circle the wagons," i.e., develop a seige mentality to retain esprit de corps 3. Strengthen expertise	1. Change leadership at each stage in the decline process 2. Reorganize at each stage 3. Cut programs run by weak subunits 4. Shift programs to another agency 5. Get temporary exemptions from personnel and budgetary regulations which limit discretion
Economic/ Technical	(Organizational Atrophy) 1. Increase hierarchical control 2. Improve productivity 3. Experiment with less costly service delivery systems 4. Automate 5. Stockpile and ration resources	1. Renegotiate long-term contracts to regain flexibility 2. Install rational choice techniques like zero-base budgeting and evaluation research 3. Mortgage the future by deferring maintenance and downscaling personnel quality 4. Ask employees to make voluntary sacrifices like taking early retirements and deferring raises 5. Improve forecasting capacity to anticipate further cuts 6. Reassign surplus facilities to other users 7. Sell surplus property, lease back when needed 8. Exploit the exploitable

brought in to make the cuts, take the flak, and move on to another organization. By rotating managers into and out of the declining organization, interpersonal loyalties built up over the years will not interfere with the cutback process. This is especially useful in implementing a higher level decision to terminate an organization where managers will make the necessary cuts knowing that their next assignments will not depend on their support in the organization to be terminated.

The "exploit the exploitable" tactic also calls for further explanation. Anyone familiar with the personnel practices of universities during the 1970s will recognize this tactic. It has been brought about by the glutted market for academic positions which has made many unlucky recent Ph.D.s vulnerable and exploitable. This buyers' market has coincided neatly with the need of universities facing steady states and declining enrollments to avoid long-term tenure commitments to expensive faculties. The result is a marked increase in part-time and non-tenure track positions which are renewed on a semester-to-semester basis. So while retrenchment is smoothed and organization flexibility increased, it is attained at considerable cost to the careers and job security of the exploited teachers.

Cutback management is a two-crucible problem: besides selecting tactics for either resisting or smoothing decline, if necessary, management must also select who will be let go and what programs will be curtailed or terminated. Deciding where to make cuts is a test of managerial intelligence and courage because each choice involves trade-offs and opportunity costs that cannot be erased through the generation of new resources accrued through growth.

As with most issues of public management involving the distribution of costs, the choice of decision rules to allocate cuts usually involves the trade-off between equity and efficiency.[35] In this case, "equity" is meant to mean the distribution of cuts across the organization with an equal probability of hurting all units and employees irrespective of impacts on the long-term capacity of the organization. "Efficiency" is meant to mean the sorting, sifting, and assignment of cuts to those people and units in the organization so that for a given budget decrement, cuts are allocated to minimize the long-term loss in total benefits to the organization as a whole, irrespective of their distribution.

Making cuts on the basis of equity is easier for managers because it is socially acceptable, easier to justify, and involves few decision-making costs. "Sharing the pain" is politically expedient because it appeals to common sense ideals of justice. Further, simple equity decision making avoids costs from sorting, selecting, and negotiating cuts.[36] In contrast, efficiency cuts involve costly triage analysis because the distribution of pain and inconvenience requires that the value of people and subunits to the organization have to be weighed in terms of their expected *future* contributions. In the public sector, of course, things are never quite this clear cut because a host of constraints like career status, veteran's preference, bumping rights, entitlements, and mandated programs limit managers from selecting optimal rules for making cuts. Nevertheless, the values of equity and efficiency are central to allocative decision making and provide useful criteria for judging the appropriateness of cutback rules. By applying these criteria to five of the most commonly used or proposed cutback methods—seniority, hiring freezes, even-percentage-cuts-across-the-board, productivity criteria, and zero-base budgeting—we are able to make assessments of their efficacy as managerial tools.

Seniority is the most prevalent and most maligned of the five decision rules. Seniority guarantees have little to do with either equity or efficiency, *per se*. Instead, they are directed at another value of public administration; that is, the need to provide secure career-long employment to neutrally competent civil servants.[37] Because seniority is likely to be spread about the organization unevenly, using seniority criteria for making cuts forces managers to implicitly surrender control over the impact of cuts on services and the capacity of subunits. Furthermore, since seniority usually dictates a "last-in-first-out" retention system, personnel cuts using this decision rule tend to inflict the greatest harm to minorities and women who are recent entrants in most public agencies.

A *hiring freeze* is a convenient short-run strategy to buy time and preserve options. In the short run it hurts no one already employed by the organization because hiring freezes rely on "natural attrition" through resignations, retirements, and death to diminish the size of an organization's work force. In the long run, however, hiring freezes are hardly the most equitable or efficient way to scale down organizational size. First, even though natural and self selection relieves the stress on managers, it also takes control over the decision of whom and where to cut away from management and thereby reduces the possibility of intelligent long range cutback planning. Second, hiring freezes are more likely to harm minorities and women who are more likely to be the next hired rather than the next retired. Third, attrition will likely occur at different rates among an organization's professional and technical specialties. Since resignations will most likely come from those employees with the most opportunities for employment elsewhere, during a long hiring freeze an organization may find itself short on some critically needed skills yet unable to hire people with these skills even though they may be available.

Even-percentage-cuts-across-the-board are expedient because they transfer decision-making costs lower in the organization, but they tend to be insensitive to the needs, production functions, and contributions of different units. The same percentage cut may call for hardly more than some mild belt tightening in some large unspecialized units but when translated into the elimination of one or two positions in a highly specialized, tightly integrated small unit, it may immobilize that unit.

Criticizing *productivity criteria* is more difficult but nevertheless appropriate, especially when the concept is applied to the practice of cutting low producing units and people based on their *marginal product* per increment of revenue. This method is insensitive to differences in clients served, unit capacity, effort, and need. A more appropriate criterion is one that cuts programs, organization units, and employees so that the *marginal utility* for a decrement of resources is equal across units, individuals, and programs thereby providing for *equal sacrifices* based on the *need* for resources. However, this criterion assumes organizations are fully rational actors, an assumption easily dismissed. More likely, cuts will be distributed by a mix of analysis and political bargaining.

Aggregating incompatible needs and preferences is a political problem and this is why *zero-base budgeting* gets such high marks as a method for making decisions about resource allocation under conditions of decline. First, ZBB is future directed; instead of relying on an "inviolate-base-plus-increment" calculus, it allows for the analysis of both existing and proposed new activities. Second, ZBB allows for trade-offs between programs or units below their present funding levels. Third, ZBB allows a ranking of decision packages by political bargaining and negotiation so that attention is concentrated on those packages or activities most likely to be affected by cuts.[38] As a result, ZBB allows both analysis and politics to enter into cutback decision making and therefore can incorporate an expression of the *intensity of need* for resources by participating managers and clients while also accommodating estimates of how cuts will affect the *activity levels* of their units. Nevertheless, ZBB is not without problems. Its analytic component is likely to be expensive—especially so under conditions of austerity—and to be subject to all the limitations and pitfalls of cost-benefit analysis, while its political component is likely to be costly in political terms as units fight with each other and with central management over rankings, trade-offs, and the assignment of decrements.[39]

These five decision rules illustrate how strategic choices about cutback management can be made with or without expediency, analysis, courage, consideration of the organization's long-term health, or the effect of cuts on the lives of employees and clients. Unfortunately, for some employees and clients, and the public interest, the choice will usually be made by managers to "go along" quietly with across-the-board cuts and exit as soon as possible. The alternative for those who would prefer more responsible and toughminded decision making *to facilitate long run organizational survival* is to develop in managers and employees strong feelings of organizational loyalty and loyalty to clients, to provide disincentives to easy exit, and to encourage participation so that dissenting views on the location of cuts could emerge from the ranks of middle management, lower level employees, and clients.[40]

Ponderables

The world of the future is uncertain, but scarcity and trade-offs seem in evitable. Boulding has argued, "in a stationary society roughly half the society will be experiencing decline while the other half will be experiencing growth."[41] If we are entering an era of general slowdown, this means that the balance in the distribution between expanding and contracting sectors, regions, and organizations will be tipped toward decline. It means that we will need a governmental capacity for developing trade-offs between growing and declining organizations and for intervening in regional and sectorial economies to avoid the potentially harmful effects of radical perturbations from unmanaged decline.

So far we have managed to get along without having to make conscious trade-offs between sectors and regions. We have met declines on a "crisis-to-crisis" basis through emergency legislation and financial aid. This is a strategy that assumes declines are special cases of temporary disequilibrium, bounded in time and space, that are usually confined to a single organization, community, or region. A broad scale long-run *societal level* decline, however, is a problem of a different magnitude and to resolve it, patch work solutions will not suffice.

There seem to be two possible directions in which to seek a way out of immobility. First is the authoritarian possibility; what Robert L. Heilbroner has called the rise of "iron governments" with civil liberties diminished and resources allocated throughout society from the central government without appeal.[42] This is a possibility abhorrent to the democratic tradition, but it comprises a possible future—if not for the United States in the near future, at least for some other less affluent nations. So far we have had little experience with cutting back on rights, entitlements, and privileges; but scarcity may dictate "decoupling" dependent and less powerful clients and overcoming resistance through violent autocratic implementation methods.

The other possible future direction involves new images and assumptions about the nature of man, the state and the ecosystem. It involves changes in values away from material consumption, a gradual withdrawal from our fascination with economic growth, and more efficient use of resources—especially raw materials. For this possibility to occur, we will have to have a confrontation with our propensity for wishful thinking that denies that some declines are permanent. Also required is a widespread acceptance of egalitarian norms and of anti-growth and no growth ideologies which are now only nascent, and the development of a political movement to promote their incorporation into policy making.[43] By backing away from our obsession with growth, we will also be able to diminish the "load" placed on central governments and allow for greater decentralization and the devolvement of functions.[44] In this way, we may be able to preserve democratic rights and processes while meeting a future of diminished resources.

However, the preferable future might not be the most probable future. This prospect should trouble us deeply.

Notes

1. The intellectual foundations of this essay are too numerous to list. Three essays in particular sparked my thinking: Herbert Kaufman's *The Limits of Organizational Change* (University, Ala.: The University of Alabama Press, 1971) and *Are Government Organizations Immortal?* (Washington, D.C.: The Brookings Institution, 1976) and Herbert J. Gans, "Planning for Declining and Poor Cities," *Journal of the American Institute of Planners* (September, 1975), pp. 305-307. The concept of "cutback planning" is introduced in the Gans article. My initial interest in this subject stemmed from my work with a panel of the National Academy of Public Administration on a NASA-sponsored project that produced *Report of the Ad Hoc Panel on Attracting New Staff and Retaining Capability During a Period of Declining Manpower Ceilings.*

2. For an explication of the concept of "organizational slack" see Richard M. Cyert and James G. March, *A Behavioral Theory of the Firm* (Englewood Cliffs, N.J.: Prentice-Hall, 1963), pp. 36-38. They argue that because of market imperfections between payments and demands "there is ordinarily a disparity between the resources available to the organization and the payments required to maintain the coalition. This difference between total resources and total necessary payments is what we have called *organizational slack.* Slack consists in payments to members of the coalition in excess of what is required to maintain the organization. . . . Many forms of slack typically exist: stockholders are paid dividends in excess of

those required to keep stockholders (or banks) within the organization; prices are set lower than necessary to maintain adequate income from buyers; wages in excess of those required to maintain labor are paid; executives are provided with services and personal luxuries in excess of those required to keep them; subunits are permitted to grow without real concern for the relation between additional payments and additional revenue; public services are provided in excess of those required. . . . Slack operates to stabilize the system in two ways: (1) by absorbing excess resources, it retards upward adjustment of aspirations during relatively good times; (2) by providing a pool of emergency resources, it permits aspirations to be maintained (and achieved) during relatively bad times."

3. See William G. Scott, "The Management of Decline," *The Conference Board RECORD* (June, 1976), pp. 56-59 and "Organization Theory: A Reassessment," *Academy of Management Journal* (June, 1974), pp. 242-253; also Rufus E. Miles, Jr., *Awakening from the American Dream: The Social and Political Limits to Growth* (New York: Universal Books, 1976).

4. See Daniel M. Fox, *The Discovery of Abundance: Simon N. Patten and the Transformation of Social Theory* (Ithaca, N.Y.: Cornell University Press, 1967).

5. See Andrew Glassberg, "Organizational Responses to Municipal Budget Decreases," *Public Administration Review,* July/August, 1978; and Edward H. Potthoff, Jr., "Pre-planning for Budget Reductions," *Public Management* (March, 1975), pp. 13-14.

6. See Donella H. Meadows, Dennis L. Meadows, Jorgen Randers, and William W. Behrens III, *The Limits to Growth* (New York: Universe Books, 1972); also Robert L. Heilbroner, *An Inquiry into the Human Prospect* (New York: W.W. Norton, 1975), and *Business Civilization in Decline* (New York: W.W. Norton, 1976).

7. See Advisory Commission on Intergovernmental Relations, *City Financial Emergencies: The Intergovernmental Dimension* (Washington, D.C.: U.S. Government Printing Office, 1973).

8. Kenneth E. Boulding, "The Management of Decline," *Change* (June, 1975), pp. 8-9 and 64. For extensive analyses of cutback management in the same field that Boulding addresses, university administration, see: Frank M. Bowen and Lyman A. Glenny, *State Budgeting for Higher Education: State Fiscal Stringency and Public Higher Education* (Berkeley, Calif.: Center for Research and Development in Higher Education, 1976); Adam Yarmolinsky, "Institutional Paralysis," *Special Report on American Higher Education: Toward an Uncertain Future* 2 Vol., *Daedalus* 104 (Winter, 1975), pp. 61-67; Frederick E. Balderston, *Varieties of Financial Crisis* (Berkeley, Calif.: Ford Foundation, 1972); The Carnegie Foundation for the Advancement of Teaching, *More Than Survival* (San Francisco: Jossey-Bass, 1975); Earl F. Cheit, *The New Depression in Higher Education* (New York: McGraw-Hill, 1975) and *The New Depression in Higher Education—Two Years Later* (Berkeley, Calif.: The Carnegie Commission on Higher Education, 1973); Lyman A. Glenny, "The Illusions of Steady States," *Change* 6 (December/January 1974-75), pp. 24-28; and John D. Millett, "What is Economic Health?" *Change* 8 (September 1976), p. 27.

9. Scott, "Organizational Theory: A Reassessment," p. 245.

10. Paul R. Schulman, "Nonincremental Policy Making: Notes Toward an Alternative Paradigm," *American Political Science Review* (December, 1975), pp. 1354-1370.

11. See Naomi Caiden and Aaron Wildavsky, *Planning and Budgeting in Poor Countries* (New York: John Wiley & Sons, 1974).

12. See James W. Vaupel, "Muddling Through Analytically," in Willis D. Hawley and David Rogers (eds.), *Improving Urban Management* (Beverly Hills, Calif.: Sage Publications, 1976), pp. 124-146.

13. See Richard M. Cyert's contribution to this symposium, "The Management of Universities of Constant or Decreasing Size."

14. See National Academy of Public Administration, *Report,* and Glassberg, "Organizational Response to Municipal Budget Decreases."

15. See NAPA *Report* and *Cancelled Careers: The Impact of Reduction-In-Force Policies on Middle-Aged Federal Employees,* A Report to the Special Committee on Aging, United

States Senate (Washington, D.C.: U.S. Government Printing Office, 1972).

16. See Albert O. Hirschman, *Exit, Voice and Loyalty: Responses to Decline in Firms, Organizations and States* (Cambridge, Mass.: Harvard University Press, 1970); also Mancur Olson, *The Logic of Collective Action* (Cambridge, Mass.: Harvard University Press, 1965).

17. The distinctive features of public organizations are discussed at greater length in Hal G. Rainey, Robert W. Backoff, and Charles H. Levine, "Comparing Public and Private Organization," *Public Administration Review* (March/April, 1976), pp. 223-244.

18. See Robert Behn's contribution to this symposium, "Closing a Government Facility," Barry Mitnick's "Deregulation as a Process of Organizational Reduction" and Herbert A. Simon, Donald W. Smithburg, and Victor A. Thompson, *Public Administration* (New York: Knopf, 1950) for discussions of the survival tactics of threatened bureaucrats.

19. This scheme is similar to those presented in Daniel Katz and Robert L. Kahn, *The Social Psychology of Organizations* (John Wiley & Sons, 1966), p. 166, and Gary L. Wamsley and Mayer N. Zald, *The Political Economy of Public Organizations: A Critique and Approach to the Study of Public Administration* (Lexington, Mass.: D.C. Heath, 1973), p. 20.

20. See Schulman, "Nonincremental Policy Making," and Charles O. Jones, "Speculative Augmentation in Federal Air Pollution Policy-Making," *Journal of Politics* (May, 1974), pp. 438-464.

21. See Robert Behn, "Closing the Massachusetts Public Training Schools," *Policy Sciences* (June, 1976), pp. 151-172; Valarie J. Bradley, "Policy Termination in Mental Health: The Hidden Agenda," *Policy Sciences* (June, 1976), pp. 215-224; and David J. Rothman, "Prisons, Asylums and Other Decaying Institutions," *The Public Interest* (Winter, 1972), pp. 3-17. A similar phenomena is occurring in some of the fields of regulation policy where deregulation is being made more politically feasible by a combination of technical and economic changes. See Mitnick, "Deregulation as a Process of Organizational Reduction," *Public Administration Review,* July/August 1978.

22. Peter deLeon, "Public Policy Termination: An End and a Beginning," an essay prepared at the request of the Congressional Research Service as background for the Sunset Act of 1977.

23. There are many variations on the themes of Sunset. Gary Brewer's "Termination: Hard Choices—Harder Questions," *Public Administration Review,* July/August 1978, identifies a number of problems central to most sunset proposals.

24. For two treatments of this phenomena in the literature of organization theory see Barry M. Staw and Eugene Szwajkowski, "The Scarcity-Munificence Component of Organizational Environments and the Commission of Illegal Acts," *Administrative Science Quarterly* (September, 1975), pp. 345-354, and Barry Bozeman and E. Allen Slusher, "The Future of Public Organizations Under Assumptions of Environmental Stress," paper presented at the Annual Meeting of the American Society for Public Administration, Phoenix, Arizona, April 9-12, 1978.

25. See Thomas Muller, *Growing and Declining Urban Areas: A Fiscal Comparison* (Washington, D.C.: Urban Institute, 1975).

26. See Richard P. Nathan and Charles Adams, "Understanding Central City Hardship," *Political Science Quarterly* (Spring, 1976), pp. 47-62; Terry Nichols Clark, Irene Sharp Rubin, Lynne C. Pettler, and Erwin Zimmerman, "How Many New Yorks? The New York Fiscal Crisis in Comparative Perspective" (Report No. 72 of Comparative Study of Community Decision-making, University of Chicago, April, 1976); and David T. Stanley, "The Most Troubled Cities," a discussion draft prepared for a meeting of the National Urban Policy Roundtable, Academy for Contemporary Problems, Summer, 1976.

27. See Richard Child Hill, "Fiscal Collapse and Political Struggle in Decaying Central Cities in the United States," in William K. Tabb and Larry Sawers (eds.), *Marxism and the Metropolis* (New York: Oxford University Press, 1978); and H. Paul Friesema, "Black Control of Central Cities: The Hollow Prize," *Journal of the American Institute of Planners* (March, 1969), pp. 75-79.

28. See David T. Stanley, "The Most Troubled Cities" and "The Survival of Troubled Cities," a

paper prepared for delivery at the 1977 Annual Meeting of the American Political Science Association, The Washington Hilton Hotel, Washington, D.C., September 1-4, 1977; and Martin Shefter, "New York City's Fiscal Crisis: The Politics of Inflation and Retrenchment," *The Public Interest* (Summer, 1977), pp. 98-127.

29. See Kaufman, *Are Government Organizations Immortal?* and "The Natural History of Human Organizations," *Administration and Society* (August, 1975), pp. 131-148; I have been working on this question for some time in collaboration with Ross Clayton. Our partially completed manuscript is entitled, "Organizational Aging: Progression or Degeneration." See also Edith Tilton Penrose, "Biological Analogies in the Theory of the Firm," *American Economic Review* (December, 1952), pp. 804-819 and Mason Haire, "Biological Models and Empirical Histories of the Growth of Organizations" in Mason Haire (ed.), *Modern Organization Theory* (New York: John Wiley & Sons, 1959), pp. 272-306.

30. For a fuller explanation of "smoothing" or "leveling," see James D. Thompson, *Organizations in Action* (New York: McGraw-Hill, 1967), pp. 19-24.

31. For recent analyses of related phenomena see Joel D. Aberbach and Bert A. Rockman, "Clashing Beliefs Within the Executive Branch: The Nixon Administration Bureaucracy," *American Political Science Review* (June, 1976), pp. 456-468 and Hugh Heclo, *A Government of Strangers: Executive Politics in Washington* (Washington, D.C.: The Brookings Institution, 1977).

32. See James G. March and Johan P. Olsen, *Ambiguity and Choice in Organizations* (Bergen, Norway: Universitetsforlaget, 1976); and Michael D. Cohen, James G. March, and Johan P. Olsen, "A Garbage Can Model of Organizational Choice," *Administrative Science Quarterly* (March, 1972), pp. 1-25.

33. See Charles Perrow, *Organizational Analysis: A Sociological View* (Belmont, Calif.: Wadsworth Publishing Company, 1970) and Chris Argyris and Donald A. Schon, *Theory in Practice: Increasing Professional Effectiveness* (San Francisco, Calif.: Jossey-Bass, 1974) for discussions of the distinction between espoused and operative (i.e., "theory-in-use") strategies.

34. For extensive treatments of the tactics of bureaucrats, some of which are listed here, see Frances E. Rourke, *Bureaucracy, Politics, and Public Policy* (second edition, Boston: Little, Brown and Company, 1976); Aaron Wildavsky, *The Politics of the Budgetary Process* (second edition, Boston: Little, Brown and Company, 1974); Eugene Lewis, *American Politics in a Bureaucratic Age* (Cambridge, Mass.: Winthrop Publishers, 1977); and Simon, Smithburg and Thompson, *Public Administration.*

35. See Arthur M. Oken, *Equality and Efficiency: The Big Tradeoff* (Washington, D.C.: The Brookings Institution, 1975).

36. For a discussion of the costs of interactive decision making see Charles R. Adrian and Charles Press, "Decision Costs in Coalition Formation," *American Political Science Review* (June, 1968), pp. 556-563.

37. See Herbert Kaufman, "Emerging Conflicts in the Doctrine of Public Administration," *American Political Science Review* (December, 1956), pp. 1057-1073 and Frederick C. Mosher, *Democracy and the Public Service* (New York: Oxford University Press, 1968). Seniority criteria also have roots in the widespread belief that organizations ought to recognize people who invest heavily in them by protecting long time employees when layoffs become necessary.

38. See Peter A. Pyhrr, "The Zero-Base Approach to Government Budgeting," *Public Administration Review* (January/February, 1977), pp. 1-8; Graeme M. Taylor, "Introduction to Zero-base Budgeting," *The Bureaucrat* (Spring, 1977), pp. 33-55.

39. See Brewer, "Termination: Hard Choices—Harder Questions"; Allen Schick, "Zero-base Budgeting and Sunset: Redundancy or Symbiosis?" *The Bureaucrat* (Spring, 1977), pp. 12-32 and "The Road From ZBB," *Public Administration Review* (March/April, 1978), pp. 177-180; and Aaron Wildavsky, "The Political Economy of Efficiency," *Public Administration Review* (December, 1966), pp. 292-310.

40. See Hirschman, *Exit, Voice and Loyalty,* especially Ch. 7, "A Theory of Loyalty," pp.

76-105. Despite the attractiveness of "responsible and toughminded decision making" the constraints on managerial discretion in contraction decisions should not be underestimated. At the local level, for example, managers often have little influence on what federally funded programs will be cut back or terminated. They are often informed after funding cuts have been made in Washington and they are expected to make appropriate adjustments in their local work forces. These downward adjustments often are also outside of a manager's control because in many cities with merit systems, veteran's preference, and strong unions, elaborate rules dictate who will be dismissed and the timing of dismissals.

41. Boulding, "The Management of Decline," p. 8.
42. See Heilbroner, *An Inquiry into the Human Prospect;* also Michael Harrington, *The Twilight of Capitalism* (New York: Simon & Schuster, 1976).
43. For a discussion of anti-growth politics see Harvey Molotch, "The City as a Growth Machine," *American Journal of Sociology* (September, 1976), pp. 309-332.
44. Richard Rose has made a penetrating argument about the potential of governments to become "overloaded" in "Comment: What Can Ungovernability Mean?" *Futures* (April 1977), pp. 92-94. For a more detailed presentation, see his "On the Priorities of Government: A Developmental Analysis of Public Policies," *European Journal of Political Research* (September 1976), pp. 247-290. This theme is also developed by Rose in collaboration with B. Guy Peters in *Can Governments Go Bankrupt?* (New York: Basic Books, 1978).

PART II

Considerations in Designing the Enterprise: Five Guiding Foci

1. Herbert A. Simon, "The Proverbs of Administration"
2. Rufus E. Miles, "Considerations for a President Bent on Reorganization"
3. Frederic N. Cleaveland, "Administrative Decentralization in the U.S. Bureau of Reclamation"
4. Philip M. Marcus and Dora Marcus, "Control in Modern Organizations"
5. O. Glenn Stahl, "Straight Talk About Label Thinking"

AGAIN, Herbert A. Simon provides our opening selection—his well-known "The Proverbs of Administration." This is just as it should be, for that selection has been a seminal one in public administration. Basically, Simon's "Proverbs" convincingly demonstrates the serious logical and empirical inadequacies of the traditional theory of organization, the "bureaucratic principles." For example, he shows that two of its major prescriptions—those dealing with unity of command and specialization—imply exactly opposite courses of action. Simon was not the first to call attention to the theory's inadequacies,[1] nor was he the last. But his argument is the clear winner for vigorous and relentless exposition, at least in this observer's view.

Although Simon's work was not sufficient to destroy what he calls the "more common 'principles' in the literature of administration," his warnings and those of others have had a visible impact—generally on what was called organization analysis and theory, or OA & T, and specifically on those contributing to the *Public Administration Review*. The four other selections in Part II, in fact, variously reflect such an impact on both thought and practice.

These four selections can be introduced briefly. The first two selections constitute a bird's-eye-view-of-the-worm and a worm's-eye-view-of-the-bird, respectively. Thus, Rufus E. Miles writes for the loftier perspective in his "Considerations for a President Bent on Reorganization." His thoughtful piece seeks to provide a generalized perspective appropriate at the level of the president of the United States. The selection well represents the better work in the OA & T tradition—anxious to learn from experience, cautious in generalization, and neither rigidly committed to the bureaucratic principles for organization nor doctrinaire about rejecting them. Several of Miles' prescriptions have a bite to them, nonetheless, as they flatly reject some of the "principles" criticized by Simon. For example, Miles urges the usefulness of a relatively broad span of control, that is, of a large number of subordinates reporting to a common superior. In this basic way does Miles join in Simon's critique.

Frederic N. Cleaveland provides a somewhat different example of the same critical posture. His "Administrative Decentralization in the U.S. Bureau of Reclamation" has its basic focus on the "work level," on lower organization levels. A direct contrast helps fix Cleaveland's focus. The "principles" prescribe a "tall" and centralized organization, and this top-down view is well-designed to induce a monopoly of power or influence at the top levels of organization. But this centralization also can impede the processes of hewing wood and carrying water, as much experience and the bulk of the organization behavior literature establish in great detail. Adopting a bottom-up perspective, in large part, Cleaveland draws attention to the benefits of decentralization, at least for certain kinds of missions beyond some early and chaotic stages of development. This drawing of attention does not propose to "give away the store," be it noted. Cleaveland develops the family of trade-offs involved in the choice of a mode of allocating authority, trade-offs that can differ for various parts of an organization at one point in time or another.

Philip M. Marcus and Dora Marcus extend Cleaveland's basic argument in their "Control in Modern Organizations." They draw on a vital line of OB research, and develop its implications for OA & T, or organization analysis and theory, as well as for organization development, or OD. Basically, they define four types of "control curves," and summarize the behavioral research relevant to the kinds of personal adaptations and organization performances that are likely to be induced by one control curve or another.

Again, the "principles" central to so much management thought and practice come off as lacking in specificity, and often as pointing in precisely the wrong direction. Those principles prescribe *a* control curve for all or most conditions, but that curve under a broad range of conditions tends to generate awkward individual adaptations that show up in inadequate organizational performance and diminished employee satisfaction. This theme represents a major contribution of the OB approach that will eventually be well-integrated into a comprehensive organization theory.

Marcus and Marcus notwithstanding, much remains undone. Consider the many other ways in which the "proverbs" or "principles," often reflected in the early OA & T approach, have established dominant positions in theory and practice. One such crucial position involves line-staff relationships, telling attention to which is directed by O. Glenn Stahl's "Straight Talk About Label Thinking." Again, Stahl probes at central weaknesses in the "principles." They prescribe the unabridged centrality of line officials or, to say the same thing differently, they propose a narrow view of control and command. This leaves staff officials—in what amounts to analysis by residual definition—with what is left over, or "service." In complex organizations, Stahl proposes, such simplicisms can seriously impede matters. He gets right to the heart of it—"I submit that what is 'service' at one point may be 'control' at another." And so it should be, he no doubt would add.

The common principles of organization encourage neglect of the subtle issues involved in a concept of control that encompasses the two sides of staff activities, Stahl implies, and organizations will be worse off for avoidance of the real issue for theory and practice. That issue? It involves defining what Stahl in another place[2] calls a "network of authority" that reflects aspects of both service and control. To which all three major approaches to organization theory and practice would say, fervently: Amen, brother. Amen. Specifically, later work in the OA & T tradition sees line/staff relationships as a frequent storm-center.[3] Moreover, descriptive OB studies add strong support to that correct global view, as well as provide useful clinical detail.[4] And OD interventions have sought to ease line/staff relationships. One approach relies on learning designs that encourage the development of skills and attitudes that can reduce some of the trauma induced by the typical structuring of line/staff activities.[5]

Notes

1. Perhaps the earliest major critique is Francis W. Coker's "Dogmas of Administrative Reform," *American Political Science Review,* Vol. 16 (August, 1922), pp. 399-411.
2. O. Glenn Stahl, "Network of Authority," *Public Administration Review,* Vol. 18 (Winter, 1958), pp. ii-iv.
3. Ernest Dale and Lyndall F. Urwick, *Staff in Organization* (New York: McGraw-Hill, 1960), esp. pp. 89-109.
4. See, for example, Melville Dalton, *Men Who Manage* (New York: Wiley, 1959).
5. E.g., William G. Dyer, Robert F. Maddocks, J. Weldon Moffitt, and William J. Underwood, "A Laboratory-Consultation Model for Organization Change," pp. 307-323, in W. Warner Burke and Harvey A. Hornstein, editors, *The Social Technology of Organization Development* (Fairfax, Va.: NTL Learning Resources Corp., 1972).

HERBERT A. SIMON

The Proverbs of Administration

A fact about proverbs that greatly enhances their quotability is that they almost always occur in mutually contradictory pairs. "Look before you leap!"—but "He who hesitates is lost."

This is both a great convenience and a serious defect—depending on the use to which one wishes to put the proverbs in question. If it is a matter of rationalizing behavior that has already taken place or justifying action that has already been decided upon, proverbs are ideal. Since one is never at a loss to find one that will prove his point—or the precisely contradictory point, for that matter—they are a great help in persuasion, political debate, and all forms of rhetoric.

But when one seeks to use proverbs as the basis of a scientific theory, the situation is less happy. It is not that the propositions expressed by the proverbs are insufficient; it is rather that they prove too much. A scientific theory should tell what is true but also what is false. If Newton had announced to the world that particles of matter exert either an attraction or a repulsion on each other, he would not have added much to scientific knowledge. His contribution consisted in showing that an attraction was exercised and in announcing the precise law governing its operation.

Most of the propositions that make up the body of administrative theory today share, unfortunately, this defect of proverbs. For almost every principle one can find an equally plausible and acceptable contradictory principle. Although the two principles of the pair will lead to exactly opposite organizational recommendations, there is nothing in the theory to indicate which is the proper one to apply.[1]

It is the purpose of this paper to substantiate this sweeping criticism of administrative theory, and to present some suggestions—perhaps less concrete than they should be—as to how the existing dilemma can be solved.

Some Accepted Administrative Principles

Among the more common "principles" that occur in the literature of administration are these:

1. Administrative efficiency is increased by a specialization of the task among the group.

2. Administrative efficiency is increased by arranging the members of the group in a determinate hierarchy of authority.

3. Administrative efficiency is increased by limiting the span of control at any point in the hierarchy to a small number.

4. Administrative efficiency is increased by grouping the workers, for purposes of control, according to (a) purpose, (b) process, (c) clientele, or (d) place. (This is really an elaboration of the first principle but deserves separate discussion).

Since these principles appear relatively simple and clear, it would seem that their application to concrete problems of administrative organization would be unambiguous and that their validity would be easily submitted to empirical test. Such, however, seems not to be the case. To show why it is not, each of the four principles just listed will be considered in turn.

Specialization. Administrative efficiency is supposed to increase with an increase in specialization. But is this intended to mean that *any* increase in specialization will increase efficiency? If so, which of the following alternatives is the correct application of the principle in a particular case?

1. A plan of nursing should be put into effect by which nurses will be assigned to districts and do all nursing within that district, including school examinations, visits to homes or school children, and tuberculosis nursing.

2. A functional plan of nursing should be put into effect by which different nurses will be assigned to school examinations, visits to homes of school children, and tuberculosis nursing. The present method of generalized nursing by districts impedes the development of specialized skills in the three very diverse programs.

Both of these administrative arrangements satisfy the requirement of specialization—the first provides specialization by place; the second, specialization by function. The principle of specialization is of no help at all in choosing between the two alternatives.

It appears that the simplicity of the principle of specialization is a deceptive simplicity—a simplicity which conceals fundamental ambiguities. For "specialization" is not a condition of efficient administration; it is an inevitable characteristic of all group effort, however efficient or inefficient that effort may be. Specialization merely means that different persons are doing different things—and since it is physically impossible for two persons to be doing the same thing in the same place at the same time, two persons are always doing different things.

The real problem of administration, then, is not to "specialize," but to specialize in that particular manner and along those particular lines which will lead to administrative efficiency. But, in thus rephrasing this "principle" of administration, there has been brought clearly into the open its fundamental ambiguity: "Administrative efficiency is increased by a specialization of the task among the group in the direction which will lead to greater efficiency."

Further discussion of the choice between competing bases of specialization will be undertaken after two other principles of administration have been examined.

Unity of Command. Administrative efficiency is supposed to be enhanced by arranging the members of the organization in a determinate hierarchy of authority in order to preserve "unity of command."

Analysis of this "principle" requires a clear understanding of what is meant by the term "authority." A subordinate may be said to accept authority whenever he permits his behavior to be guided by a decision reached by another, irrespective of his own judgment as to the merits of that decision.

In one sense the principle of unity of command, like the principle of specialization, cannot be violated; for it is physically impossible for a man to obey two contradictory commands—that is what is meant by "contradictory commands." Presumably, if unity of command is a principle of administration, it must assert something more than this physical impossibility. Perhaps it asserts this: that it is undesirable to place a member of an organization in a position where he receives orders from more than one superior. This is evidently the meaning that Gulick attaches to the principle when he says,

> The significance of this principle in the process of co-ordination and organization must not be lost sight of. In building a structure of co-ordination, it is often tempting to set up more than one boss for a man who is doing work which has more than one relationship. Even as great a philosopher of management as Taylor fell into this error in setting up separate foremen to deal with machinery, with materials, with speed, etc., each with the power of giving orders directly to the individual workman. The rigid adherence to the principle of unity of command may have its absurdities; these are, however, unimportant in comparison with the certainty of confusion, inefficiency and irresponsibility which arise from the violation of the principle.[1]

Certainly the principle of unity of command, thus interpreted, cannot be criticized for any lack of clarity or any ambiguity. The definition of authority given above should provide a clear test whether, in any concrete situation, the principle is observed. The real fault that must be found with this principle is that it is incompatible with the principle of specialization. One of the most important uses to which authority is put in organization is to bring about specialization in the work of making decisions, so that each decision is made at a point in the organization where it can be made most expertly. As a result, the use of authority permits a greater degree of expertness to be achieved in decision making than would be possible if each operative employee had himself to make all the decisions upon which his activity is predicated. The individual fireman does not decide whether to use a two-inch hose or a fire extinguisher; that is decided for him by his officers, and the decision is communicated to him in the form of a command.

However, if unity of command, in Gulick's sense, is observed, the decisions of a person at any point in the administrative hierarchy are subject to influence through only one channel of authority; and if his decisions are of a kind that require expertise in more than one field of knowledge, then advisory and informational services must be relied upon to supply those premises which lie in a field not recognized by the mode of specialization in the organization. For example, if an accountant in a school department is subordinate to an educator, and if unity of command is observed, then the finance department cannot issue direct orders to him regarding the technical, accounting aspects of his work. Similarly, the director of motor vehicles in the public works department will be unable to issue direct orders on care of motor equipment to the fire-truck driver.[3]

Gulick, in the statement quoted above, clearly indicates the difficulties to be faced if unity of command is not observed. A certain amount of irresponsibility and confusion are almost certain to ensue. But perhaps this is not too great a price to pay for the increased expertise that can be applied to decisions. What is needed to decide the issue is a principle of administration that would enable one to weigh the relative advantages of the two courses of action. But neither the principle of unity of command nor the principle of specialization is helpful in adjudicating the controversy. They merely contradict each other without indicating any procedure for resolving the contradiction.

If this were merely an academic controversy—if it were generally agreed and had been generally demonstrated that unity of command must be preserved in all cases, even with a loss in expertise—one could assert that in case of conflict between the two principles, unity of command should prevail. But the issue is far from clear, and experts can be ranged on both sides of the controversy. On the side of unity of command there may be cited the dictums of Gulick and others.[4] On the side of specialization there are Taylor's theory of functional supervision, Macmahon and Millett's idea of "dual supervision," and the practice of technical supervision in military organization.[5]

It may be, as Gulick asserts, that the notion of Taylor and these others is an "error." If so, the evidence that it is an error has never been marshalled or published—apart from loose heuristic arguments like that quoted above. One is left with a choice between equally eminent theorists of administration and without any evidential basis for making that choice.

What evidence there is of actual administrative practice would seem to indicate that the need for specialization is to a very large degree given priority over the need for unity of command. As a matter of fact, it does not go too far to say that unity of command, in Gulick's sense, never has existed in any administrative organization. If a line officer accepts the regulations of an accounting department with regard to the procedure for making requisitions, can it be said that, in this sphere, he is not subject to the authority of the accounting department? In any actual administrative situation authority is zoned, and to maintain that this zoning does not contradict the principle of unity of command requires a very different definition of authority from that used here. This subjection of the line officer to the accounting department is no different, in principle, from Taylor's recommendation that in the matter of work programming a workman be subject to one foreman, in the matter of machine operation to another.

The principle of unity of command is perhaps more defensible if narrowed down to the following: In case two authoritative commands conflict, there should be a single determinate person whom the subordinate is expected to obey; and the sanctions of authority should be applied against the subordinate only to enforce his obedience to that one person.

If the principle of unity of command is more defensible when stated in this limited form, it also solves fewer problems. In the first place, it no longer requires, except for settling conflicts of authority, a single hierarchy of authority. Consequently, it leaves unsettled the very important question of how authority should be zoned in a particular organization (i.e., the modes of specialization) and through what channels it should be exercised. Finally, even this narrower concept of unity of command conflicts with the principle of specialization, for whenever disagreement does occur and the organization members revert to the formal lines of authority, then only those types of specialization which are represented in the hierarchy of authority can impress themselves on decision. If the training officer of a city exercises only functional supervision over the police training officer, then in case of disagreement with the police chief, specialized knowledge of police problems will determine the outcome while specialized knowledge of training problems will be subordinated or ignored. That this actually occurs is shown by the frustration so commonly expressed by functional supervisors at their lack of authority to apply sanctions.

Span of Control. Administrative efficiency is supposed to be enhanced by limiting the number of subordinates who report directly to any one administrator to a small number—say six. This notion that the "span of control" should be narrow is confidently asserted as a third incontrovertible principle of administration. The usual common-sense arguments for restricting the span of control are familiar and need not be repeated here. What is not so generally recognized is that a contradictory proverb of administration can be stated which, though it is not so familiar as the principle of span of control, can be supported by arguments of equal plausibility. The proverb in question is the following: Administrative efficiency is enhanced by keeping at a minimum the number of organizational levels through which a matter must pass before it is acted upon.

This latter proverb is one of the fundamental criteria that guide administrative analysts in procedures simplification work. Yet in many situations the results to which this principle leads are in direct contradiction to the requirements of the principle of span of control, the principle of unity of command, and the principle of specialization. The present discussion is concerned with the first of these conflicts. To illustrate the difficulty, two alternative proposals for the organization of a small health department will be presented— one based on the restriction of span of control, the other on the limitation of number of organization levels:

1. The present organization of the department places an administrative overload on the health officer by reason of the fact that all eleven employees of the department report directly to him and the further fact that some of the staff lack adequate technical training. Consequently, venereal disease clinic treatments and other details require an undue amount of the health officer's personal attention.

It has previously been recommended that the proposed medical officer be placed in charge of the venereal disease and chest clinics and all child hygiene work. It is further recommended that one of the inspectors be designated chief inspector and placed in charge of all the department's inspectional activities and that one of the nurses be designated as head nurse. This will relieve the health commissioner of considerable detail and will leave him greater freedom to plan and supervise the health program as a whole, to conduct health education, and to coordinate the work of the department with that of other community agencies. If the department were thus organized, the effectiveness of all employees could be substantially increased.

2. The present organization of the department leads to inefficiency and excessive red tape by reason of the fact that an unnecessary supervisory level intervenes between the health officer and the operative employees, and that those four of the twelve employees who are best trained technically are engaged largely in "overhead" administrative duties. Consequently, unnecessary delays occur in securing the approval of the health officer on matters requiring his attention, and too many matters require review and re-review.

The medical officer should be left in charge of the venereal disease and chest clinics and child hygiene work. It is recommended, however, that the position of chief inspector and head nurse be abolished and that the employees now filling these positions perform regular inspectional and nursing duties. The details of work scheduling now handled by these two employees can be taken care of more economically by the secretary to the health officer, and, since broader matters of policy have, in any event, always required the personal attention of the health officer, the abolition of these two positions will eliminate a wholly unnecessary step in review, will allow an expansion of inspectional and nursing services, and will permit at least a beginning to be made in the recommended program of health education. The number of persons reporting directly to the health officer will be increased to nine, but since there are few matters requiring the coordination of these employees, other than the work schedules and policy questions referred to above, this change will not materially increase his work load.

The dilemma is this: in a large organization with complex interrelations between members, a restricted span of control inevitably produces excessive red tape, for each contact between organization members must be carried upward until a common superior is found. If the organization is at all large, this will involve carrying all such matters upward through several levels of officials for decision and then downward again in the form of orders and instructions—a cumbersome and time-consuming process.

The alternative is to increase the number of persons who are under the command of each officer, so that the pyramid will come more rapidly to a peak, with fewer intervening levels. But this, too, leads to difficulty, for if an officer is required to supervise too many employees, his control over them is weakened.

If it is granted, then, that both the increase and the decrease in span of control has some undesirable consequences, what is the optimum point? Proponents of a restricted span of control have suggested three, five, even eleven, as suitable numbers, but nowhere have they explained the reasoning which led them to the particular number they selected. The principle as stated casts no light on this very crucial question. One is reminded of current arguments about the proper size of the national debt.

Organization by Purpose, Process, Clientele, Place. Administrative efficiency is supposed to be increased by grouping workers according to (a) purpose, (b) process, (c) clientele, or (d) place. But from the discussion of specialization it is clear that this principle is internally inconsistent; for purpose, process, clientele, and place are competing bases of organization, and at any given point of division the advantages of three must be sacrificed to secure the advantages of the fourth. If the major departments of a city, for example, are organized on the basis of major purpose, then it follows that all the physicians, all the lawyers, all the engineers, all the statisticians will not be located in a single department exclusively composed of members of their profession but will be distributed among the various city departments needing their services. The advantages of organization by process will thereby be partly lost.

Some of these advantages can be regained by organizing on the basis of process *within* the major departments. Thus there may be an engineering bureau within the public works department, or the board of education may have a school health service as a major division of its work. Similarly, within smaller units there may be division by area or by clientele: e.g., a fire department will have separate companies located throughout the city, while a welfare department may have intake and case work agencies in various locations. Again, however, these major types of specialization cannot be simultaneously achieved, for at any point in the organization it must be decided whether specialization at the next level will be accomplished by distinction of major purpose, major process, clientele, or area.

. The conflict may be illustrated by showing how the principle of specialization according to purpose would lead to a different result from specialization according to clientele in the organization of a health department.

1. Public health administration consists of the following activities for the prevention of disease and the maintenance of healthful conditions: (1) vital statistics; (2) child hygiene—prenatal, maternity, postnatal, infant, preschool, and school health programs; (3) communicable disease control; (4) inspection of milk, foods, and drugs; (5) sanitary inspection; (6) laboratory service; (7) health education.

One of the handicaps under which the health department labors is the fact that the department has no control over school health, that being an activity of the county board of education, and there is little or no coordination between that highly important part of the community health program and the balance of the program which is conducted by the city-county health unit. It is recommended that the city and county open negotiations with the board of education for the transfer of all school health work and the appropriation therefor to the joint health unit. . . .

2. To the modern school department is entrusted the care of children during almost

the entire period that they are absent from the parental home. It has three principal responsibilities toward them: (1) to provide for their education in useful skills and knowledge and in character; (2) to provide them with wholesome play activities outside school hours; (3) to care for their health and to assure the attainment of minimum standards of nutrition.

One of the handicaps under which the school board labors is that fact that, except for school lunches, the board has no control over child health and nutrition, and there is little or no coordination between that highly important part of the child development program and the balance of the program which is conducted by the board of education. It is recommended that the city and county open negotiations for the transfer of all health work for children of school age to the board of education.

Here again is posed the dilemma of choosing between alternative, equally plausible, administrative principles. But this is not the only difficulty in the present case, for a closer study of the situation shows there are fundamental ambiguities in the meanings of the key terms—"purpose," "process," "clientele," and "place."

"Purpose" may be roughly defined as the objective or end for which an activity is carried on; "process" as a means for accomplishing a purpose. Processes, then, are carried on in order to achieve purposes. But purposes themselves may generally be arranged in some sort of hierarchy. A typist moves her fingers in order to type; types in order to reproduce a letter; reproduces a letter in order that an inquiry may be answered. Writing a letter is then the purpose for which the typing is performed; while writing a letter is also the process whereby the purpose of replying to an inquiry is achieved. It follows that the same activity may be described as purpose or as process.

This ambiguity is easily illustrated for the case of an administrative organization. A health department conceived as a unit whose task it is to care for the health of the community is a purpose organization; the same department conceived as a unit which makes use of the medical arts to carry on its work is a process organization. In the same way, an education department may be viewed as a purpose (to educate) organization, or a clientele (children) organization; the forest service as a purpose (forest conservation), process (forest management), clientele (lumbermen and cattlemen utilizing public forests), or area (publicly owned forest lands) organization. When concrete illustrations of this sort are selected, the lines of demarcation between these categories become very hazy and unclear indeed.

"Organization by major purpose," says Gulick, ". . . serves to bring together in a single large department all of those who are at work endeavoring to render a particular service."[6] But what is a particular service? Is fire protection a single purpose, or is it merely a part of the purpose of public safety?—or is it a combination of purposes including fire prevention and fire fighting? It must be concluded that there is no such thing as a purpose, or a unifunctional (single-purpose) organization. What is to be considered a single function depends entirely on language and techniques.[7] If the English language has a comprehensive term which covers both of two subpurposes it is natural to think of the two together as a single purpose. If such a term is lacking, the two subpurposes become purposes in their own right. On the other hand, a single activity may contribute to several objectives, but since they are technically (procedurally) inseparable, the activity is considered a single function or purpose.

The fact, mentioned previously, that purposes form a hierarchy, each subpurpose contributing to some more final and comprehensive end, helps to make clear the relation between purpose and process. "Organization by major process," says Gulick, ". . . tends to bring together in a single department all of those who are at work making use of a given special skill or technology, or are members of a given profession."[8] Consider a simple skill of this kind—typing. Typing is a skill which brings about a means-end coordination of muscular movements, but at a very low level in the means-end hierarchy. The content of the typewritten letter is indifferent to the skill that produces it. The skill consists merely in the ability to hit the letter *"t"* quickly whenever the letter *"t"* is required by the content and to hit the letter *"a"* whenever the letter *"a"* is required by the content.

There is, then, no essential difference between a "purpose" and a "process," but only a distinction of degree. A "process" is an activity whose immediate purpose is at a low level in the hierarchy of means and ends, while a "purpose" is a collection of activities whose orienting value or aim is at a high level in the means-end hierarchy.

Next consider "clientele" and "place" as bases of organization. These categories are really not separate from purpose, but a part of it. A complete statement of the purpose of a fire department would have to include the area served by it: "to reduce fire losses on property in the city of X." Objectives of an administrative organization are phrased in terms of a service to be provided and an area for which it is provided. Usually, the term "purpose" is meant to refer only to the first element, but the second is just as legitimately an aspect of purpose. Area of service, of course, may be a specified clientele quite as well as a geographical area. In the case of an agency which works on "shifts," time will be a third dimension of purpose—to provide a given service in a given area (or to a given clientele) during a given time period.

With this clarification of terminology, the next task is to reconsider the problem of specializing the work of an organization. It is no longer legitimate to speak of a "purpose" organization, a "process" organization, a "clientele" organization, or an "area" organization. The same unit might fall into any one of these four categories, depending on the nature of the larger organizational unit of which it was a part. A unit providing public health and medical services for school-age children in Multnomah County might be considered (1) an "area" organization if it were part of a unit providing the same service for the state of Oregon; (2) a "clientele" organization if it were part of a unit providing similar services for children of all ages; (3) a "purpose" or a "process" organization (it would be impossible to say which) if it were part of an education department.

It is incorrect to say that Bureau A is a process bureau; the correct statement is that Bureau A is a process bureau *within* Department X.' This latter statement would mean that Bureau A incorporates all the processes of a certain kind in Department X, without reference to any special subpurposes, subareas, or subclientele of Department X. Now it is conceivable that a particular unit might incorporate all processes of a certain kind but that these processes might relate to only certain particular subpurposes of the department purpose. In this case, which corresponds to the health unit in an education department mentioned above, the unit would be specialized by both purpose and process. The health unit would be the only one in the education department using the medical art (process) and concerned with health (subpurpose).

Even when the problem is solved of proper usage for the terms "purpose," "process," "clientele," and "area," the principles of administration give no guide as to which of these four competing bases of specialization is applicable in any particular situation. The British Machinery of Government Committee had no doubts about the matter. It considered purpose and clientele as the two possible bases of organization and put its faith entirely in the former. Others have had equal assurance in choosing between purpose and process. The reasoning which leads to these unequivocal conclusions leaves something to be desired. The Machinery of Government Committee gives this sole argument for its choice:

Now the inevitable outcome of this method of organization [by clientele] is a tendency to Lilliputian administration. It is impossible that the specialized service which each Department has to render to the community can be of as high a standard when its work is at the same time limited to a particular class of persons and extended to every variety of provision for them, as when the Department concentrates itself on the provision of the particular service only by whomsoever required, and looks beyond the interest of comparatively small classes.[10]

The faults in this analysis are obvious. First, there is no attempt to determine how *a* service is to be recognized. Second, there is a bald assumption, absolutely without proof, that a child health unit, for example, in a department of child welfare could not offer services of "as high a standard" as the same unit if it were located in a department of health. Just how the shifting of the unit from one department to another would improve or damage the quality of its work is not explained. Third, no basis is set forth for adjudicating the competing claims of purpose and process—the two are merged in the ambiguous term "service." It is not necessary here to decide whether the committee was right or wrong in its recommendation; the important point is that the recommendation represented a choice, without any apparent logical or empirical grounds, between contradictory principles of administration.

Even more remarkable illustrations of illogic can be found in most discussions of purpose *vs.* process. They would be too ridiculous to cite if they were not commonly used in serious political and administrative debate.

For instance, where should agricultural education come: in the Ministry of Education, or of Agriculture? That depends on whether we want to see the best farming taught, though possibly by old methods, or a possibly out-of-date style of farming, taught in the most modern and compelling manner. The question answer itself.[11]

But does the question really answer itself? Suppose a bureau of agricultural education were set up, headed for example, by a man who had had extensive experience in agricultural research or as administrator of an agricultural school, and staffed by men of similarly appropriate background. What reason is there to believe that if attached to a Ministry of Education they would teach old-fashioned farming by new-fashioned methods, while if attached to a Ministry of Agriculture they would teach new-fashioned farming by old-fashioned methods? The administrative problem of such a bureau would be to teach new-fashioned farming by new-fashioned methods, and it is a little difficult to see how the departmental location of the unit would affect this result. "The question answers itself" only if one has a rather mystical faith in the potency of bureau-shuffling as a means for redirecting the activities of an agency.

These contradictions and competitions have received increasing attention from students of administration during the past few years. For example, Gulick, Wallace, and Benson have stated certain advantages and disadvantages of the several modes of specialization, and have considered the conditions under which one or the other mode might best be adopted.[12] All this analysis has been at a theoretical level—in the sense that data have not been employed to demonstrate the superior effectiveness claimed for the different modes. But though theoretical, the analysis has lacked a theory. Since no comprehensive framework has been constructed within which the discussion could take place, the analysis has tended either to the logical one-sidedness which characterizes the examples quoted above or to inconclusiveness.

The Impasse of Administrative Theory. The four "principles of administration" that were set forth at the beginning of this paper have now been subjected to critical analysis. None of the four survived in very good shape, for in each case there was found, instead of an unequivocal principle, a set of two or more mutually incompatible principles apparently equally applicable to the administrative situation.

Moreover, the reader will see that the very same objections can be urged against the customary discussions of "centralization" *vs.* "decentralization," which usually conclude, in effect, that "on the one hand, centralization of decision-making functions is desirable; on the other hand, there are definite advantages in decentralization."

Can anything be salvaged which will be useful in the construction of an administrative theory? As a matter of fact, almost everything can be salvaged. The difficulty has arisen from treating as "principles of administration" what are really only criteria for describing and diagnosing administrative situations. Closet space is certainly an important item in the design of a successful house;

yet a house designed entirely with a view to securing a maximum of closet space—all other considerations being forgotten—would be considered, to say the least, somewhat unbalanced. Similarly, unity of command, specialization by purpose, decentralization are all items to be considered in the design of an efficient administrative organization. No single one of these items is of sufficient importance to suffice as a guiding principle for the administrative analyst. In the design of administrative organizations, as in their operation, over-all efficiency must be the guiding criterion. Mutually incompatible advantages must be balanced against each other, just as an architect weighs the advantages of additional closet space against the advantages of a larger living room.

This position, if it is a valid one, constitutes an indictment of much current writing about administrative matters. As the examples cited in this chapter amply demonstrate, much administrative analysis proceeds by selecting a single criterion and applying it to an administrative situation to reach a recommendation; while the fact that equally valid, but contradictory, criteria exist which could be applied with equal reason, but with a different result, is conveniently ignored. A valid approach to the study of administration requires that *all* the relevant diagnostic criteria be identified; that each administrative situation be analyzed in terms of the entire set of criteria; and that research be instituted to determine how weights can be assigned to the several criteria when they are, as they usually will be, mutually incompatible.

An Approach to Administrative Theory

This program needs to be considered step by step. First, what is included in the description of administrative situations for purposes of such an analysis? Second, how can weights be assigned to the various criteria to give them their proper place in the total picture?

The Description of Administrative Situations. Before a science can develop principles, it must possess concepts. Before a law of gravitation could be formulated, it was necessary to have the notions of "acceleration" and "weight." The first task of administrative theory is to develop a set of concepts that will permit the description, in terms relevant to the theory, of administrative situations. These concepts, to be scientifically useful, must be operational; that is, their meanings must correspond to empirically observable facts or situations. The definition of "authority" given earlier in this paper is an example of an operational definition.

What is a scientifically relevant description of an organization? It is a description that, so far as possible, designates for each person in the organization what decisions that person makes and the influences to which he is subject in making each of these decisions. Current descriptions of administrative organizations fall far short of this standard. For the most part, they confine themselves to the allocation of *functions* and the formal structure of *authority*.

They give little attention to the other types of organizational influence or to the system of communication.[13]

What does it mean, for example, to say: "The department is made up of three bureaus. The first has the function of _____, the second the function of _____, and the third the function of _____?" What can be learned from such a description about the workability of the organizational arrangement? Very little, indeed. For from the description there is obtained no idea of the degree to which decisions are centralized at the bureau level or at the departmental level. No notion is given as to the extent to which the (presumably unlimited) authority of the department over the bureau is actually exercised or by what mechanisms. There is no indication of the extent to which systems of communication assist the coordination of the three bureaus or, for that matter, to what extent coordination is required by the nature of their work. There is no description of the kinds of training the members of the bureau have undergone or of the extent to which this training permits decentralization at the bureau level. In sum, a description of administrative organizations in terms almost exclusively of functions and lines of authority is completely inadequate for purposes of administrative analysis.

Consider the term "centralization." How is it determined whether the operations of a particular organization are "centralized" or "decentralized"? Does the fact that field offices exist prove anything about decentralization? Might not the same decentralization take place in the bureaus of a centrally located office? A realistic analysis of centralization must include a study of the allocation of decisions in the organization and the methods of influence that are employed by the higher levels to affect the decisions at the lower levels. Such an analysis would reveal a much more complex picture of the decision-making process than any enumeration of the geographical locations of organizational units at the different levels.

Administrative description suffers currently from superficiality, oversimplification, lack of realism. It has confined itself too closely to the mechanism of authority and has failed to bring within its orbit the other, equally important, modes of influence on organizational behavior. It has refused to undertake the tiresome task of studying the actual allocation of decision-making functions. It has been satisfied to speak of "authority," "centralization," "span of control," "function," without seeking operational definitions of these terms. Until administrative description reaches a higher level of sophistication, there is little reason to hope that rapid progress will be made toward the identification and verification of valid administrative principles.

Does this mean that a purely formal description of an administrative organization is impossible—that a relevant description must include an account of the content of the organization's decisions? This is a question that is almost impossible to answer in the present state of knowledge of administrative theory. One thing seems certain: content plays a greater role in the application of administrative principles than is allowed for in the formal administrative theory of the present time. This is a fact that is beginning to be recognized in the literature of administration. If one examines the chain of publications extending from Mooney and Reilley, through Gulick and the President's Committee controversy, to Schuyler Wallace and Benson, he sees a steady shift of emphasis from the "principles of administration" themselves to a study of the *conditions* under which competing principles are respectively applicable. Recent publications seldom say that "organization should be by purpose," but rather that "under such and such conditions purpose organization is desirable." It is to these conditions which underlie the application of the proverbs of administration that administrative theory and analysis must turn in their search for really valid principles to replace the proverbs.

The Diagnosis of Administrative Situations. Before any positive suggestions can be made, it is necessary to digress a bit and to consider more closely the exact nature of the propositions of administrative theory. The theory of administration is concerned with how an organization should be constructed and operated in order to accomplish its work efficiently. A fundamental principle of administration, which follows almost immediately from the rational character of "good" administration, is that among several alternatives involving the same expenditure that one should always be selected which leads to the greatest accomplishment of administrative objectives; and among several alternatives that lead to the same accomplishment that one should be selected which involves the least expenditure. Since this "principle of efficiency" is characteristic of any activity that attempts rationally to maximize the attainment of certain ends with the use of scarce means, it is as characteristic of economic theory as it is of administrative theory. The "administrative man" takes his place alongside the classical "economic man."[4]

Actually, the "principle" of efficiency should be considered a definition rather than a principle: it is a definition of what is meant by "good" or "correct" administrative behavior. It does not tell *how* accomplishments are to be maximized, but merely states that this maximization is the aim of administrative activity, and that administrative theory must disclose under what conditions the maximization takes place.

Now what are the factors that determine the level of efficiency which is achieved by an administrative organization? It is not possible to make an exhaustive list of these, but the principal categories can be enumerated. Perhaps the simplest method of approach is to consider the single member of the administrative organization and ask what the limits are to the quantity and quality of his output. These limits include (a) limits on his ability to perform and (b) limits on his ability to make correct decisions. To the extent that these limits are removed, the administrative organization approaches its goal of high efficiency. Two persons, given the same skills, the same objectives and values, the same knowledge and information, can rationally decide only upon the same course of action. Hence, administrative theory must be interested in the factors that will determine with what skills, values, and knowledge the organization member undertakes his work. These are the "limits" to rationality with which the principles of administration must deal.

On one side, the individual is limited by those skills, habits, and reflexes which are no longer in the realm of the conscious. His performance, for example, may be limited by his manual dexterity or his reaction time or his strength. His decision-making processes may be limited by the speed of his mental processes, his skill in elementary arithmetic, and so forth. In this area, the principles of administration must be concerned with the physiology of the human body and with the laws of skill-training and of habit. This is the field that has been most successfully cultivated by the followers of Taylor and in which has been developed time-and-motion study and the therblig.

On a second side, the individual is limited by his values and those conceptions of purpose which influence him in making his decisions. If his loyalty to the organization is high, his decisions may evidence sincere acceptance of the objectives set for the organization; if that loyalty is lacking, personal motives may interfere with his administrative efficiency. If his loyalties are attached to the bureau by which he is employed, he may sometimes make decisions that are inimical to the larger unit of which the bureau is a part. In this area the principles of administration must be concerned with the determinants of loyalty and morale, with leadership and initiative, and with the influences that determine where the individual's organizational loyalties will be attached.

On a third side, the individual is limited by the extent of his knowledge of things relevant to his job. This applies both to the basic knowledge required in decision making—a bridge designer must know the fundamentals of mechanics—and to the information that is required to make his decisions appropriate to the given situation. In this area, administrative theory is concerned with such fundamental questions as these: What are the limits on the mass of knowledge that human minds can accumulate and apply? How rapidly can knowledge be assimilated? How is specialization in the administrative organization to be related to the specializations of knowledge that are prevalent in the community's occupational structure? How is the system of communication to channel knowledge and information to the appropriate decision-points? What types of knowledge can, and what types cannot, be easily transmitted? How is the need for intercommunication of information affected by the modes of specialization in the organization? This is perhaps the *terra incognita* of administrative theory, and undoubtedly its careful exploration will cast great light on the proper application of the proverbs of administration.

Perhaps this triangle of limits does not completely bound the area of rationality, and other sides need to be added to the figure. In any case, this enumeration will serve to indicate the kinds of considerations that must go into the construction of valid and noncontradictory principles of administration.

An important fact to be kept in mind is that the limits of rationality are variable limits. Most important of all, consciousness of the limits may in itself alter them. Suppose it were discovered in a particular organization, for example, that organizational loyalties attached to small units had frequently led to a harmful degree of intra-organizational competition. Then, a program which trained members of the organization to be conscious of their loyalties, and to subordinate loyalties to the smaller group to those of the large, might lead to a very considerable alteration of the limits in that organization.[15]

A related point is that the term "rational behavior," as employed here, refers to rationality when that behavior is evaluated in terms of the objectives of the larger organization; for, as just pointed out, the difference in direction of the individual's aims from those of the larger organization is just one of those elements of nonrationality with which the theory must deal.

A final observation is that, since administrative theory is concerned with the nonrational limits of the rational, it follows that the larger the area in which rationality has been achieved the less important is the exact form of the administrative organization. For example, the function of plan preparation, or design, if it results in a written plan that can be communicated interpersonally without difficulty, can be located almost anywhere in the organization without affecting results. All that is needed is a procedure whereby the plan can be given authoritative status, and this can be provided in a number of ways. A discussion, then, of the proper location for a planning or designing unit is apt to be highly inconclusive and is apt to hinge on the personalities in the organization and their relative enthusiasm, or lack of it, toward the planning function rather than upon any abstract principles of good administration.[16]

On the other hand, when factors of communication or faiths or loyalty are crucial to the making of a decision, the location of the decision in the organization is of great importance. The method of allocating decisions in the army, for instance, automatically provides (at least in the period prior to the actual battle) that each decision will be made where the knowledge is available for coordinating it with other decisions.

Assigning Weights to the Criteria. A first step, then, in the overhauling of the proverbs of administration is to develop a vocabulary, along the lines just suggested, for the description of administrative organization. A second step, which has also been outlined, is to study the limits of rationality in order to develop a complete and comprehensive enumeration of the criteria that must be weighed in evaluating an administrative organization. The current proverbs represent only a fragmentary and unsystematized portion of these criteria.

When these two tasks have been carried out, it remains to assign weights to the criteria. Since the criteria, or "proverbs," are often mutually competitive or contradictory, it is not sufficient merely to identify them. Merely to know, for example, that a specified change in organization will reduce the span of control is not enough to justify the change. This gain must be balanced against the possible resulting loss of contact between the higher and lower ranks of the hierarchy.

Hence, administrative theory must also be concerned with the question of the weights that are to be applied to these criteria—to the problems of their relative importance in any concrete situation. This question is not one that can be solved in a vacuum. Arm-chair philosophizing about administration—of which the present paper is an example—has gone about as far as it can profitably go in this particular direction. What is needed now is empirical research and experimentation to determine the relative desirability of alternative administrative arrangements.

The methodological framework for this research is already at hand in the principle of efficiency. If an administrative organization whose activities are susceptible to objective evaluation be subjected to study, then the actual change in accomplishment that results from modifying administrative arrangements in these organizations can be observed and analyzed.

There are two indispensable conditions to successful research along these lines. First, it is necessary that the objectives of the administrative organization under study be defined in concrete terms so that results, expressed in terms of these objectives, can be accurately measured. Second, it is necessary that sufficient experimental control be exercised to make possible the isolation of the particular effect under study from other disturbing factors that might be operating on the organization at the same time.

These two conditions have seldom been even partially fulfilled in so-called "administrative experiments." The mere fact that a legislature passes a law creating an administrative agency, that the agency operates for five years, that the agency is finally abolished, and that a historical study is then made of the agency's operations is not sufficient to make of that agency's history an "administrative experiment." Modern American legislation is full of such "experiments" which furnish orators in neighboring states with abundant ammunition when similar issues arise in their bailiwicks, but which provide the scientific investigator with little or nothing in the way of objective evidence, one way or the other.

In the literature of administration, there are only a handful of research studies that satisfy these fundamental conditions of methodology—and these are, for the most part, on the periphery of the problem of organization. There are, first of all, the studies of the Taylor group which sought to determine the technological conditions of efficiency. Perhaps none of these is a better example of the painstaking methods of science than Taylor's own studies of the cutting of metals.[17]

Studies dealing with the human and social aspects of administration are even rarer than the technological studies. Among the more important are the whole series of studies on fatigue, starting in Great Britain during World War I and culminating in the Westinghouse experiments.[18]

In the field of public administration, almost the sole example of such experimentation is the series of studies that have been conducted in the public welfare field to determine the proper case loads for social workers.[19]

Because, apart from these scattered examples, studies of administrative agencies have been carried out without benefit of control or of objective measurements of results, they have had to depend for their recommendations and conclusions upon *a priori* reasoning proceeding from "principles of administration." The reasons have already been stated why the "principles" derived in this way cannot be more than "proverbs."

Perhaps the program outlined here will appear an ambitious or even a quixotic one. There should certainly be no illusions, in undertaking it, as to the length and deviousness of the path. It is hard to see, however, what alternative remains open. Certainly neither the practitioner of administration or the theoretician can be satisfied with the poor analytic tools that the proverbs provide him. Nor is there any reason to believe that a less drastic reconversion than that outlined here will rebuild those tools to usefulness.

It may be objected that administration cannot aspire to be a "science"; that by the nature of its subject it cannot be more than an "art." Whether true or false, this objection is irrelevant to the present discussion. The question of how "exact" the principles of administration can be made is one that only experience can answer. But as to whether they should be logical or illogical there can be no debate. Even an "art" cannot be founded on proverbs.

Notes

1. Lest it be thought that this deficiency is peculiar to the science—or "art"—of administration, it should be pointed out that the same trouble is shared by most Freudian psychological theories, as well as by some sociological theories.
2. Luther Gulick, "Notes on the Theory of Organization," in Luther Gulick and L. Urwick (eds.), *Papers on the Science of Administration* (Institute of Public Administration, Columbia University, 1937), p. 9.
3. This point is discussed in Herbert A. Simon, "Decision-Making and Administrative Organization," 4 *Public Administration Review* 20-21 (Winter, 1944).
4. Gulick, "Notes on the Theory of Organization," p. 9; L. D. White, *Introduction to the Study of Public Administration* (Macmillan Co., 1939), p. 45.
5. Frederick W. Taylor, *Shop Management* (Harper & Bros., 1911), p. 99; Macmahon, Millett, and Ogden, *The Administration of Federal Work Relief* (Public Administration Service, 1941), pp. 265-68; and L. Urwick, who describes British army practice in "Organization as a Technical Problem," Gulick and Urwick (eds.), *op. cit.,* pp. 67-69.
6. *Op. cit.,* p. 21.
7. If this is correct, then any attempt to prove that certain activities belong in a single department because they relate to a single purpose is doomed to fail. See, for example, John M. Gaus and Leon Wolcott, *Public Administration and the U.S. Department of Agriculture* (Public Administration Service, 1940).
8. *Op. cit.,* p. 23.
9. This distinction is implicit in most of Gulick's analysis of specialization. However, since he cites as examples single departments within a city, and since he usually speaks of "grouping activities" rather than "dividing work," the relative character of these categories is not always apparent in this discussion (*op. cit.,* pp. 15-30).
10. *Report of the Machinery of Government Committee* (H. M. Stationery Office, 1918).
11. Sir Charles Harris, "Decentralization," 3 *Journal of Public Administration* 117-33 (April, 1925).
12. Gulick, "Notes on the Theory of Organization," pp. 21-30; Schuyler Wallace, *Federal*

Departmentalization (Columbia University Press, 1941); George C. S. Benson, "International Administrative Organization," 1 *Public Administration Review* 473-86 (Autumn, 1941).

13. The monograph by Macmahon, Millett, and Ogden, *op. cit.,* perhaps approaches nearer than any other published administrative study to the sophistication required in administrative description. See, for example, the discussion on pp. 233-36 of headquarters-field relationships.

14. For an elaboration of the principle of efficiency and its place in administrative theory see Clarence E. Ridley and Herbert A. Simon, *Measuring Municipal Activities* (International City Managers' Association, 2nd ed., 1943), particularly Chapter I and the preface to the second edition.

15. For an example of the use of such training, see Herbert A. Simon and William Divine, "Controlling Human Factors in an Administrative Experiment," 1 *Public Administration Review* 487-92 (Autumn, 1941).

16. See, for instance, Robert A. Walker, *The Planning Function in Urban Government* (University of Chicago Press, 1941), pp. 166-75. Walker makes out a strong case for attaching the planning agency to the chief executive. But he rests his entire case on the rather slender reed that "as long as the planning agency is outside the governmental structure . . . planning will tend to encounter resistance from public officials as an invasion of their responsibility and jurisdiction." This "resistance" is precisely the type of nonrational loyalty which has been referred to previously, and which is certainly a variable.

17. F. W. Taylor, *On the Art of Cutting Metals* (American Society of Mechanical Engineers, 1907).

18. Great Britain, Ministry of Munitions, Health of Munitions Workers Committee, *Final Report* (H.M. Stationery Office, 1918); F. J. Roethlisberger and William J. Dickson, *Management and the Worker* (Harvard University Press, 1939).

19. Ellery F. Reed, *An Experiment in Reducing the Cost of Relief* (American Public Welfare Administration, 1937); Rebecca Staman, "What Is the Most Economical Case Load in Public Relief Administration?" 4 *Social Work Technique* 117-21 (May-June, 1938); Chicago Relief Administration, *Adequate Staff Brings Economy* (American Public Welfare Association, 1939); Constance Hastings and Saya S. Schwartz, *Size of Visitor's Caseload as a Factor in Efficient Administration of Public Assistance* (Philadelphia County Board of Assistance, 1939); Simon *et al., Determining Work Loads for Professional Staff in a Public Welfare Agency* (Bureau of Public Administration, University of California, 1941).

RUFUS E. MILES, JR.

Considerations for a President
Bent on Reorganization

President Carter spoke often during his campaign of his intention to reorganize the federal government. Previous presidents, especially Lyndon Johnson and Richard Nixon, carried with them into the White House similar convictions that the effectiveness of the United States government could be substantially improved through reorganization. Each appointed study commissions with sweeping mandates. Two such commissions were appointed by Johnson and one by Nixon; all recommended major regroupings of federal functions.[1] Yet most of such restructuring never occurred.

President Johnson was successful in 1965 and 1966 in gaining congressional approval of two new departments—Housing and Urban Development, and Transportation—but when he tried to combine the Departments of Commerce and Labor into a single department in 1967, it was a fiasco. Thereafter, he recommended no more consolidations to Congress. In 1971, President Nixon built his State of the Union message around sweeping reorganization proposals that would have created Departments of Community Development, Human Resources, Natural Resources, and Economic Affairs, replacing the Departments of Agriculture, Interior, Commerce, Labor, Housing and Urban Development, and Health, Education, and Welfare. These sweeping changes were also pigeon-holed by Congress. The natural inference was that it was much easier to gain congressional approval for the creation of new departments than for the consolidation and abolition of existing departments.

Since neither president succeeded in bringing about any of the major consolidations their advisers counselled, was it faulty advice, congressional obstinacy, or presidential ineptitude and lack of "follow-through" that blocked their purposes? Or was it that the president and his advisers look at the subject of organization in a very different way than does Congress? None of the three advisory commissions, it should be noted, had members with congressional experience. In any event, President Carter and his advisers would do well to ponder the lessons of this experience.

The principles of organization that should guide a president in considering how to structure the federal government differ in many respects from those that normally guide the head of a huge industrial corporation, and even in some respects from those that should guide governors of states. The organization of the federal government affects and reflects many of the purposes and values of the body politic and should be thought of as one of the dynamics that shapes the future of our national society. Organization is especially important at the federal level in expressing the nation's priorities, in allocating resources, in attracting its most competent leader-executives to key positions, and in accomplishing the purposes of the president, the Congress, and the body politic. It may be useful at the outset of a new administration to offer a number of criteria—not an exhaustive list—that the president and his advisers might do well to take into account in considering major reorganization proposals. Following are 13 such criteria.

1. *Organization is an important expression of social values; are the values that deserve greatest emphasis at this stage of the nation's development given appropriate organizational recognition?*

The act of elevating the organizational status of a function, especially when it involves creating an organization that is directly answerable to the president, is, first and foremost, an expression of the importance that the president, the Congress, and the public attach to the purposes of that organization. When Congress enacted the Employment Act of 1946, creating the Council of Economic Advisers and requiring the submission to the Congress of an Annual Economic Report of the President, this represented a new expression of national concern for the management of the economy so as to achieve balanced economic growth and full employment.

A decade later, when the nation was startled by the Russian sputnik in 1957, there was a strongly expressed desire that the United States should promptly do its best to regain the lead in the space race. This led to the creation of the National Aeronautics and Space Administration, with a clearcut mission, directly answerable to the president.

When the country became increasingly distressed over the deterioration of its cities, the president decided to create a Cabinet-level Department of Housing and Urban Development (which, incidentally, had a mission that exceeded its capacity) to reflect the importance that the society attached to the purposes assigned to the Department. The same was true when a Department of Transportation was created. In declaring his war against poverty, President Johnson created the Office of Economic Opportunity and put it in the Executive Office of the President.

When the American people became deeply concerned in the late 1960s over the deterioration of the environment, two new agencies were created, both directly answerable to the president: the Council on Environmental Quality and the Environmental Protection Agency. When the energy crisis descended on the world, the Federal Energy Agency was created, again directly answerable to the president. *Each of these new agencies was created to reflect a new national priority.*

Expression of national priority is the foremost purpose for creating a new Cabinet department or agency directly answerable to the president. It is the first criterion by which any major organizational proposal should be judged: Does the function to be elevated deserve a higher national priority than it has had, or, conversely, do functions that are to be submerged deserve relatively lower priority than they have had? Submergence may sometimes be a worthwhile price for improved coordination, but the costs need to be carefully weighed in relation to the benefits.

In the pre-election period, President Carter expressed himself as being strongly in favor of a new Cabinet-level department to consolidate energy functions and develop a coherent energy policy for the nation. He also said, though with less emphasis, that he favored a Cabinet-level Department of Education,[2] presumably to reflect what he believes to be the high level of importance that the country now accords, and should continue to accord, to education. These are the only two functions so far identified as deserving the kind of emphasis that only Cabinet status can give. The first will almost certainly come into being in the near future. It will be a matter of major interest to see whether President Carter will continue to hold to his high valuation of education and elevate its organizational status to the Cabinet level.

2. *Organizations should be placed in a favorable environment for the performance of their central missions.*

Accidents of history, or the vagaries of politics have resulted in placing various organizations in settings hostile to them, or where their major problems are not treated with suitable understanding and emphasis. One major purpose of government reorganization is to correct such conditions and place agencies where they can perform more effectively. This was a major reason why the Office of Education was taken out of the Department of the Interior in 1939 and placed in the newly formed Federal Security Agency (the forerunner of the current Department of Health, Education, and Welfare).

It was why the Public Health Service was moved in the same year from the Treasury Department to the Federal Security Agency. It was the reason for moving the Food and Drug Administration from the Department of Agriculture to the Federal Security Agency. It was the rationale for the removal from the Atomic Energy Commission of the responsibilities for overseeing the safety of the nuclear industry which conflicted with its responsibilities for the development and promotion of the multiple uses of nuclear energy. In the process, the Atomic Energy Commission was abolished and the Nuclear Regulatory Commission was created, directly answerable to the president, separate from a newly created Energy Research and Development Administration. Numerous other examples could be adduced.

The fact that an agency is suitably placed in one decade may not mean that it is appropriately placed one or two decades later. Conditions can change rapidly, and when they do, organizational shifts may become logical and desirable.

The water pollution control function that was vested in the Public Health Service in the 1950s and was elevated briefly to agency status within the Department of HEW in the mid-1960s was transferred in the late 1960s to the Interior Department, and was finally made a major component of the new Environmental Protection Agency when it was created at the beginning of the 1970s. Agencies should be placed in settings that are most conducive to the achievement of their central missions.

3. *Organization affects the allocation of resources.*

Other factors equal, the higher the organizational level of any agency, the stronger the voice of its chief in advocating its cause and its fiscal needs in the highest councils of government. A third echelon official rarely can plead his case before the president, and does not often swing much weight with the Office of Management and Budget. The fact of being low in the hierarchy tends unconsciously to establish in the minds of those who make budget recommendations to the president an assumption that the function deserves a smaller share of the nation's fiscal resources than if it were organizationally directly answerable to the president.

Not only does the organizational *level* influence resource allocation, but so does organizational *placement*. The most conspicuous example of this is the effect of the "uncontrollable" parts of the HEW budget on the "controllable" parts. The "uncontrollable" increases in the HEW budget (the term "relatively uncontrollable" is defined in the president's 1977 budget as meaning those expenditures that are required by law and cannot be reduced without changes in law) have risen from $45 billion in 1970 to $132 billion in the 1977 budget. This is an average annual increase of approximately 15 percent, primarily to cover needs for Social Security, Medicare, Medicaid, and public assistance. *These annual increases are greater than the total budgetary allocation for education programs administered by HEW.* Most of the education programs fall within the controllable category, the small part of HEW's budget. When uncontrollable requirements are increasing so rapidly, the pressures are unavoidably great to hold down or cut back the controllable parts of the department's budget. Organizational setting and status inescapably affect budget allocations.

4. *Organization by reasonably broad purpose serves the president best, not so narrow as to be overly responsive to specific clientele groups, nor so broad as to be unmanageable.*

The president and the public are usually best served when Cabinet officers' are put in charge of organizations whose purposes are sufficiently broad so that they exceed the span of concern of any single clientele group. One of the functions of Cabinet officers should be to aid the president in his always difficult task of making all clientele groups understand that resources are limited, that not all programs can be of highest priority, or of equal priority, and that governance is the process of making hard choices in a manner that will enlist confidence in the fairness of the decision-making process and the decision makers themselves, even when the clienteles do not agree with the decisions. This role can be better performed when the portfolio of a Cabinet officer is broad enough to encompass a substantial range of programs and clientele groups, some of which are competing with one another for attention and resources.

On the other hand, a president is poorly served when the portfolio of assignments to a Cabinet officer is so broad as to exceed the capacity of all but a Superman (or perhaps even him) to perform them effectively. If the scope of a department is excessively broad, certain responsibilities that the president and the nation may wish to treat as being of first order of importance will inescapably slip to second or third order and effective leadership of these functions will then become virtually impossible. The advantage gained by breadth of perspective is then more than offset by failure of effective performance. Emphasis should therefore be placed on a *reasonably* broad set of purposes and responsibilities, *not the broader the better.*

5. *Wide span of control has significant advantages in improving administration and reducing unnecessary layers of bureaucracy.*

While presidents may prefer Cabinet departments that are few in number, broad in scope, and large in size, there are various advantages to having a dozen or more of lesser size and range. An organizational structure that is in the form of a steep pyramid, with narrow spans of control at each echelon, requires long lines of communication causing distortions of purpose, and it escalates administrative costs. It also increases problems of coordination. Anthony Downs in his *Inside Bureaucracy*[3] illuminates this point forcefully. His principles are worth quoting:

The foregoing analysis underlies our statement of three principles of organizational control. The first is the Law of Imperfect Control: *No one can fully control the behavior of a large organization.* The second is the Law of Diminishing Control: *The larger any organization becomes, the weaker is the control over its actions exercised by those at the top.* The third is the Law of Decreasing Coordination: *The larger any organization becomes, the poorer is the coordination among its actions.*

These principles argue for avoiding gigantic departments, unless there is an overriding reason for their existence, as is true in the case of the Department of Defense. A Department of Human Resources (the Nixonian model that would greatly enlarge the existing Department of Health, Education, and Welfare) and even HEW in its present form have no such compelling rationale. No other country in the world, and no state in the United States groups so many important functions together in a single department. HEW is now the dinosaur of the federal establishment; it has grown too large to survive long in its present form.

Span of control also has important political implications. Wide span of control satisfies many constituencies; narrow span of control satisfies few. Wide span of control puts more key program administrators organizationally close to the president, thus making the program constituencies feel that their cases are being heard and understood by the president. Depending on the president, this may or may not be an advantage. If he wishes to fend off as many officials as possible who might be classified as special pleaders, he is likely to prefer a small number of officials directly answerable to him; if he can take the time and wants to hear what they have to say, he will enlarge the range of important membership in his official family. But from the standpoint of the Congress and its constituencies, there is no question but that wide span of control is preferable.

6. *Organizational form and prestige are especially important at the federal level in attracting and retaining first-rate leader-managers.*

The principal attraction high government posts have to offer is the combination of prestige and power (opportunity to influence outcomes and be of service to the nation). Both prestige and power diminish rapidly as the number of echelons between the president and any official increases. Frustration sets in when opportunities to influence outcomes become disappointing. Since many are making a financial sacrifice to come to Washington, the psychic rewards must be substantial (or the appointees have independent means, or both) in order to keep them at their posts very long.

In large business corporations, salaries and other benefits can be scaled in such a way as to attract and hold the high quality talent needed to run the company. In government, this is not possible. At the beginning of 1977 the salary of a Cabinet officer was $63,000 and the next highest level was $44,600. The salary of lower level officials, such as the Commissioner of Education, was $37,800, well under that of many large city school superintendents. The practical upper limit upon all executive salaries except those of the president and Cabinet secretaries, is the salary paid to congressmen. This level is not likely to be adjusted upward for inflation for a number of years. With the exception of Cabinet positions (and even these are not an exception for some people) federal salaries have been a negative inducement to many first-rate, potential appointees. Other factors must be sufficiently attractive to offset the negative inducement.

Holding on to the services of first-rate officials is harder than attracting them in the first place. The turnover of officials below the Cabinet level should be cause for greater concern than it is. Assistant secretaries and other comparable officials average between 18 months and two years. It takes six months to a year for most such officials to learn to perform their jobs reasonably well. About half the time, therefore, the typical presidential appointee is performing below an acceptable level of performance. Often, too, there are long gaps between the departure of one official and the arrival of his replacement. This is an unhealthy situation. It is important, therefore, to make as many officials as possible feel they are a part of the president's team, close enough to feel the aura of the White House and loyalty to the president and his program.

Because of these factors, it is in the president's interest and in the public interest to have a rather large number of Cabinet posts. A small number of Cabinet positions would sharply diminish the attractiveness of the lower positions to the nation's ablest people. Cabinet posts have a magnetic appeal, which lower level positions cannot come close to matching. A comparatively wide span of control is, therefore, in the president's interest and in the public interest because it enables the president to attract and hold more first-rate appointees than any other form of organization.

Increasing the number of Cabinet officers need not be inconsistent with a reduction in the number of organizational entities directly answerable to the president. There are now 11 Cabinet departments; increasing the number by one or two (or more if the need be) could be more than offset by reducing the number of small independent agencies under the president. Some of these could be incorporated within existing or future departments.

7. Balance is important in government organization: excessive concentration of important responsibilities in one agency diminishes the effective performance of most of them.

Balance is an underrated criterion by which to judge the merit of organizational proposals. An organization like HEW that has over 300 programs and expenditures of $145 billion (with a projection for 1977 of $165 billion), which is well over half of the federal expenditures for domestic programs, is inherently suspect as an organizational model, and as earlier mentioned, would be made even more unbalanced with the rest of the government by converting it into a Department of Human Resources. Such overconcentration produces a situation in which some parts of the secretary's responsibilities are bound to be given short shrift and conducted in a less than distinguished manner, to say the least.

The Department of Health, Education, and Welfare—the department that is most conspicuously out of balance with the others—is also the fastest growing department and the one most in need of major legislative leadership in respect to extremely complex issues. Two such issues, alone, are among the most difficult challenges of legislative design and effective administration ever faced by the federal government: welfare reform and health insurance. Each is incredibly complex in its economic, political, and administrative ramifications. It is vital that in respect to each, mistakes be reduced to a minimum. Once made, mistakes of legislative design that affect the "uncontrollable" parts of the budget are both extremely costly and hard to rectify. There are also such pressing matters as tightening up the administration by state governments of the Medicaid program—no easy task—and the downward revision of the benefit formula under Social Security to keep future costs from going through the roof. With such complicated and vital responsibilities in the lap of the secretary, how is it possible for him to give appropriate attention to dozens of other issues in the fields of education; food, drug, and vaccine regulation; mental health; the aging; child abuse; and on and on?

Administering so huge an array of programs is also complicated by the nature of congressional relationships. The Congress would not tolerate a concentration of power in one substantive committee that would parallel the concentration of responsibilities vested in HEW. Congress is much more mindful of the principle of balance and divides power and responsibility more evenly among its committees. Consequently, HEW must deal with many different committees, a fact that markedly complicates the congressional relationships of HEW. A coordinated approach to the manifold problems and programs of HEW is virtually impossible because of both volume and proliferation among congressional committees and subcommittees.

Finally, balance is important in dealing with the organized groups of society that have a strong interest in the outcomes of the various federal programs. The greater the number of groups, the less access they have to the secretary. They must concentrate their communications and lobbying on lower level officials. And the greater the number of lower level officials with little or no access to the secretary, the more unmanageable the department becomes.

8. *When purposes overlap, one must be designated as dominant; otherwise responsibility is unclear.*

No matter what principles of organization are followed, it is inevitable that programs and purposes will overlap. The concerns of the Department of State overlap with those of the Department of Defense. The concerns of the CIA overlap with both. The responsibilities of the Treasury Department in collecting Social Security taxes and writing checks overlap with those of the Social Security Administration of HEW that keeps all the records and deals with the public. Similar overlaps occur throughout the government. Many are inevitable because purposes cannot be defined so as to put them in tight compartments.

Whenever a program function cuts across two or more major purposes, it is necessary to decide, first, which purpose is dominant in order to decide where to put the unit, organizationally, and second, how to coordinate such cross-cutting functions. For example, there are scores of fellowship programs throughout the government that have been created to develop the skilled manpower needed to assure the success of the mission-oriented agencies such as Defense, NASA, Agriculture, the new Energy Research and Development Administration, the National Institutes of Health, etc. These are obviously educational programs as well as being defense, space, energy, and health programs. But the decision has been made that these are primarily mission-oriented programs, and only secondarily educational programs. They are placed organizationally, therefore, in the mission agencies.

It could be administratively disastrous to remove these programs (and the veterans educational benefit programs) from their respective agencies and put them in a centralized educational agency or department simply because they channel funds to educational institutions and their students. It would soon be found that such a centralized "education" agency was an administrative bottleneck between the mission agencies and the educational institutions and their students, causing unnecessary delays and marked increases in the number of administrative employees and consequent costs, all because the secondary purpose had been mistaken for the dominant purpose. The clarity with which the dominant purpose is identified and the function placed accordingly has much to do with the efficiency of governmental administration.

9. *When purposes overlap, a system of coordination must be established.*

The most difficult task of public management is not deciding how the functions of government should be divided among organizational units, but how the functions can and should be effectively coordinated after they have been divided. All government is a complex set of matrices; if work is divided on one set of principles or axes, it must be coordinated on another. This is the basic reason for the classic organization by line and staff, a useful, almost indispensable method of coordination but not the full answer to the need for coordinating related functions.

A discussion of the various means of achieving coordination would be beyond the purview of this article. It is one area of public administration which has often baffled the experts. One new attempt to cope with this problem is contained in Chapter IX of *A Cabinet Department of Education: Analysis and Proposal* (1976), published by the American Council on Education, from which this article is adapted.

10. *Programs should be grouped on the basis of their affinity or the potential for cross-fertilization.*

The grouping of programs within an organization should depend, in part, on the importance of the actual and potential interrelationships between them. If there are or should be numerous such interrelationships, the argument for putting them together in the same department is strong. If a bureau has few important relationships, within the setting where it currently is located, and if its relationships with bureaus that are currently located in another department are far more important, and should be developed and encouraged, then it is a good candidate for transfer. The food stamp program, now in the Department of Agriculture, is a good example of a program that should be administered by the same department that is responsible for welfare and income maintenance, namely, HEW. Yet this would run into the problem of further enlarging an already gargantuan department. The answer to this may be to split off whatever portion of HEW may now have few relations with the rest of the department, and group it with other organizational units with which it has affinity. The Education Division of HEW would seem to meet this criterion.

11. *Reorganizations have traumatic effects which should be carefully weighed.*

Reorganizations vary widely in the degree to which they disrupt the skein of human relationships that are the communications and nerve networks of every organization. Some reorganizations cause little or no disruption, while others are traumatic. The creation of the Department of Health, Education, and Welfare in 1953, out of what had previously been the Federal Security Agency, was one of the easiest reorganizations ever performed. Only the name was changed, the administrator was made a Cabinet secretary, and three new positions were added. The cost, in administrative disruption, was close to zero. Other reorganizations have involved much reshuffling of people from one organizational and physical location to another, necessitating a whole new set of human relationships, superiors getting acquainted with new subordinates and vice versa, old habits and trusted communications patterns terminated and new ones initiated. Such were the reorganizations of the Office of Education in 1965, and the Public Health Service in 1968. Reorganizations of the latter type require much time for healing.

Traumatic reorganizations may be analogized to surgical operations. It is important that their purposes be carefully assessed and a thoughtful judgment reached that the wielding of the surgical knife is going to achieve a purpose that, after a period of recuperation, will be worth the trauma inflicted. And the surgical knife should not be wielded again and again before the healing process from earlier incisions has been completed. Yet this is what sometimes happens in government reorganizations. Agencies are kept in a constant state of disruption by having presidential appointees who may average two years of service, or less, conclude that the organizational structure left by their predecessors is not sound because the results being produced are not satisfactory. Hence, they feel they must reorganize. The problem may not be organizational at all, or not primarily organizational, and it may be partly a problem of too much reorganization. Repetitive reorganization without proper initial diagnosis is like repetitive surgery without proper diagnosis: obviously an unsound and unhealthy approach to the cure of the malady.

It is essential, therefore, that the initial diagnosis of any malfunctioning be carefully made, that reorganizations be designed to achieve clearly defined purposes, and that they be no more disruptive than they need to be to accomplish their overriding purpose. In medicine this is known as minimal or conservative surgery.

12. *Reorganizations that require congressional approval or acquiescence should be carefully weighed to make sure that they are worth the expenditure of political capital required and have a reasonable chance of approval.*

By no means the least of the criteria for judging the desirability of a reorganization proposal is the assessment of its political costs and its likelihood of approval by Congress. Congress and the president (and the president's advisers) have different perspectives on the subject of organization. Power is divided differently in Congress than it is in the Executive Branch, and reorganizations that would shift power from one committee to another, or that would demote, relatively speaking, an organizational unit in which powerful committee chairmen and members have a special interest run the hazard of being defeated, ignored, or amended in a manner that would seem unacceptable to the president. Even though the president presides over the Executive Branch, the Constitution gives Congress a significant role in the design of the executive structure. The president must respect the congressional role and the interests of Congress as he considers his own priorities in the matter of reorganization.

A few reorganizations may have low political costs. There are a number of such reorganization options open to the president. The more difficult problem arises when the political costs begin to rise because of the pressure groups that would be offended and the congressmen and their staffs whose bailiwicks would be adversely affected. When the political costs are substantial, the president should be appraised of this fact in advance and, obviously, should not seek reorganizations that will be politically expensive unless he is prepared to spend a substantial amount of political capital in gaining their approval. Reorganization plans submitted and turned down or ignored (if they require affirmative legislation) are humiliating, the more so if the president's own party controls Congress. It is important, therefore, before drawing a trial balance on a series of models of reorganization to examine the positions that the key interest groups and congressmen (and staffs) are likely to take on the various models, and cast them into the balance in arriving at judgments as to both desirability and feasibility.

13. *Economy as a ground for major reorganization is a will-o'-the-wisp.*

Last and least important among the criteria for judging among reorganization models is the matter of whether dollar savings can be accomplished. It is extremely difficult to predict how much, if anything, can be saved by a major reorganization, and it is impossible to prove, after the fact, how much, if any, has been saved. The comparison that must be made in a continually shifting context is the amount that a new organizational pattern will cost compared to what would have been required under the former organization. Since it is never possible to know what costs would have been without the reorganization, such calculations are close to meaningless. The rationale that lies behind most reorganizations is that the new structure will increase the *effectiveness* of government, not reduce its costs.

Almost invariably, reorganizations that elevate the status of a subordinate organization to a higher level, especially those that create new Cabinet departments or new agencies directly answerable to the president, result in larger staffs for the new secretary or agency head, and those staffs are more highly paid than when the organization was at a lower level. Indeed, that is one of the purposes of such elevation. If a function needs stronger leadership, one important way in which such leadership can become effective is by creating higher and more prestigious positions and providing such leaders with the opportunity to surround themselves with first-rate staff. It would be a mistake to pretend or predict that these officials are going to be so competent, managerially speaking, that they will be able to reduce the costs of the subordinate units of the organization in sufficient degree to more than offset the added costs of the larger and higher paid staff at the top. It *could happen;* the likelihood is great that it will not. *The officials in such an organization have far greater interest in accomplishing more effectively the missions assigned to their agencies than they do in reducing the staff.*

Even more unlikely is that savings will be made by creating larger aggregations of agencies and putting a new superstructure over them. The additional layer is almost certain to cost more money. To the extent that savings are achievable in the federal government through improved management, they are likely to be made through changes in policies and procedures, not organization.

Thus, it would be a mistake to place the subject of economy high on a list of important criteria for judging the desirability of any proposed reorganization. It is, of course, necessary to consider estimated costs in relation to possible benefits, but these estimates should rarely, if ever, be a controlling consideration.

Obviously, almost no reorganization proposal is likely to rank high in respect to all of these criteria. Some of the criteria pull in opposite directions. But all deserve to be thought about as various reorganization plans are being considered.

Notes

1. The two Johnson task forces were headed by Don K. Price (report submitted in November 1964 and declassified by the Lyndon Baines Johnson Library in 1976) and by Ben W. Heineman (report submitted in sections during 1967 and declassified by the Lyndon B. Johnson Library in 1976). The Nixon task force, chaired by Roy Ash, reported in 1970 (its full report has not yet been made public, but its basic recommendations were converted into a broad set of reorganization proposals made by President Nixon in 1971). For a full explication of the Nixon proposals see *Papers Relating to the President's Departmental Reorganization Program* (Washington, D.C.: U.S. Government Printing Office, 1971). A revised version of this document was also issued in 1972.
2. Candidate Carter took this position in a statement of his position on a wide variety of issues, published by his campaign headquarters, and also in specific response to a questionnaire sent to all candidates by the National Education Association.
3. See Anthony Downs, *Inside Bureaucracy,* the Rand Corporation (Boston: Little Brown and Co., 1967), p. 271.

FREDERIC N. CLEAVELAND

Administrative Decentralization in the U.S. Bureau of Reclamation

In recent years Americans have become increasingly concerned with the greater concentration of power in Washington. More than a few ballots were marked for the candidate of the "challenger" party on last November 4 for no more specific reason than that the party in power had become identified with centralization. Yet there is considerable evidence of an important trend over the last decade toward the decentralization of administration in federal departments and agencies. Whether this trend came because of or in spite of the party in power is not the concern of this article. Its purpose is to consider briefly how one agency, the Bureau of Reclamation, moved during this period from a highly centralized to a decentralized and regionalized organization, and then to analyze and discuss some of its experiences with administrative decentralization.

There are several points to be made at the beginning by way of delimitation. First, this discussion will not be concerned with political decentralization, with the virtues and defects of a federal structure of government, but only with administrative decentralization within a government agency. Second, the unwary must be forewarned lest they assume that decentralization is synonymous with the existence of a large force of field officials. No more poignantly conclusive evidence to the contrary can be offered than the case of the New England postmaster who, following a severe snow storm which had catapulted a tree branch through the roof of his post office, sat the next day amidst a snow drift within the building and penned a note to Washington requesting permission to use money from his service fund to have the hole in the roof repaired.[1] The Post Office Department has headquarters in Washington and a far-flung field force, but this postmaster knew only too well that the Post Office Department is not decentralized. Delegation of authority to the field is the stuff of which decentralization is made. Third, this article is concerned primarily with decentralization by area rather than along functional lines.[2]

Balance in Administrative Decentralization

There are clearly important values to be attained by centralization just as there are equally important, although sometimes competing, values to be gained by decentralization. Losing the values of centralization can be considered one of the costs of administrative decentralization. The problem, then, can be posed as one of weighing values and costs in order to strike the "right" balance. One mark of the competent executive is his ability to perceive this optimum equilibrium between decentralization and centralization where maximum values are attained at minimum costs. Clearly, centralization and decentralization in public administration are matters of degree and not absolutes. As James W. Fesler has remarked: "The task is one of statesmanship in achieving the proper balance, . . . not one of standing up to be counted either for centralization or for decentralization."[3]

Many different aspects of the search for this balance in headquarters-field relations are worthy of investigation. Only three important aspects will be considered here: finding balance in the formulation and adaptation of policy, in the supervision of operations, and in improving administrative efficiency.[4] In each of these areas the values and costs of decentralization can be stated as a troublesome dilemma confronting the administrator. The job of finding effective equilibrium among the alternatives in these dilemmas cannot be left to chance, or to the natural wisdom and good will of the participants. There is bound to be a "headquarters" point of view and a "field" point of view, each sincerely and ardently held, and generally in conflict. Effective equilibrium is likely to grow out of accommodation of both points of view.

The three critical dilemmas to be considered in this discussion may be defined briefly as follows:

The Policy Dilemma: flexible adjustment to local conditions vs. national uniformity. Decentralization ensures that important decisions will be made close to the area directly affected. John Gaus has long pleaded for such "an ecological approach to public administration," emphasizing the logic of the situation, building "quite literally from the ground up."[5] While it encourages experimentation to meet local needs more adequately, it also challenges national uniformity in the interpretation and application of policy. The influence of local pressures may force decisions contrary to national interests. Headquarters personnel are still fully responsible for the consequences of decisions made in the field; therefore, there must be controls over the exercise of discretionary authority by field officials. Yet, can controls be designed consistent with the goals of decentralization?

The Dilemma of Supervision: area integration vs. technical control. Decentralizing along areal lines provides a sound basis for integrating field activities under a regional generalist with the same kind of management responsibility for his limited area that the bureau chief carries for the whole national program. Such integration makes for more effective teamwork, economy in housekeeping staff, and better coordination in service to the public, but it weakens the control and influence of functional specialists. It is absurd to say that the soils technician in the field should look to a regional general administrator for direction of his work rather than to the soils specialists at headquarters. The only guarantee for high quality performance lies in direct supervision and control exercised by outstanding specialists at headquarters.

The Efficiency Dilemma: simplified channels and speed vs. the avoidance of administrative errors. An agency, through decentralization, can greatly simplify its administrative procedures, cutting down the volume of headquarters-field communication and speeding up the process of decision making. Headquarters can then concentrate upon its major responsibility of formulating top policy and maintaining liaison with the Congress, while field officials can experiment with field organization and administrative techniques, finding ways to use their resources more efficiently. But such decentralization opens the floodgates to local abuses and errors of judgment. Favoritism in appointments and promotions, illegal purchases, substandard work performance, and waste may all be occurring without detection. The only way to avoid such evils is to multiply controls—have more inspections, detailed manuals for field guidance, conferences, and a stream of reports from the field. But such devices subvert the meaning of decentralization, greatly increase the work load on headquarters, and destroy field initiative.

These three dilemmas encompass many of the most serious difficulties the Bureau of Reclamation has encountered in its search for balance in decentralization. This search in recent years has been significantly conditioned by the program heritage and organizational traditions of the Bureau personnel. The following paragraphs sketch briefly some highlights in Reclamation's past and the factual story of its transition to regional decentralization.

Formative Years for Reclamation's Program and Organization, 1902-1942

Federal reclamation of arid western lands gained acceptance as sound public policy around the turn of the century in an area of contagious optimism. Sponsors and supporters of the Reclamation Act of 1902 (32 *Stat.* 388) were in large part farsighted conservationists and sincere democrats caught up in the enthusiasm of the Progressive Movement. To many the program was first an extension of the homestead policy, designed to recover vast acres of the public domain for settlement by homesteaders. The legislation created a revolving fund out of proceeds to be derived from the sale of western public lands and authorized the Secretary of the Interior to use this fund in locating and constructing irrigation works in the 17 western states and territories. Settlers on reclamation projects could purchase no more than 160 acres and were to repay into the fund the proportionate cost of developing their acreage.

From 1902 to 1924 major attention was given to the trial-and-error process of perfecting an organization for carrying out the new program.⁴ The Reclamation Service, as it was called, experimented briefly with a field organization built on separate "districts" for the major river basins, then moved to five large regions each under a single supervising engineer. At the headquarters level, the Service tried single leadership and board leadership with first a five-man commission and then a three-member group. The commission provided broader consideration of policy matters but failed to furnish the essential unified direction for an active construction program. In 1915, therefore, a central field office was established in Denver, Colorado, to direct operations within policies established by the commission sitting in Washington. At the same time the regional structure was abandoned and all project engineers and other field officials (except district counsel) were required to report to the director of the reclamation service through the chief of construction, as the head of the Denver office was designated. Denver thus became the real operational headquarters of the organization. In time there was a return to single leadership, and in 1923 the service was redesignated the Bureau of Reclamation and its head, the commissioner of reclamation.

During these two decades of organizational experimentation, major emphasis in operations had been given to the engineering aspects of the program. The immediate job in 1902 was to build dams and dig canals. These engineering structures tended to become ends in themselves in the minds of many on the Bureau's staff. Indeed it required the near exhaustion of the reclamation fund and acute distress among the settlers to bring the Bureau and the Congress to grips with the economic and social aspects of the reclamation program. The Bureau obtained its first nonengineer commissioner (an Idaho businessman) in 1923 in order to place more emphasis on working out the economic problems, and a few weeks later the secretary set up a Committee of Special Advisers to study Bureau policies and operations. The so-called "Fact Finders' Report"[7] issued by this committee led to the establishment of a director of farm economics at Denver and to the extension of the authority of the director of finance over all "business operations" at the project level. The objective was to work more closely with project settlers on agricultural problems and also to try to improve their repayment record. Conflict developed almost at once over the confused and overlapping relationship between the chief engineer and director of finance in their supervision of project personnel. Within a year the Finance Division was moved from Denver to Washington, its nonaccounting functions transferred to the chief engineer. All employees at the project level were made responsible to a project superintendent who reported directly to the chief engineer.

It is significant that through all these organizational permutations the stature of the chief engineer grew steadily. His responsibility for directing project activities was a natural outgrowth of the initial concentration upon construction work and the lessons learned from experiments with multiheaded leadership. By 1924 there was a clear division of function between Denver and Washington. While the commissioner formulated policy, exercised overall guidance throughout the Bureau, and maintained necessary liaison with the Congress, the president, and other executive agencies, the chief engineer really controlled execution of the program. Gradually over the years the chief engineer built up a high *esprit de corps* among Reclamation engineers. These men became in a sense the elite among Bureau employees. As they developed their skills they were frequently moved about from one construction job to another, progressing to more and more responsible posts. A great majority of the Bureau's employees thus continued to look to Denver as their headquarters and the chief engineer as the one and only "chief." To many the commissioner seemed like a Washington representative of the "chief" attending to the troublesome details of financing the construction program.

From 1924 to the end of the 1930s the Bureau enjoyed considerable organizational stability, but the reclamation program, by contrast, was in a state of constant ferment. The Fact Finders' Report in 1924 launched major efforts to resolve some of the critical social and economic problems which had received only sporadic, stopgap attention earlier. At the same time the Bureau faced the possibility of working itself out of a job. Most of the relatively simple irrigation projects were already under construction and the Bureau's engineers were finding it increasingly difficult to locate areas where development was economically feasible.[3] Furthermore, the reclamation fund was largely exhausted.

Reclamation's engineers found the way out of this dilemma of diminishing financial resources and shrinking opportunities for development when they pushed ahead in their investigation of the Boulder Canyon Project on the lower Colorado River. The answer was multi-purpose planning—the harnessing of rivers for flood control, for irrigation, and for the production of hydroelectric power. Revenues from leasing power production rights or from direct sale of power would reduce the repayment obligation of the irrigators enough to make the project economically feasible. Multi-purpose planning thus opened a whole new frontier for development. Hydroelectric power became known in Bureau circles as the "paying partner" of irrigation; project investigations abandoned earlier as lacking in feasibility were resurrected and revised to follow the multiple-purpose pattern.

Economic depression and the dramatic efforts of the Roosevelt administration to deal positively with its problems also produced major changes in the reclamation program. With passage of the National Industrial Recovery Act, Reclamation suddenly found at its disposal a total of $220,000,000. This sum was roughly equivalent to the aggregate expenditure made on federal reclamation of arid lands during the first 31 years of the program (1902-1933). For the next several years the Bureau continued to receive large sums from the Public Works Administration, and in 1938 the Congress restored the reclamation fund to solvency by diverting into it certain money accrued from the income of the naval petroleum reserves (52 *Stat.* 291, 318).

Multiple-purpose planning struck a responsive note in the philosophy of more positive government articulated by President Franklin Roosevelt. Comprehensive resource development through federal leadership was recognized as a means of obtaining two major national objectives: (1) the conservation and utilization of natural resources for the benefit of the people, and (2) expanding employment and business to lift the economy out of depression. The National Resources Board, and its successors, gave great encouragement to comprehensive resource planning, refining the multiple-purpose approach by adding the emphasis upon regionalism, stressing the importance of planning water resource development along drainage basin lines. All through the 1930s the Bureau of Reclamation pursued the development of multiple-purpose projects. Studies began a decade earlier culminated in a whole series of major regional projects: the Columbia Basin Project, the Central Valley (California) Project, and the Colorado-Big Thompson transmountain diversion, all authorized between 1935 and 1940. Finally, in 1939 the Congress acted to write the general principle of multiple-purpose development into reclamation law.'

These substantive developments in the reclamation program are significant in this examination of administrative decentralization because to a considerable extent they forced the Bureau into a pattern of decentralization. The plight of project settlers demanded more and more attention to land classification, irrigation practices, farm demonstration activities—indeed to the whole economy of irrigated agriculture. Multiple-purpose projects proved more difficult to design and construct; they required more basic data. Furthermore, basin-wide planning inevitably meant closer contact (and sometimes conflict) with countless other governmental activities, federal, state, and local. Nor did the administrative and management aspects lag far behind in growing complexity. The Bureau's job in 1940 was infinitely bigger than it had been in 1924: bigger in scope—basin-wide, even region-wide—bigger in cost, more diversified in nature, and far more complicated technically. But the Bureau was still trying to carry on under its straight-line organization with authority centralized in the chief engineer. Finally, the Bureau's program was fast becoming political "dynamite." Its comprehensive projects made their impact felt upon the economy of entire regions. It was harder and harder to remain aloof from political controversy, yet Reclamation's field staff was ill trained to "build political fences," uninterested in public relations, and unaccustomed to developing local support.

The Bureau Adopts Administrative Decentralization to Meet Its Expanding Responsibilities

By the early 1940s, Secretary of the Interior Ickes and his under secretary had become convinced that the Bureau of Reclamation should be fundamentally reorganized to enable it to meet its expanding responsibilities. The reorganization effort they initiated is difficult to describe for it extended over several years and the proposed changes were installed piecemeal. Despite this halting approach, there were at least three fundamental objectives running through all the changes made: (1) to decentralize authority for work execution along regional lines; (2) to limit the authority of the chief engineer and his staff to the design and construction of new projects and major repairs or additions to existing projects; and (3) to establish a functional type of organization operating on staff and line principles with direct line authority running from the commissioner to the regional directors.

Considerable opposition developed within the Bureau to all three of these basic objectives.[10] Many both inside and outside the Denver office evidenced understandable loyalty to the existing institutional pattern. Partisan supporters of the chief engineer looked upon the whole affair as an effort to "dehorn" their "chief." One member of the chief engineer's staff later testified that there was a widespread feeling that "the engineers have been pushed back in the corner."[11] For his part Chief Engineer S. O. Harper strongly supported regionalization but only within a straight-line organization centering in the Chief Engineer's Office. Shortly before retirement in 1944 he expressed his feelings openly:

> . . . I think it [reorganization] is a fine step forward. . . . I must say, however, that I have been and always will be unalterably opposed to the change made in Denver in splitting up the single-headed organization . . . and substituting for it a five- or six-headed group with no directing head.[12]

Commissioner of Reclamation Page for his part was reluctant to carry through any reorganization calling for decentralization and the chief engineer's vigorous opposition to the proposals strengthened his convictions. But the pressure from the top was strong. When the first tentative plan did not go into the question of regional decentralization, the secretary and his departmental advisers insisted that the Bureau "should proceed immediately to regionalize its activities, leaving in Denver only service functions such as design and construction, and perhaps some central accounting or auditing duties."[13]

A plan of reorganization was finally agreed upon and approved by Secretary Ickes on December 24, 1942. It provided for (1) three major branches—investigations and planning, design and construction, and operation and maintenance; and (2) five (later six) regional offices to be established in the 17 western states. The regional offices were to concentrate on planning and development activity and supervise the operation and maintenance of completed projects. The Chief Engineer's Office, renamed Branch of Design and Construction, was responsible for designing works; and for directing, coordinating, and supervising construction and power operation and maintenance activities.

Implementing the reorganization proposals proved to be a long and difficult job requiring constant effort by the many in the Bureau who really wanted to see decentralization succeed. The commissioner in his *Annual Reports* frequently called attention to the difficulty in wartime of obtaining qualified personnel for the important regional jobs created. Yet decentralization demanded regional directors and regional staffs fully competent to carry out the heavy responsibilities assigned to them. An Office of Management Planning was established to provide technical guidance in setting up new organizational units and devising procedures. Patterns of cooperative activity had to be worked out to knit together the more complicated line and staff structure. The functional branches, except Design and Construction, were moved to Washington under the watchful eyes of the commissioner and his management staff.

In carrying out the reorganization, the Bureau made certain additional adjustments toward greater decentralization and a further narrowing of the chief engineer's authority. A separate Branch of Power Utilization was provided, taking over responsibility for the power program, except for design and construction. The regional director's responsibilities for basic program planning and budgeting were gradually clarified. As a result he had more tools with which to formulate and execute a comprehensive reclamation program in his region, for the annual budget and program plans encompassed design and construction activities. But the chief engineer was still responsible for directing these phases of the program.

As late as March, 1945, the secretary's staff management advisers were still sharply critical of what they called "two basically different organizational proposals being currently developed within the bureau."[14] One was the regional organization, and the other "an effort to maintain the previous status quo wherein all field work would be handled under the direction and control of the Chief Engineer." Despite this penetrating criticism, however, the commissioner was able to win secretarial support for his position "that the responsibility for the technical aspects of design and construction work should remain in the Chief Engineer, and therefore, authority for this work should also be vested in the Chief Engineer."[15] Secretary Ickes in approving this policy charged the commissioner and the chief engineer with joint responsibility to see that wherever practicable design and construction authority would be delegated to regional directors. This decision set the pattern and confirmed for the chief engineer the dual role of staff and line official which he fills today.

Pressure for reorganization had been set off by the significant growth of reclamation policy during depression years. This growth was basically a reaffirmation of the fundamental objectives established in the Reclamation Act of 1902—to conserve water resources for full utilization in the public interest, promoting the stability of the family farm, building and safeguarding homes. Multiple-purpose planning was a new technique developed to serve those goals. Administrative decentralization has been conceived of in the Bureau as another technique to serve those goals by relating the reclamation program more closely to the people it serves. The soundness of this conception depends very considerably on the success of Reclamation's continuing search for equilibrium in decentralization.

Reclamation's Search for Balance in Administrative Decentralization

The Bureau's experience over the past ten years provides ample evidence of the dynamic character of the process of reorganization. The significant developments have come slowly, often involving change in the attitudes of large numbers of Bureau personnel and the development of new working patterns. Recharting the formal structure is only the beginning of reorganization. The heart of reorganization lies in the process of adjustment as individuals and working groups search out a new position of equilibrium to accommodate the alterations in formal organizational environment around them. But, how has the Bureau fared in working out its adjustment to the three dilemmas of decentralized administration identified earlier? The Reclamation staff at all levels is alive with ideas on this score; it is possible here to consider only a few of them briefly, attempting to give some impressions of the search for balance.

The Policy Dilemma. Reorganization has accomplished two major changes in the division of responsibility for formulating policy: (1) responsibility for top policy decisions has been moved from Denver to Washington (for all but design and construction); and (2) major authority has been delegated to regional directors for making operating policy decisions, particularly in project planning, in scheduling and accomplishing construction, and in operating and maintaining projects. But this division of responsibility has been flexible in application; any danger of a gulf developing to separate headquarters and top policy making from those who plan and carry out the program has been avoided by bringing the regional directors increasingly into policy discussions at headquarters. Thus the broad policy framework within which the Bureau functions has become progressively more sensitive to the needs of those responsible for program execution. Not only the functional specialists, but also men informed on regional resources, conversant with regional political pressures, and aware of regional needs and desires join in advising the commissioner on policy.

The annual policy conference illustrates the kind of machinery which makes this possible. This conference brings together a group of some 15 to 18 persons —regional directors, functional division heads, and the commissioner's immediate staff—to meet in executive session for several days thrashing out major policy problems and reaching realistic conclusions. At the first such conference in 1950, regional directors and division heads submitted items for the agenda in advance. The Office of Management Planning prepared the agenda, setting up separate committees of three or four persons (including both regional officials and division heads) to consider each of the more complex problems and to lead the discussions on it. Following the conference, "study assignment groups" were set up to continue working on certain problems. Their recommendations were later circulated to all who had attended the conference with instructions to review them carefully with their staffs and submit comments.

This participation by regional and functional leaders in basic policy discussions out of which decisions come demonstrates the Bureau's continuing effort to develop its pattern of regional policies and programs within the overall framework of national policy and a national program. In this scene the regional director is the key figure, for he is at once a regional official *and* a national official (as a member of the commissioner's "board of directors"). He contributes the knowledge of his region and the practical insights of the responsible operating official. He derives from these discussions something of the Bureau-wide perspective, the consciousness of a national program into which he must fit his regional program.

It is instructive, too, to examine the relationship of regional and head-quarters officials in operating policy decisions. Here the pattern varies somewhat among the Bureau's three fields of activity (project planning, design and construction, and operation and maintenance). While major authority has been delegated to the field in all three areas the positions of the functional divisions differ. Thus the head of the functional Division of Design and Construction also has major line responsibility which circumscribes the regional director's authority in this area. Perhaps the clearest relationship has been worked out in the area of project planning investigations. Here the regional director is primarily responsible for initiating, conducting, and completing the investigation; headquarters participates most actively in the review and revision of the final report.

In most cases these investigations are begun in answer to some strong local request, frequently accompanied by funds advanced by local interests. In this situation decentralization of authority to initiate field studies ensures that local needs will receive attention in the investigation stage. The regional director must also plan the regional program of investigation work, determining priorities among studies to be made. The actual field investigation work is carried on by project planning personnel at district and area planning offices under rather close supervision by the regional planning engineer and his staff. Upon completion of the study a report is prepared for the regional director to submit to headquarters, containing the considered judgment of the regional staff as to the feasibility of the project. Before acceptance, this project plan report must "run the gauntlet" of all the other regional directors, functional division heads, and the commissioner's immediate staff.

This clearance process accomplishes several important things. First, it ensures that projects recommended for authorization have been fitted into the national reclamation program. If the regional director has succumbed to strong local pressures in initiating an investigation, this requirement of clearance at least delays action and may lift him and the Bureau "off the hook." Second, clearance makes possible better coordination within the Bureau itself. For example, the commissioner's top adviser in project operations has a chance to review the adequacy of arrangements for land classification or the calculation of repayment ability. Third, clearance provides a way for evaluating performance of an important segment of the Bureau's field staff and determining whether fundamental Bureau policies in the area of project planning are being applied properly.

On the negative side there are still complaints from some, particularly in the field, that headquarters specialists are guilty of "over-reviewing," going into too many details, and even rechecking routine mathematical calculations. This kind of review adds to the lengthy period of time required to "clear" a report through headquarters. More serious is the occasional charge that Washington officials sometimes actually redraft the substance of project plan reports in the course of reviewing them. Much of this criticism may be considered the natural resentment of field personnel to headquarters control. But even so, it suggests one area that will bear watching if the Bureau is to achieve further progress toward balance in the making of operating policy decisions.

The Supervision Dilemma. The Bureau has openly and clearly taken a stand for the principle of dual supervision. Official policy as expressed in Volume I of the *Bureau of Reclamation Manual* conceives of line responsibility in the following terms:

A. Line officers are those officials who are charged with all the responsibilities of one organizational level (or sublevel) of the Bureau, including the direction of a lower level or sublevel, if any. . . .[16]

The concept of the role of staff officers is revealed in the *Manual* statement on technical supervision:

Technical supervision . . . is the responsibility of a staff officer to see that his functional specialty is carried out properly at lower organizational levels. It is the authority to observe, appraise, interpret, and advise. It does not include the authority to issue orders or to direct any officer, line or staff, in a lower organizational level. If a staff officer believes it necessary to have orders issued, he recommends the issuance of the order by his line officer. Thus, technical supervision does not conflict with the chain of command, while at the same time it enables specialized knowledge to be transmitted readily throughout the Bureau.[17]

The effective operation of such a complicated system depends upon the good will of line and staff officials at all levels, and their continued willingness to give and take in day-to-day personal relations. There remains the confusing "twilight zone" between line and staff functions. The *Manual* hardly helps to clarify the situation when, after stating clearly that staff officers have no authority to issue orders or direct anyone at a lower organizational level, it goes on to put some teeth into staff advice, providing:

Technical advice rendered by a staff officer to a lower level of organization may not be disregarded by the line officer (or his staff representative) to whom the advice is given. The line officer must either follow the technical advice or refer the matter with his objections to a common superior for resolution. However, a staff officer may give informal advice with the understanding that it may be disregarded; it need not be specifically labeled as such so long as it is otherwise clear that the advice was rendered on that basis.[18]

Despite these difficulties in defining the staff-line relationship in meaningful terms, the Bureau has made definite progress in integrating line supervision and staff supervision. Several factors have helped in the slow process of changing the ingrained habits of the many functional specialists who were previously line officials under the chief engineer: (1) the growing stature of regional directors as demonstrated by their increasing role in major policy decisions; (2) the movement of functional divisions from Denver to Washington; and (3) the continued pressure which the commissioner, his assistant commissioners, and his management advisers have exerted upon staff officers to confine their activities to functional supervision. Rough spots still exist as, for example, the staff tendency to "over-review" field reports, or occasional cases of a headquarters division head by-passing the regional director to deal directly with a project official. There is even some evidence of similar tendencies among regional staff personnel. Nevertheless, for the most part Reclamation has moved ahead toward finding a satisfactory balance that assures basic integration of field activities through decentralization to regional directors, yet maintains uniform high standards of technical performance through expert supervision.

The same degree of progress cannot be reported, however, in fitting the chief engineer and his Division of Design and Construction effectively into this line and staff organization. Since 1943 the chief engineer has been both the commissioner's top staff specialist on engineering design and construction and the line officer responsible for directing major design work and for representing the commissioner in contract negotiations and contract administration. These dual responsibilities have three serious consequences.

First, the project construction engineer has two line bosses. He answers to the regional director for keeping work on schedule and administering routine project affairs; he is the chief engineer's representative for dealing with the contractors and thus responsible to him for supervising construction. On occasion these project heads find themselves trapped between conflicting instructions from their two bosses. They must continually fret over the practical necessity of clearing proposals with both Denver and the regional office "just to be on the safe side." Even where no overt incidents develop, the uncertainty of the situation impairs morale and saps the efficiency of the whole organization.

Second, the regional director, a responsible operating official, is denied control over a major operation for which he is still held responsible. He must live with the project and with the water users, who are in a real sense his clients; yet he cannot control the design of major engineering works or their construction. He is seriously handicapped in his efforts to hold down project costs and yet ensure adequate and sound structures. If the Denver office is guilty of "over-designing" a project now and then, as some have claimed, he still does not have clear authority to require modification of the "fancy extras."

Third, the Division of Design and Construction is forced by necessity to concern itself almost entirely with operating functions—designing specific structures and administering construction contracts. One of its primary responsibilities, according to official Bureau policy, should be to serve as the commissioner's expert staff on design, working out design standards and exercising technical supervision over field design work to improve compliance with these standards; but there is little time for such activities. Indeed, one of the explanations offered by Design and Construction officials for failure to delegate more design authority to the regions is that not enough work has yet been done on developing standard designs for reclamation structures.

The Bureau is making some progress in working toward a better balance in this situation. Much credit goes to the present chief engineer who has probably made the present system work more effectively than could any other engineer in the Bureau. His willingness to work closely with regional directors, to negotiate and compromise where necessary, has opened the way gradually to increasing delegations of design authority to the regions. The development of some design standards, particularly for the simpler and less costly items, has also helped; and some regions have aided their own cause by building up better field design staffs.

There remains the problem of stabilizing the work load of the centralized design staff. As long as the decision to delegate or not is made in Denver, there will be a great temptation to use this authority to ensure a steady work load for the Denver office. This often means fluctuation in the design work load at the regional level, making it all the more difficult to build up a staff warranting the confidence of the chief engineer's office. This design delegation issue indicates clearly that there are thorny problems yet to be resolved before an effective balance is attained between regional integration and functional supervision.

The Efficiency Dilemma. In discussing the Bureau's search for balance in administrative management there are three particular areas to be surveyed; flexibility in organizational structure, efforts to encourage self-improvement, and control techniques.

The Bureau of Reclamation has developed a rather happy balance between uniformity and flexibility in organizational structure. Regional office organization is largely standardized, reflecting rather closely the headquarters pattern. Staffing, however, tends to vary according to the charcteristics of the regional program. Below the regional level neither the organizational pattern nor the number of sub-regional levels is uniform. Regions with a heavy construction program (for example, Regions 6 and 7 directing the Bureau's program in the Missouri Valley) tend to set up district offices between the projects and the regional office. Regions with a major investigation program and little construction activity are not likely to create districts; instead, the regional office deals directly with project offices and perhaps sets up area planning offices in the field to carry on the investigations. Some regions have established river control offices to conduct research in stream flow, sedimentation, and related problems of water control; other regions carry on such activities out of the regional headquarters. Certain regions have merged the operation and maintenance staff with the project planning staff at the project level to form a division of operation and development. By permitting this flexibility the Bureau has encouraged experimentation in structural arrangements. The resulting field organizations are designed to fit the specific needs of the area, not the "chart drafters" in Washington.

The Bureau has put on a major drive over the last few years to encourage regional self-improvement through systematic self-analysis.[19] Freedom to experiment with different patterns of organization is a worthwhile policy only if the regions are continually studying their work, their structure, and their performance with a constant eye to self-improvement. A number of interesting techniques for self-evaluation through management audits have been developed.

Region 2 (Central Valley) has experimented with joint technical-administrative reviews of field offices, initiated and conducted by the technical supervisory personnel in the regional divisions. By systematically interviewing the field office staff, the audit team of regional supervisors attempts to assess the quality of supervision and assistance given by its own division and at the same time evaluate operating performance in the field office. The audit is focused upon identifying and solving problems, but perhaps its most important result is greater management consciousness among the technical specialists conducting the survey and those being interviewed. During the first trial year 11 such reviews were conducted in Region 2 with significant progress toward improving supervisory techniques as well as operating methods.

In Region 5 another type of audit, the "self-analysis survey," has proved very useful in examining in detail the total performance of a project staff from top management to the ditch riders. The total job to be done on the project is analyzed and broken down into its component parts or "activity factors." These factors become the units of measurement and evaluation. For top management the list might include such items as planning, organization, and public relations. With the help of the project head and his advisers, the activity factors are weighted to show their importance to the total job. Next, each factor is analyzed in consultation with those responsible for carrying it on. Check points, or indicators, reflecting quality of performance are identified and measured to disclose strengths and weaknesses in performance. The ratio between these strengths and weaknesses, and the relative weight of the factor, are combined to give a rough quantitative indication of how well the activity is performed. This process is valuable not because it produces a precise score evaluating performance, but because it forces project officials to think systematically and analytically about their work. Weaknesses are disclosed and ways to overcome them can be identified more readily. The whole staff is afforded a comprehensive view of project operation leading to better coordination. Such self-analysis, if undertaken conscientiously, is almost certain to yield dividends in greater efficiency.

The Bureau also employs what it calls "staffing standards analysis" as a tool of self-evaluation. Each operating office and regional office is arranged on a master staffing analysis chart, showing for each type of work performed the present staff and its ratio to total employees in each office and to average work load. The line official in charge of an office can read the chart horizontally to find the staffing pattern in each functional unit throughout his organization. The staff officer by reading vertically can analyze staffing patterns for personnel engaged in his special function throughout the Bureau or any particular region. While the work-staff analysis chart does not pretend to present more than an over-simplified picture that ignores exceptional local conditions, it does provide kinds of comparative data tremendously valuable to every manager in his self-appraisal.

The other side of this coin of field initiative in self-improvement is the maintenance of Bureau-wide controls to guard against administrative errors. The heart of the Bureau's system of control is the machinery for program planning, designed to produce annually a six-year program setting forth the work to be done, the funds required to do it, and the dates for beginning and completing each phase. Field officers, under direct supervision from the regional staff, develop the data and lay out the program plan. Though it is reviewed carefully in the regional office and at headquarters, it remains primarily a field product. Once set up and approved, this program document becomes the standard used by region and headquarters to evaluate field performance. Where actions are not taken on schedule, this fact serves as evidence of potential trouble, calling for careful study either by the local office (self-analysis and trouble-shooting) or by the regional or headquarters staff. There is fairly general agreement throughout the field that this six-year program is probably the most useful single report or document developed in the Bureau of Reclamation.

In addition to control through programming, the Bureau relies upon conferences of all kinds, upon the *Manual,* and upon a system of field inspections and audits as control devices.

Conferences of functional staff personnel are used to clarify and interpret official policy, to concentrate attention upon the development of performance standards, and, of course, to encourage a sharing of ideas and techniques. During the fiscal year 1951, seven divisions conducted conferences attended by headquarters personnel, their regional staffs, and sometimes by representatives from certain district and project offices.

The Bureau of Reclamation *Manual* is now in better shape to serve as a control device than heretofore. Credit goes to the Office of Management Planning for the job of reducing the former "twelve-foot bookshelf" of printed administrative regulations to comprehensible size. Today's *Manual* is only one-sixth as large, a real achievement in condensation. Of course, any codification of standing orders, accepted practices, and procedures has its limitations. It is not difficult to find criticism, especially in the field, that the *Manual* has been written by unrealistic technicians and has led to the substitution of "official" procedure for commonsense judgment. Such criticism is valuable as a constant spur to keep the *Manual* simple and direct. It must be written in language which means something to field personnel if it is to be an effective guide for and control over their activities.

There is an ever-present danger of overemphasizing control machinery in a decentralized organization. The Bureau has already built up an elaborate structure of review and clearance procedures, field inspections, and audits of various kinds which reduce the time and energy resources of field, regional, and headquarters personnel. It is easy for controls to become ends in themselves, especially to those who design the control machinery or make the inspections and audits. There is only one criterion to measure the worth of any control device: what does it contribute to the accomplishment of the organization's primary mission? And those who judge its worth should be the line officials directly responsible for accomplishing that mission, and not functional specialists. The control structure in any organization, Reclamation included, requires continuing attention from top management. The Bureau appears to have found a satisfactory balance, but controls can quickly mushroom unless watched closely.

Conclusion

Reclamation's progress since 1943 toward workable decentralization has been noteworthy. Many Bureau officials believe the expanded program of the postwar years could not possibly have been planned and carried out successfully by the highly centralized organization of 1940.

Regional decentralization has distributed the supervisory work load; it has located planning authority in the hands of regional directors sensitive to the needs of their regions and in a position to develop balanced development programs based on priorities within those regions. Yet broad policy is still within national control and that control is made more flexible by the active participation of both regional and functional leadership in the development of basic policy. Major headway has been made in reconciling field integration of Bureau activities and adequate technical control, except in the area of project design and construction. Here, although working relationships have improved steadily, there remain seeds of conflict and confusion constituting a continual drag on effective performance. It is to be hoped that the search for a solution to this problem will be pushed aggressively. Finally, in the area of administrative efficiency the Bureau has shown considerable originality. The regions and field offices have responded constructively to encouragement from headquarters, experimenting in organizational forms and techniques of self-criticism and self-improvement. This vitality of regional and field personnel is the best safeguard against "over-building" control machinery.

In short, the experience of the Bureau of Reclamation in seeking effective equilibrium in decentralized administration should prove a valuable guide to other agencies contemplating decentralization.

Notes

1. C. Lester Walker, "So They're Re-doing the Post Office," 202 *Harper's* 39 (June, 1951).
2. Decentralization along functional lines implies that each functional division in the organization maintains its own field service, staffed and directed by specialists, carrying on their own activities independent of the field staffs of other functional divisions in the same agency. Decentralization by area calls for reproducing in each major field-service area a miniature of the central headquarters. The head of this "regional" office is usually charged with directing and coordinating the same functions that the bureau chief is responsible for, but the regional head's authority applies only within his limited geographic area. Macmahon, Millet, and Ogden in their study of federal work relief used the terms decentralization by specialty and decentralization by hierarchy, respectively. Arthur W. Macmahon, John D. Millett, and Gladys Ogden, *The Administration of Federal Work Relief* (published for the Committee on Public Administration of the Social Science Research Council by Public Administration Service, 1941), pp. 244-45.
3. *Area and Administration* (University of Alabama Press, 1949), p. 62.
4. There is a considerable body of literature on administrative decentralization, including a number of efforts to describe its advantages and disadvantages. The following have proved particularly useful in this discussion: George C. S. Benson, "A Plea for Administrative Decentralization," 7 *Public Administration Review* 170-78 (Summer, 1947); James W. Fesler, "Field Organization" in Fritz Morstein Marx, *Elements of Public Administration* (Prentice-Hall, 1946), pp. 264-93; James W. Fesler, *Area and Administration* (University of Alabama Press, 1949), especially pp. 49-72; M. George Goodrick, "Integration vs. Decentralization in the Federal Field Service," 9 *Public Administration Review* 272-77 (Autumn, 1949); John D. Millett, "Field Organization and Staff Supervision" in L. D. White and Others, *New Horizons in Public Administration* (University of Alabama Press, 1945), pp. 96-118; and David B. Truman, *Administrative Decentralization* (University of Chicago Press, 1940), especially pp. 1-20.
5. John M. Gaus, *Reflections on Public Administration* (University of Alabama Press, 1947), p. 9.
6. See Murray L. Cross, *Organization and Development of Bureau Organization* (U.S. Bureau of Reclamation, Office of the Chief Counsel, undated). This typewritten manuscript contains an excellent account of the Bureau's organizational development in the early years.
7. *Federal Reclamation by Irrigation, A Report Submitted to the Secretary of the Interior by the Committee of Special Advisers on Reclamation* (S. Doc. No. 92, 68th Cong., 1st sess.). This outstanding report is generally recognized as a major turning point in the evolution of reclamation policy.
8. The Reclamation Act itself had been made more restrictive by amendment. Originally the secretary of the Interior was given authority to determine the economic feasibility of proposed projects, to authorize them for construction, and to make expenditures from the reclamation fund for this work. When settlers on the first projects began to default on their construction payments and petition for relief, the Congress undertook belatedly to curb the tendency of the Bureau to spread itself too thin, attempting too many new projects before completing any. Thus, in 1910 Congress provided that henceforth new projects must be approved by the president before construction could begin (36 *Stat.* 835). Four years later Congress set up another control, this time in its own hands, requiring that in the future expenditures for the reclamation program should be made only out of annual appropriations by the Congress from the reclamation fund (38 *Stat.* 686).
9. 53 *Stat.* 1187. See especially Sec. 9(a). One observer has called this legislation ". . . a clearer expression of the essentially coordinated nature of all water control objectives than almost any other legislative expression of the Congress." Joseph S. Ransmeier, *The Tennessee Valley Authority* (Vanderbilt University Press, 1942), p. 27.
10. Much of this controversy was later reported in hearings held by the Harness Investigating

Committee of the 80th Congress. *Investigation of Bureau of Reclamation, Department of the Interior,* Hearings before the House Committee on Expenditures in the Executive Departments, Subcommittee . . . on Publicity and Propaganda of Federal Officials (U.S. Government Printing Office, 1948). Secretary Ickes' position is candidly revealed in a speech he made in 1946 at the Bureau of Reclamation Conference of Regional and Branch Directors with the Commissioner's Staff. He described his attitude as follows: "However, among other things, I found that the Bureau of Reclamation [in 1940] while it was supposed to be set up here in Washington was, in effect, operating from Denver . . . it struck me that we had a case of the tail wagging the dog. . . . I had two objectives in mind: One, to get away from Denver; and two, to give a localization to the operations of the Bureau which I thought would be of advantage to the Bureau and would get us better results." Quoted in the Harness Committee Hearings, pp. 651-52.

11. *Ibid.,* p. 681.
12. *Ibid.,* pp. 655-66.
13. This statement is contained in a *Memorandum* (untitled) from Under Secretary Fortas to Secretary Ickes, dated October 26, 1942.
14. *Appraisal of the Organization and Staff Proposed by the Bureau of Reclamation.* This undated and unsigned report is attached to *Organization Charts and Staffing Plan—Bureau of Reclamation,* a memorandum from Vernon D. Northrop, director, Division of Budget and Administrative Management, to Secretary Ickes, dated March 27, 1945.
15. This information is contained in a *Memorandum* (untitled) from Under Secretary Fortas to Secretary Ickes, dated April 3, 1945.
16. U.S. Department of the Interior, *Bureau of Reclamation Manual,* Vol. I, Organization and Administration, Chap. 2.3.2.
17. *Ibid.,* Vol. I, Chap. 2.3.3.
18. *Ibid.,* Vol. I, Chap. 2.3.3c.
19. See U.S. Bureau of Reclamation, Office of Management Planning, *Good Management; A Report on Improvement of Operations and Administration in the Bureau of Reclamation, Department of the Interior, FY'51* (September 4, 1951) and *Report on Management Improvement in the Bureau of Reclamation for Fiscal Years 1952 and 1953* (undated).

PHILIP M. MARCUS
DORA MARCUS

Control in Modern Organizations

Perhaps Cervantes' Don Quixote expresses a universal urge in his words, "I would have nobody to control me, I would be absolute." Never possible even in a feudal age, such aspirations today seem all the more unreal in the face of the pervasiveness of modern organizations. Yet control need not be exercised to bring misery to men, and recent research or organizational theory has examined the implications of control for the sometimes competing goals of individual adjustment and organizational performance.

In pre-World War II organization theory, efficiency was assumed to result from specialization of task and strict adherence to a hierarchic chain of command.[1] While much theoretical literature of this period contains broad and useful hypotheses on organization behavior, its propositions are often highly abstract and difficult to apply to specific organizational situations.[2] More recent investigations including those of the Organization Behavior Program at the Survey Research Center, have shown that greater initiative at lower levels, freer communication between levels, and less specialization may simultaneously provide an organization with a tighter control structure and a more competent and satisfied staff.[3] The research program at the University of Michigan has focused on control because of its central importance in coordinating diverse specializations and integrating groups into functioning units. After examining some of the theoretical aspects of control, we will dwell on some representative findings concerning the control structures of various organizations.

Some Theoretical Aspects of Control

Coordination in an organization is effected by the organization's control structure. What must be coordinated includes not only the various organizational units representing division of labor, or specialization, but also the diverse capabilities, temperaments, and attitudes of the people employed. Control may be defined as "that process in which a person (or group of persons or organization of persons) determines, i.e., intentionally affects, what another person (or group, or organization) will do."[4] This definition is sufficiently inclusive to encompass unilateral control, whereby one person or group influences another, or bilateral control, whereby two parties mutually affect each other.

An attempt to clarify aspects of organizational control has been made by Arnold S. Tannenbaum and Robert L. Kahn in their development of the "control graph,"[5] (see Figure 1), which depicts two aspects of control operative within an organization. The horizontal axis represents hierarchical levels in an organization. The vertical axis represents the amount of control that each level exercises.[6]

Plotting control in this manner provides a picture of the *distribution*, as well as the *amount* of control at various levels. The distribution of control is the amount of control exercised by *each* level in the organization. The sum of levels of control at all hierarchical levels may be considered the *total amount of control* operative in an organization. The *total amount* of control exercised in an organization is a variable frequently neglected in the literature. Control is most often viewed in terms of the position or person(s) exercising it.[7] Thus, there are analyses of "authoritarian" or "democratic" structures, or, in other words, analyses of the *distribution* of control. Such a conceptualization assumes that if control is redistributed and increased at the lower levels it is decreased at the top. But control removed from an upper level may result in a reduction of total control in the organization. For example, if executives, for some reason, issue fewer directives, it cannot be assumed that the discretion of lower echelons will necessarily be increased; it is more likely that fewer organizational demands will be met. Reducing the amount of total control beyond a certain level may endanger the coordination and effective functioning of an entire organization.

FIGURE 1
Control Curves for Four Different Types of Organizations

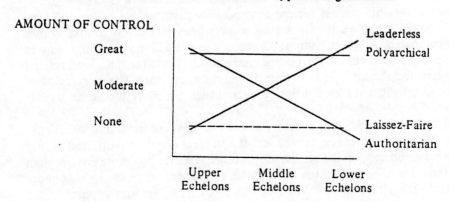

AMOUNT OF CONTROL

Great

Moderate

None

Leaderless
Polyarchical

Laissez-Faire
Authoritarian

Upper Echelons   Middle Echelons   Lower Echelons

Different types of organizational control structure may be depicted on the control graph. An authoritarian organization would be represented by a negatively sloped line; a democratic or laissez-faire organization by a low flat line; and a polyarchical organization by a high flat line. Obviously, no organization would conform perfectly to any curve.

Although the *total amount* and the *distribution* of control are conceptually independent, subsequent research has not clearly indicated their empirical independence. In the Center study of the League of Women Voters,[8] the correlation between total amount of control and distribution of control was very small and statistically insignificant. David Bowers'[9] also found a very low correlation between total control and distribution of control in his study of insurance agencies. On the other hand, a study of a large delivery company revealed a high and significant correlation between the two variables.[10]

In an analysis of membership participation in four labor unions it was reported that the membership as a whole exercised more influence than their presidents, i.e., the control curves tended to be positively sloped.[11] But when officers of the two most effective unions were compared with those of the other two, the membership reported that the more effective officers exercised more control. Members also reported that they exercised more control in the effective unions than in ineffective ones, thus affirming the assumption that effectiveness is related to the total amount of control exercised in an organization. Generally, all other organizations studied had negatively sloped control curves, i.e., officers were perceived as exercising more control than employees.

Self-ratings by the rank and file as to control they exercised showed variations among organizations.[12] On a five point scale of influence, for example, the lower skilled workers in a national delivery company felt they exerted the least control of the four hierarchical levels. League of Women Voters' members and insurance salesmen rated the amount of influence they exercised in their respective organizations about equally, and slightly above mid-points for the scale. Rank and file union members estimated their total influence to be very near the top of the scale.

In several studies respondents were asked to rate the amount of influence they *should have* (ideal control) in their organization as well as the amount of influence they did possess (actual control). The distributions of *ideal* and *actual* control responses for these studies have been plotted on control graphs and compared. A comparison of 32 stations in the delivery company showed negatively sloped curves for both actual and ideal control, i.e., workers felt they had and should have less control than their superiors. The workers' ideal curve also indicated they felt both they and their superiors should have more control.

In the League of Women Voters study, the ideal control curve was higher than the actual control curve; the actual and ideal slopes also differed in that members reported, on the one hand, that their officers had more control than the rank and file, and on the other hand, that members ought to have more control than either the president or the board. The amount of control the members thought the board should exercise was much greater than the amount they would grant the president, suggesting that League members see the role of president primarily as expediter, or representative to outside groups. In conclusion, it should be reported that most respondents of the organizations studied want more control, not only for themselves, but for others within the organization.

Control and Individual Adjustment

Distribution of control significantly affects individual behavior and adjustment to organizational life. Several studies made by the Center test the hypothesis that *morale* and *loyalty* to an organization and *participation* in it are high for those who desire to exercise control and are able to do so. Two experimental programs were set up in a clerical organization.[13] One was patterned after a *democratic model,* i.e., responsibility was increased and greater authority delegated to lower level personnel. At group meetings, decisions were made as to work distribution, length of recess, right to leave department during working hours, etc. The other experimental program was established along more *autocratic* lines, i.e., the clerks' routines were regulated more rigidly by "scientific management" principles, and decisions were made by upper level company officials. Results indicated that more clerks preferred the democratic model. However, there were persons in both programs who would have been more satisfied with the other type of control structure. What is needed is the integration of personality predispositions with the organizational pattern of control.

In the study of the League of Women Voters, loyalty to the League was measured by two questionnaire items concerning the degree of effort the respondent would make to prevent local leagues from failing from membership apathy or community opposition.[14] The amount of influence and control exercised by League members was measured by a question concerning the influence exercised by members and officers. When the loyalty index was related to the control measure, it indicated that the more control League members exercised, the more loyalty they felt toward the organization.

Employees of 32 delivery stations were asked to rate the level of morale in their stations.[15] The mean of their responses regarding morale was computed for each station and was found to correlate with the measure of employee influence. Total control (i.e., the total amount of influence exerted within an organization) is also related to loyalty and morale. The delivery stations study showed that stations with more total control had higher employee morale. But this was also true for the four labor unions studied. No such relationship was found in the League study.

Control and Organizational Effectiveness

Because goals vary from organization to organization and are often intangible, development of adequate measures of organizational effectiveness has been very difficult. Data on productivity, turnover, and absenteeism do not provide entirely satisfactory indices.[16] Measures of organizational effectiveness were related to measures of control in a number of studies. For example, in the study of the delivery stations, productivity records and ratings from questionnaire responses concerning the degree of intraorganizational strain and flexibility were used to determine effectiveness. Scores were assigned to each station. These scores correlated with scores on total control, but were found to be unrelated to the distribution of control.

In the study of the League of Women Voters, judges were asked to rate the individual leagues on a number of matters, e.g., success in fund-raising, quality of League publications, impact on the community, etc. Both total control and the distribution of control were found to be related to organizational effectiveness. The more influence exerted by lower levels of the League, the greater the effectiveness; the more reciprocal influence among all organizational levels, the greater the effectiveness.

In both studies, total control was related to organizational effectiveness; the distribution of control was found related to effectiveness only in the League study. This suggests that the total amount of control exercised in an organization is more crucial than the distribution of control.

The League, however, must substitute psychological remunerations for the financial and status rewards offered to members of other organizations. The exercise of influence and control in League affairs is perhaps a major factor in maintaining the interest and activity of the membership and the effectiveness of the League as an organization.

Data from a nationwide survey of 30 automobile dealerships—highly competitive and reliant "individual enterprise" among their salesmen—suggest that the amount and distribution of control are more important in an organizational structure which emphasizes cooperation and coordination of its parts than in one which stresses competition and individual initiative.[17] Using sales records as a measure of effectiveness, it was discovered that there was no correlation with measure of total control or distribution of control.

Size may be another factor affecting the relationship between control and effectiveness. When the units of an organization are small and scattered, as are automobile dealerships, there is less likelihood of close personal ties. Group cohesiveness built upon these ties would not be enhanced, nor would norms governing production be sustained as motivating forces for the participants. Consequently, lower organizational effectiveness may result. In contrast, larger work units allow small subgroups to form among individuals with shared values and attitudes. Overlapping membership in small groups provides links with the larger organization and promotes greater member morale and loyalty, which, in turn, increases organizational effectiveness.[18]

Control and Consensus

Consensus may be defined as uniformity in perceptions and attitudes.[19] Members of an organization may agree, for example, upon what jobs need to be done and the best ways of doing them. Such agreement among organizational participants produces judgments as to appropriate behavior and application of sanctions against those who do not conform. Consensus gives rise, then, to shared norms which govern the behavior and activities of members of an organization. Consensus should thus be positively related to organizational effectiveness.

A number of areas of consensus have been identified as relevant to work groups, including work group standards, morale, adequacy of supervisory planning, general work group consensus, and amount of influence desired for various levels. In the stations of the delivery company, no significant correlations were found between *the distribution of control* and these variables. However, another variable, degree of trust and confidence in the supervisor, was significantly related. Even when the averages of these items were computed across hierarchical levels, they did not yield a relationship to the distribution of control. When the measures of consensus were correlated with *total amount of control* within each station, a different picture emerged. Four of these measures were found to be significantly related to total control: morale; trust and confidence in the supervisor; adequacy of supervisory planning; and general work group consensus. No relationship was found between work group standards or the influence desired for various levels and total control. When the amount of consensus *between* levels was analyzed, it was found that work group standards and morale were correlated with total control, while influence desired for various levels was not. Further, a general measure of consensus was found to relate to total control, but not to the distribution of control.

This indicates that total control, or the composite of mutual influence within a station, is related to the amount of consensus both between levels in the hierarchy and within the work group. Consensus is necessary to the coordination and attainment of the goals of large scale organizations. Consensus makes possible a greater amount of decentralization of responsibility and delegation of tasks and, for this reason, is crucial to the effective operation of an organization.

Findings concerning control and consensus in the delivery company stations are consistent with those of the study of four labor unions. Twenty-four different items were used to measure union norms, including the willingness to do picket duty, the international's role, various passive and active sanctions, attitudes of member's friends, spouse, etc. In general, active members of the union showed a higher consensus on most of these norms than inactives. The four locals were ranked on their overall uniformity in nine content areas (representing a categorization of the 24 original items) and there was a very high correlation among the areas. Locals high in one area of uniformity tended to be high in others. A strong positive relationship was found when these measures were correlated with amount of total control in each local.

Results from Experimental Studies

While some of the studies described yield findings of interest and potential value, it may be argued that the practical application of these findings is somewhat limited, that it would be an extremely difficult task to introduce new patterns of control into organizational settings. However, experimental studies are available which demonstrate that control variables and some of their correlates are capable of being implemented.

One such study conducted in a large white-collar organization has already been mentioned. In both the democratic and the autocratic experimental divisions, attempts to change the level of control and decision making, albeit in different directions, were successful. Along with the delegation of decision making, the amount of job involvement and company loyalty increased among members of the participative groups. The experimenters also reported that these employees continued to perform their jobs even in the absence of supervisors, and attitudes toward company management and high-producing workers became more favorable. The reverse was found among members of the hierarchically controlled groups. These employees reported a decrease in job involvement, less loyalty to the company, and less feeling of job responsibility in the absence of their supervisors. Turnover also increased as did negative attitudes toward management and high producers.

Yet productivity increased among both groups. In fact, the amount of increase was greater in the hierarchical groups than in the participative groups. While it is difficult to judge what the long run effects will be, it is suggested that effectiveness will decrease in the hierarchical groups because of the hostility and resentment developed toward high producers and management. ". . .[T]urnover and the adverse attitudes created by the hierarchically-controlled program tend typically to affect productivity adversely over a long period of time."[20]

Another experimental study cited earlier was conducted in a large manufacturing plant over a three-year period. Results of measures taken just prior to induced change indicated that all plant departments which had been selected to undergo no change, scored higher than the experimental departments on 11 independent variables. These variables involved various aspects of employee participation in decision making, peer interaction and influence, supportive behavior, and emphasis on the work group.[21] Measures taken at the end of the study revealed that all but one of the initial differences in variables reversed themselves. The experimental departments showed substantial improvement on ten of the variables,[22] while the others experienced negative change on seven variables.[23]

An analysis of the dependent variables in this study revealed a more or less consistent pattern with that of the independent variables, i.e., generally favoring the experimental departments. An increase in measures of machine efficiency and employee satisfaction was found for the experimental groups, and a decrease in both variables was found for the control groups. While both the experimental and control departments increased in absentee rates, the increase was greater in the control groups.

Conclusion

The research described in these pages suggests that the concept of *total control* must be closely considered in a study of organizational behavior. Whether the criterion of a good organization is that of productivity or the intelligent utilization of human resources, the findings indicate that with greater *total control* there is a greater sharing in control at all levels, morale is higher, consensus regarding work is greater, and organizational effectiveness is facilitated.

It is virtually impossible for upper echelons to integrate and coordinate the lower levels in organizations characterized by increasing specialization, because persons in the upper echelons lack sufficient technical understanding. In fact, the subordinates who carry out the directives are often in a better position to make wise decisions.

In short, both organizational characteristics and humane considerations require that some control be delegated to the lower echelons. A greater amount of total control, whereby subordinates can actually influence their supervisors, will heighten, not lower, the organization's performance. However, when subordinates obtain a measure of expertise but are given no control, morale and willingness to contribute to the organization decrease. Dissatisfactions manifest themselves in high turnover and absentee rates, and in lower efficiency and production.

The comparisons made earlier between actual and ideal control curves showed that subordinates do not want more control and influence for themselves at the expense of higher levels in the organization. Rather, they desire more control for all levels over job activities, so that individuals know what is expected of them and what rewards or punishments they may receive. As society becomes increasingly dependent upon organization services, it needs also to become increasingly sensitive to the critical implications of control for individual adjustment and organizational performance.

Notes

1. A thorough critical evaluation of the early organization literature can be found in James G. March and Herbert A. Simon, *Organizations* (Wiley and Sons, 1958).
2. Examples of these abstract propositions are Robert Michel's "iron law of oligarchy" and Max Weber's "routinization of charisma."
3. Some of these more recent theorists would include Rensis Likert, Chris Argyris, Douglas McGregor and W. F. Whyte. Georges Friedmann, writing of the industrial situation in

Europe, has come to very similar conclusions about the more traditional approaches to administration.

4. Arnold S. Tannenbaum, "Control in Organizations: Individual Adjustment and Organizational Performance," 2 *Administrative Science Quarterly* 236-257 (September 1962).

5. Arnold S. Tannenbaum and Robert L. Kahn, *Participation in Union Locals* (Row, Peterson, 1958).

6. The measure employed to derive these control curves is usually some variation of the following questionnaire item:

   "In general, how much influence do you think the following groups or persons actually have in determining the policies and actions in (organization's name)?"

   The question is asked for each group or level in the organization and the response categories range from "no influence" to "a very great deal of influence." "Total control" is usually derived by summing the amount exercised at all levels. The distribution of control is calculated by subtracting the control exercised by the upper echelons from that exercised by the lower.

7. A few social scientists have begun to explore the possibility of social control as a non-fixed entity. It is quite explicit in Talcott Parsons, "On the Concept of Influence," 27 *Public Opinion Quarterly* 59-62 (Spring 1963). David Riesman implicitly makes a similar assumption in his analysis of the American power structure. David Riesman, "Who Has the Power?," in R. Bendix and S. M. Lipset (editors), *Class, Status and Power* (The Free Press, 1953), pp. 154-162. For a thorough discussion of control, see Rolf Dahrendorf, *Class and Class Conflict in Industrial Society* (Stanford University Press, 1959), pp. 157-240.

8. Arnold S. Tannenbaum, "Control and Effectiveness in a Voluntary Organization," 68 *American Journal of Sociology* 33-46 (July 1961).

9. David G. Bowers, "Organizational Control in an Insurance Company," *Sociometry* 27, 2 (June 1964).

10. Clagett G. Smith and Ogus Ari, "Organization Control Structure and Member Consensus," 69 *American Journal of Sociology* 623-638 (May 1964).

11. Tannenbaum and Kahn, *op. cit.*

12. When making cross-organizational comparisons such as these self ratings, one of the limitations of the control graph should be kept in mind. The horizontal axis on the control graph representing the hierarchical levels varies for each graph since it depends upon the structure of each organization.

13. Nancy C. Morse and Everett Reimer, "The Experimental Change of a Major Organizational Variable," 52 *The Journal of Abnormal and Social Psychology* 120-129 (January 1956).

14. Clagett G. Smith and Arnold S. Tannenbaum, "Organizational Control Structure: A Comparative Analysis," *Human Relations* 299-316 (in press, 1963).

15. Bernard Indik, Basil Georgopoulos, and Stanley E. Seashore, "Superior-Subordinate Relationships and Performance," 14 *Personnel Psychology* 357-374 (1961).

16. Basil Georgopoulos and Arnold S. Tannenbaum, "A Study of Organizational Effectiveness," 22 *American Sociological Review* 534-540 (1957).

17. Martin Patchen, Stanley E. Seashore, and William Eckerman, "Some Dealership Characteristics Related to Change in New Car Sales Volume," Unpublished report (Institute for Social Research, 1961).

18. The relevance of work group size and its implications for social activity is explored in S. M. Lipset, M. A. Trow, and J. S. Coleman, *Union Democracy* (The Free Press, 1956), pp. 150-175. Stanley E. Seashore (*Group Cohesiveness in the Industrial Work Group*, Institute for Social Research, 1954), however, found a curvilinear relationship between size and group cohesiveness; small groups tended to have very low or very high cohesiveness scores. It is clear, then, that more research is needed to clarify this important point.

19. Clagett G. Smith and Ogus Ari, *op. cit.*

20. Rensis Likert, *New Patterns of Management* (McGraw-Hill, 1961), p. 68.

21. Of the 11 independent variables, only five differences between control and experimental

departments were statistically significant. See Seashore and Bowers, *op. cit.*, Tables 3 and 4, pp. 73-74.
22. Of these ten independent variables, eight were found to be statistically significant.
23. Of these seven independent variables, four were found to be statistically significant.

O. GLENN STAHL

Straight Talk About Label Thinking

To assail certain management controls in government administration as interferences with "operating" programs is one of the fashions of the day that matured during the war. One of the recent written examples is the thought-provoking article, "A Dangerous Tendency in Government," by Willard N. Hogan, which appeared in the Summer 1946 issue of *Public Administration Review*. But most of the shouting is oral and less carefully thought out. The complaints and attacks (and occasionally even the fears) center in varying degrees on budget, personnel, accounts and audits, management planning or analysis, and housekeeping services, which are deplored as unwarranted "obstructions" to authority and responsibility for carrying out programs successfully. (Curiously, there is little reference to the inhibitions and distortions that sometimes result from the formalism and legalistic reasoning insisted on by some lawyers. These seem to have been accepted so long that they are more hallowed than modern management techniques.) Many of these criticisms of the reasons for management controls, or of the ways in which they are exercised, contain constructive observations. But in great part the criticisms are superficial.

Executives and students of administration are continually stressing the point that management "staff" activities are services to the operating objectives of an organization; that the outfit was created to do a certain "job"; and that budget, personnel, management planning, public relations, fiscal control, and housekeeping operations are incidental. Such activities are there to help get that "job" done. They are, in the broadest sense, services.

Of course, the mere statement of the point presents a truism that no one can deny. The surprising thing is the degree to which shallow or specious conclusions are arrived at in its name. Much of the difficulty arises out of over-simplification. From the way this point is sometimes ridden one can almost picture the proverbial general in the Pentagon, master of all he surveys and sufficient unto himself, barking his commands and finding life in a complex organization sublimely simple. The reasoning is almost like this: any school-boy should know that if something is to be a "service" then it can't be a "control." The dictionary just doesn't permit such things.

There is a name for such reasoning: it is "label thinking."

The Role of Staff

I submit that what is "service" at one point may be "control" at another. Let us see what this means by an example. A top executive has the necessary responsibility and authority to carry out a given program. His organization is divided into six major branches. In addition to other appropriate staff advisers, the top executive has a management chief or chiefs under whom are found the usual management activities. These management people are directly responsible to the top executive. They "serve" him. Nevertheless, the top executive is a very busy man. He expects his management people to be broad gauged and program conscious. Therefore, he asks them to represent him and act for him in varying degrees on personnel, budgetary, and comparable matters. When they are in contact with program officers at any point below the chief executive, they are either advising, providing the "know how," or controlling administration. To some extent, they are acting as line officials in their respective fields of specialization.

And what is so frightening about this? They are no more "specialists" than the various program officials themselves. It is the only way by which the busy top executive can maintain the controls he must maintain if he is to exercise real leadership and influence in the organization. If there is any problem, it is a problem of education of management staff and program staff alike.

It is popular in government for a program man to complain that a management man is not acting in his "service" capacity because he disagrees with or disapproves a proposal of the program man. This complaint was particularly loud among able and zealous experts brought into the federal government during the war to do something big in their field of specialization and to do it fast. Undoubtedly their complaints were often justified. They may have encountered some pretty unimaginative management men. But to assume that a personnel, budget, or other management specialist should jump through hoops at every wish or whim of every program official at any point down the line is not so much a recognition of the proper "service" relationship of these management people as it is a denial of the authority of a superior level in the line—the level in the hierarchy above the program official and to which he is responsible—the level at which the management specialists are employed expressly for the purpose of informing, guiding, helping, and, if necessary, restraining him, for the good of the program and by the general order or delegation of the superior officer.

These are simply some of the tools by which and through which the top executive manages. If his organization is big or far flung, he also may delegate many personnel and budget and similar management decisions directly to principal program officials who in turn, if size and operations require it, have management specialists on their own staffs to help them control the organization below. But, in any event, the top manager still needs basic policy control and certain common denominator or general procedure types of control at his own level; and if he needs them and has them, we expect him to use them and operate through them. They are "staff" or "service" to him. But they are "control" to those below. The men who exercise the controls represent management in their respective areas to all below their chief. A great deal of the thoughtless "griping" directed against management specialists is the chafing of subordinate officials at the rightful and necessary guidance and controls imposed by their proper superiors.

The idea of staff assistance does not require access to one's superiors chiefly through staff officers; actually program heads may see the line chief more frequently than his lieutenants. That depends on the subject matter. Program men are free, of course, to persuade or influence their superior officer on management matters, but that is not best done by "taking it out on" the management people who represent him. One federal agency in a statement announcing a reorganization handled the problem this way:

As in all cases of line and staff organization there is no question of the line or the staff being superior one to the other. They simply perform different and necessary functions for the Administrator.

The Complaints

What are some of the typical specific complaints?

1. *Negative restrictions get you down.* There are so many points at which government officials are prevented from doing something that they often get a feeling of frustration. A private businessman is a free agent by comparison. Many of these restrictions go too far. Many of them are unwise. Many (for example, the straitjacketing of the procurement system to ensure fair competition, the mysticism of federal budget "green sheets," the rigidity of the compensation system, the pretense of complex civil service categories that establish varying degrees of "status" for employees, to name only a few) are anachronisms, relics of conditions in government no longer significant. These should be fundamentally reconstituted. Negative restrictions, however, are not bad merely because they are negative. Most are desirable, if not always in form, at least in objective. Tangible evidence is rarely forthcoming of programs which have genuinely suffered because some individual could not be hired or fired, because somebody didn't get paid enough, or because there was not enough money or space or something else for some minor aspect of the program. The cases where real damage can be shown because of such action or lack of action are probably few and far between. Nevertheless, it is largely these individual minor experiencs that lead to the general charges of obstruction. A charge is valid only when the general nature of the restriction is bad,

and the situation is not remedied by spanking the management specialist and putting him in his servile place.

2. *You can't fire anybody.* This is one of those popular notions which arises from the human difficulties involved in any removal from office and the desire to blame inaction on something outside one's self. Actually, what most federal officials need in order to fire an incompetent employee is courage, plain ordinary courage, which is the same thing needed to fire an incompetent employee in private industry or anywhere else. It would not make for an effective working force, it would not make employees secure and productive, if they were to get the feeling that they could be removed from office on a summary basis. The limitations that appeals procedures and the like impose upon executives in this matter are far less a hindrance to elimination of incompetent personnel than they are a guarantee of the psychological security which a good staff needs.

3. *The boss acts too much through his leg men.* This point has been fairly well covered above. The answer is that he has to act through staff men of one kind or another. If they are narrow or obstructionist by nature, that is not a problem of organization but of personnel selection and training.

Hogan, for example, cites the power of the Bureau of the Budget in determining whether departmental proposals and plans are "in accord with the program of the President" and refers to these controls as "placed outside the line of operating responsibility" (p. 237). If the president does not use this staff agency for this purpose, he would have to use staff assistants or some new setup created for the purpose. Surely it is not suggested that he look after all these details himself. Or is it suggested that these "proposals and plans" do not need review and coordination? Few operating heads are so self-abnegating that they will not grasp at any opportunity to further their programs without regard to the president's wishes. Experienced bureaucrats know how to play special interest groups and congressional committees against the president's program if they feel it is necessary. This is not often a vicious thing; it usually grows out of an intense conviction of righteousness. But it is underhanded and it does circumvent real control by the chief executive of his administrative machine. He needs the Bureau of the Budget for precisely that kind of control.

4. *Management men are too zealous for their specialties.* Of course, these specialists are often wrong in degree or in direction at any time or in the case of any individual. But so are "program" men! They are all human beings. The problem that grows out of the zeal of expert interest and specialization is not solved by insisting on the exclusive rights of various specialties within a program to operate without substantial outside management controls, but by preparing specialists and experts of all stripes to be generalists and executives.

5. *Management people often exercise an unconscious or willful control over program policy.* Again, is this not a matter largely of individuals and of individual situations? Is not control by indirection and subtle sabotage evidenced just as frequently in the so-called "program" line and by subordinate operating officials as it is by management zealots? Ask any department head.

More Important Dangers

Emphasis on management controls as the villain in the piece distracts attention from much more fundamental and serious dangers in big government. Some of these have already been implied, but they may be recapitulated.

1. *The tendency toward autonomy and resistance to coordination by operating programs.* People who have worked in Washington know how intense and widespread this tendency is. It flows from perfectly understandable human causes. It ranges from the resistance of the armed forces to integration in a common department of national defense to the continuous effort of bureaus and offices to operate independently within the various departments. The examples are frequent of bureaus that would like to run their own shows without regard to tying their programs into related programs of other bureaus. And the occasions are frequent when a budget examination, job classification review, personnel selection approval, or organization analysis will force them to do what they should have done but didn't.

2. *Separatism fostered by support of special interest groups.* This is a corollary to and something of a restatement of the preceding point. It is evidenced in conflicting interests that may even reach public attention: for example, the conflicts over prices between the Department of Agriculture, with primary interest in a producer group, and the Office of Price Administration, with primary interest in a consumer group. The experienced bureaucrat sees it time and again between agencies and often, also, within almost every large agency.

3. *Over-formalized procedures.* This point has been most recently evidenced by passage of the Administrative Procedure Act. Blachly and Oatman have so thoroughly discredited the usefulness and wisdom of this restrictive legislation that it need only be cited here.[1]

4. *The limitations of the expert.* Here I am borrowing the title of a brilliant article by Harold J. Laski,[2] in which he calls attention to the tendency of specialists to assume that their expertise cloaks them with authority in all fields. "The expert . . . sacrifices the insight of common sense to the intensity of his experience." He fails to see around his subject. "He too often, also, fails to see his results in their proper perspective." As for caste spirit: "The inability of doctors to see light from without is notorious; and a reforming lawyer is at least as strange a spectacle as one prepared to welcome criticism of his profession from men who do not practice it. There is, in fact, no expert group which does not tend to deny that truth may possibly be found outside the boundary of its private Pyrenees" (p. 103). So Laski cautions against over-reliance on expertise in government. Are not his warnings at least as applicable to program men as they are to management men?

Remedies

No very penetrating analysis is needed to demonstrate that these dangers can be most effectively combated by activities and processes which develop perspective and coordination. Management controls themselves are often good counterirritants. It is desirable to concentrate authority in persons who are responsible for given programs of work but they must be equipped to carry it out. The real need, as I observe it, is in the preparation of men in all fields for executive leadership and for the mastery of management techniques. Many top administrators do not know how to use their "staff." As Laski puts it:

> . . . The wisdom that is needed for the direction of affairs is not an expert technic but a balanced equilibrium. It is a knowledge of how to use men, a faculty of judgment about the practicability of principles. It consists not in the possession of specialized knowledge, but in a power to utilize its results at the right moment, and in the right direction (pp. 105-106).

Laski stresses that the leader, the executive, the statesman, to be successful and worthy of authority, must coordinate his specialism "with the total sum of human knowledge," must see his expertise in perspective, must represent "common sense" in relation to the special field of work being administered.

The ideal may be to dispense with "staff" and with specialized management services entirely whenever operators and administrators are self-sufficient in this perspective and mastery, but we are far from that ideal.

Some exceptional men acquire the overall view through experience; others have been aided by a liberal education. We need a systematic effort in our whole educational system to turn out experts who have been exposed to such general understanding and wisdom that they may orient their specialization properly in the world's work. But a premium should not be placed on "generalism." An administrator is not made by a liberal education alone. Most executive posts below those of "cabinet" rank inescapably require statisticians, doctors, lawyers, scientists, economists—in short, experts—if understanding direction is to be achieved. But *specialists must be trained in more than their specialties.*

Many of the limitations of experts can be traced to a narrow, specialized education. Only the person with very unusual personal gifts can overcome the caste spirit, the provincialism, of the expert. On the theory that experts cannot escape administrative responsibility at some time in their careers if they are to rise above mediocrity, chemists and lawyers and doctors and statisticians and similar specialists should be expected to have in their professional curriculums certain minimums of the social sciences, social psychology, literature, and English, and a liberal dose of administration or management science. Few vocations are without the need for executive capacity and an understanding of how to lead and to work with people. This necessary "liberal" base to all preparation for vocations is never wasted; it also serves the needs of good citizenship.

We cannot expect formal education to provide the full training that is needed. One of the most difficult objectives to achieve in government organizations is acceptance of the idea that executives should be prepared for administrative responsibility. There is more resistance to this kind of training than to almost any other. The higher up in the scale we go, the greater the resistance. Among popular notions are the following: it is "belittling" to suggest that an executive needs training; or, he has gained it by experience; or, he can rely on somebody else to "administer" while he "plans" or "deals with the interests." This is some of the most meretricious balderdash that ever rang down the halls of bureaucracy. How many of the characteristics and attitudes needed are born in a man or acquired through the trial and error learning of one man's experiences? Very few indeed. They are concepts based on analysis of the experiences of many. One does not just come by them naturally through occupation of the position "next in line."

The major step that can be taken by bureaucracy—by forward-looking imaginative bureaucracy—is to insist that all potential executives participate in comprehensive training in management and leadership before they are considered equipped for major directive responsibility. For very top policy-making posts we rely on the selection policy of individual presidents, but there are thousands of jobs in the federal service of major executive importance to which this training requirement might well be applied.

This in-service training should be undertaken regardless of the individual's previous background. A broad education or experience cannot be relied on to have developed the necessary outlook. Such training cannot be a "short course" affair. It must be a progressive and systematic series of steps, beginning perhaps with intensive training in supervision for first-line supervisors, including emphasis on human relationships and how to get people to work together. The program could next add refinements of supervisory principles and practices and exploration of the purposes and uses of various management techniques, such as budget planning, organization planning, personnel administration, property and materials control, and fiscal accounting. The training might also include public relations and the legal aspects of administration. The plan should provide for higher and higher requirements for progress to successive levels of administrative responsibility. Thus, about three different stages of training for executives could be planned—one for minor supervisors, one for middle supervisors, and one for major executives. No one would be selected for a job above a certain level unless he had succeeded in the necessary training.

An example of the practicability of management training on a large scale is that sponsored by the British Ministry of Labour for business executives. It recognizes that "few men, having a practical and chiefly technical background, can be expected to have acquired the fundamentals of business management as well." The syllabus, planned by the British government and offered in technical colleges in industrial centers, is described as "coming to grips with everyday business affairs" and dealing "with the fundamentals of the human side of business, the relations of management and staff," and the accounting, financial, and statistical aspects of business.[3]

Conclusion

The purpose of this article is not to say that management specialties do not need improvement. They need continuous and intensive improvement. But the problem cannot be dismissed by saying that these specialties should be viewed as "services" rather than "controls." Reform of management organization and methods needs to be seen in perspective. It is granted that we can't avoid big government; let us therefore focus attention on its big shortcomings and obstructions, which management techniques were in part developed to correct. Then we may feel we are sharpening the tools to deal with the fundamental bugaboos of complex organization.

Notes

1. "Sabotage of the Administrative Process," 6 *Public Administration Review,* 213-227 (1946).
2. 162 *Harper's Magazine,* 101-110 (1930).
3. British Ministry of Labour, "England's Business Training Scheme," 25 *Personnel Journal,* 121-26 (1946).

PART III

Dynamics of Organizations-in-Life: Seven Ways of Responding to Experience, and Guiding It

1. Marshall Dimock, "Revitalized Program Management"
2. Frederick C. Mosher, "Some Observations About Foreign Service Reform: 'Famous First Words' "
3. Clara Penniman, "Reorganization and the Internal Revenue Service"
4. Robert T. Golembiewski and Alan Kiepper, "MARTA: Toward an Effective, Open Giant"
5. Larry Kirkhart and Orion F. White, Jr., "The Future of Organization Development"
6. James S. Balloun and John F. Maloney, "Bearing the Cost Service Squeeze: The Project Team Approach to Cost Improvement"
7. David A. Tansik and Michael Radnor, "An Organization Theory Perspective on the Development of New Organizational Functions"

SO WHAT has experience taught us about organizing and reorganizing? And how can we go about responding proactively to that experience, as contrasted with perpetually reliving it?

Marshall Dimock shows us the way, in terms of basic strategy. He has spent an adulthood observing organizations, and he shares with us his convictions in "Revitalized Program Management." In sum, he sees organizations as going through four stages. Entrepreneurship characterizes the first stage, which tends to be exciting but untidy. Things get done, but feelings and relationships tend to be bulldozed by the willful entrepreneur, whether in a business or a public agency. Soon enough, an administrative stage sets in, and its hallmarks are steadiness and order. The costs can soon outweigh the advantages, however, particularly if the leadership emphasizes orderliness too much at the expense of innovation. If this occurs, Dimock warns, objectionable features of bureaucracy can set in. Technique can come to dominate purpose. A fourth stage then becomes needed—organizational renaissance or renewal—but its development remains highly problematic.

Dimock has no doubt about our present phase, in general, in both business and especially government. Our organizations wallow in the third stage, and this poses *the* challenge to organizational theory and praxis. We need to induce more or less continuing renaissance or renewal if we can; and we must aspire toward them even if striving will often remain the only reward.

How to load the odds in favor of renaissance or renewal in our organizations? Dimock proposes a short list of changes needed to trigger movement from bureaucracy to enterprise, and the six additional selections below provide broader as well as more detailed assessments of what needs to be done, and how.

Those six selections provide diverse perspective on how to increase an organization's coping success. For openers, Frederick C. Mosher provides valuable guidance in "Some Observations About Foreign Service Reform: 'Famous First Words.' " His basic admonition deserves to be up-front, stage-center. Organizational reform is far easier in those cases in which no fundamental changes in personnel systems are involved. But, Mosher implies, reforms often will involve not only structural change but also will benefit from (if they do not critically depend upon) supportive changes in the personnel systems which have been used to select, train, socialize, and evaluate those human products who make both "new" and "old" structures work, for better or worse. This central point gets neglected in many structural reforms, in which too little attention gets directed at the attitudinal and behavioral changes required by structural change.[1]

The experience of the State Department with various attempted reforms implies a valuable generalization, Mosher notes, concerning the probability of change in personnel systems. That conclusion? The change-effort will be long and arduous, and that places a low probability on its success, especially in the absence of a vital sense of the realities concerning the centrality of attitudinal and behavioral change. Current substantive issues tend to preoccupy the attention of decision makers in organizations such as the State Department, and that means attention to the long-run reform of personnel systems will seldom have high enough priority for sufficiently long periods of time from enough of the most relevant actors to get done a sufficiency of what requires doing.

Although Mosher does not promise any rose gardens relative to reorganization, failure and despair can be avoided, or at least their effects can be delayed or blunted. Clara Penniman provides one example in her "Reorganization and the Internal Revenue Service." She makes two basic points. First, executive leadership certainly can go a long way toward tilting the odds toward success. President Truman's surprise decision to remove all but the top IRS position from political patronage no doubt had a powerful impact on events, both in generating political acceptance of the broad purpose as well as in internally motivating the multitudinous adjustments that had to be made in the IRS organization.

Second, as Organization ↔ Environment theorists have urged, organization structure should reflect a dynamic balance. As environments shift, Penniman advises, organizational adjustments might be necessary. Substantial decentralization in the IRS case seemed to have improved both morale and productivity. But headquarters must remain vigilant. Ideally, for example, greater centralization might later become appropriate—or at least politically expedient—if initial delegations have to be fine tuned in response to violations of policy in field units. Such violations could include bribery, extreme variations in local practices, and so on. As Penniman notes: ". . . the victory is never finally won." So the top dogs also must learn new tricks if reorganization is to succeed. How to exercise quality control even as they delegate substantial operating responsibilities? The point is a central one, and not one that can be coped with easily or without prudent risk taking.

The success of organizing or reorganizing efforts always will depend on a basic and tenacious methodology—doing one's damndest, no holds barred. However, the rapid evolution of organization development (or OD) perspectives and techniques provides an increasingly firm hand-hold for grappling with the unruly dynamics. OD applications—for rough purposes, the disciplining of behavioral science findings to a relatively specific set of values—can usefully guide many organizing efforts. OD is often referred to as the "laboratory approach to planned change," and is illustrated in Robert T. Golembiewski and Alan Kiepper's "MARTA: Toward an Effective, Open Giant."

Essentially, "MARTA" reports on a specific kind of organizational start-up—one way of helping build an appropriate culture at work *via* a range of learning designs that are consistent with a relatively specific set of values or norms. Start-up constitutes a magic moment in organization life, the selection implies, and one too seldom emphasized in the public sector.[2] Moreover, the article reflects how psychological time can be speeded-up —how processes can be substantially telescoped to permit the kind of quick reaction time required by organizations such as MARTA, the Metropolitan Atlanta Rapid Transit Authority.

The MARTA selection seeks to build on OB, moreover, in a way that distinguishes its method not only from that body of literature but also from much of what gets inspired by the OA & T approach, or organization analysis and theory. How? The MARTA application illustrates one variety of "action research,"[3] guided by behavioral science theory. For example, theory points to the relevance in MARTA of a number of key processes and relationships, which were measured as part of the start-up program. In addition, specific learning designs sought to modify those relationships and processes in intended ways, reflecting the "applied behavioral sciences" bias of OD. These findings often were fed back to participants so as to reinforce intended changes in behavior and attitudes, or to indicate where mid-course corrections were appropriate. The purposes? They seek to increase participant involvement and ownership in learning and change and, thus, to enhance motivation and self-control in doing what needs to be done.

In these senses, "MARTA" emphasizes self-correcting learning. Participants evaluate their own processes in a variety of ways in action-research, in sum, and respond to that feedback so as to minimize reaction time and to maximize their sense of involvement in and ownership of the value-loaded entity that their MARTA was becoming. Some describe such organizations as self-evaluating, or self-correcting. They may also be described as self-forcing and self-enforcing.[4]

Even as the OD technology-*cum*-values served as a useful vehicle in the MARTA start-up, the continued development of the approach faces serious issues whose resolution cannot be taken for granted. Indeed, we are just beginning to learn how to frame some of these issues for future resolution. That is the basic and significant message of "The Future of Organization Development," authored by Larry Kirkhart and Orion F. White, Jr.

Kirkhart and White focus on a number of enigmas or dilemmas facing OD and, while they optimistically see light at the end of the tunnel, they do not minimize the developmental challenges of moving through that conceptual tunnel. Their argument can only be sampled here, obviously, but even that sample implies the crucial nature of the issues with which they deal. For example, OD has expanded the consciousness of many concerning the blend of "content" and "process" required in organizations. But that consciousness has not yet been reflected in the general acceptance of an appropriate evaluation of an organization's "efficiency" and "effectiveness." Traditional and limited notions still tend to dominate, and those convenient and significant simplicisms must be transcended, Kirkhart and White propose. Similarly, the authors emphasize the need to accommodate two approaches to problem solving—by participation and interaction that might lead to consensus or general agreement; and by "technical parameters," that is, by knowledge of the constraints implied by theories or "laws" relating to the physical or social worlds. That is a tough one, but the extremes-to-be-avoided seem clear enough. We need enough reliance on theory to reduce the probability that we will devote scarce effort to "reinventing the wheel," to lessen effort wasted because of an insufficient appreciation of empirical constraints or regularities. At the same time, we need to acknowledge the motivating potential inherent in participation and the involvement in decisions to which it can lead. Some would argue, in fact, that there is no such thing as a "bad decision." Decisions only have larger or smaller proportions of the appropriate people involved in their development, who are more or less supportive of those decisions. That goes a little too far for this author's tastes, but there is no denying the significance of problem solving by interaction as well as by knowledge or theory.

We cannot stop the world while these and other issues in OD get worked on, of course. Fortunately—as the MARTA case suggests, and as the earlier review of success rates helps establish—enough is now known to provide a decent chance to influence some organizational events in desired directions *via* OD.

Alternative ways also exist to encourage members of large organizations to make the kinds of adaptations that environmental changes or constraints require. The IRS relied on basic reorganization toward a more self-forcing system based on a decentralized pattern of delegation, a change motivated by powerful political pressures to improve effectiveness. MARTA emphasized the prior building of norms and attitudes that would facilitate the kind of rapid transitioning required for the timely development of a mass urban transit system, in effect anticipating the political and social pressures of a failure to do so.

James S. Balloun and John F. Maloney add to our growing inventory of learning from experience so as to guide it better, this time with emphasis on what can be described as a temporary structural arrangement—a "project team." Balloun and Maloney develop a case study of one such application in "Beating the Cost Service Squeeze: The Project Team Approach to Cost Improvement." The specific application they describe is a success story, and that should help buoy any flagging enthusiasm in the face of the potent challenges to organization renewal sketched by (among many others) Dimock and Mosher in the papers reprinted below. Balloun and Maloney are mindful of these challenges. Indeed, they root their exposition in a set of barriers in the public sector that impede cost reduction. Beyond that, they indicate how the "project team" approach can help respond adaptively to those barriers.

Another class of experiences also can help in revitalizing and restructuring organizations—how new and innovative activities can be introduced into ongoing organizations, and profitably integrated. These activities often are classified as "staff," and that in itself (recalling Stahl's contribution in Part II) implies significant problems for both introduction and integration. But the easy way out—copping out because of the likely problems—will not suffice. Growing pressures on management derive from both the magnitude and frequency of environmental changes, as well as from escalating technological complexity in generating product lines of goods and services. And these pressures require new and innovative activities. In fact, we may have to run faster to stand still in this regard, so great are the environmental and technological turbulences involved.

David A. Tansik and Michael Radnor focus on the process of such introduction and integration in their "An Organization Theory Perspective on the Development of New Organizational Functions." Their specific focus is on PPBS, or Program-Planning-Budgeting System, which was in fuller flower when they wrote but which has now found a humbler place in the firmament of managerial systems. Their specific focus merely helps isolate what they propose is a basic and generic process—a set of organizational life cycles which they offer as aids to understanding the introduction and integration of any new organizational functions, PPBS or whatever.

Viewed broadly, the selection by Tansik and Radnor in effect can be read as urging the fuller integration of the three organizational approaches sketched in the introductory essay heading this volume. PPBS, as they correctly note, comes out of the tradition identified above as organization analysis and theory; and PPBS also is essentially rooted in the centralized model of structuring work prescribed by the bureaucratic principles. Developments in organization behavior, or OB, imply the usefulness of an organization theory of greater descriptive power and comprehensiveness, however, to which Tansik and Radnor seek to contribute by their differentiation of phases in the adoption of a new function. A major result of this kind of effort, this editor concludes, would be an enhanced organization development (OD) approach. Hence, Tansik and Radnor can be viewed as supporting the same developmental progression as this volume, which can be schematized as such a movement rightward:

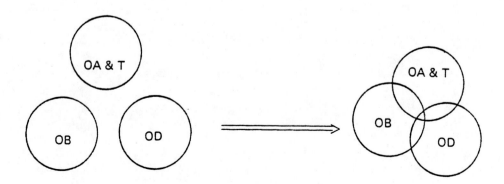

Hopefully, in the end, this volume joins in inducing precisely the kind of movement implied by Tansik and Radnor, and latent in so much of the corpus of the first 40 volumes of the *Public Administration Review* which contributes to the theory and practice of organizing and reorganizing.

Notes

1. This has been the common experience of most public reorganization efforts, for example. Dollars, effort, and planning go predominantly to the design of the model rather than its implementation.
2. For example, see Herbert A. Simon, "Birth of an Organization: The Economic Cooperation Administration," *Public Administration Review,* Vol. 13 (Autumn 1953), pp. 227-236.
3. Consult Edgar F. Huse, *Organization Development and Change* (St. Paul, Minn.: West Publishing, 1980), pp. 88-92.
4. This rich organizational notion was introduced by Leonard R. Sayles and Margaret Chandler, *Managing Large Systems* (New York: Harper and Row, 1971).

MARSHALL DIMOCK

Revitalized Program Management

The program manager, whether in industry or in government, is the production person who actually delivers goods and services to the consumer-voter. Macmahon and Millett wrote a good deal about him in *Federal Administrators* (1939) and so did Corson and Paul, more recently, in *Men Near the Top* (1966).[1] The so-called bureau chief or line executive, as Wallace Sayre was fond of pointing out in his seminar appearances, is literally at the center of all the action in public administration: he alone produces goods and services that go directly to the consumer. Consequently, as Paul Appleby used to say, all that the higher echelons do is help facilitate the result, for they produce nothing directly.[2] In recent years, however, we have tended to lose sight of these truths and in consequence are suffering a loss of vitality and momentum. At the same time, some of our national rivals, such as the Soviets,[3] are moving rapidly toward a belief that the freedom and autonomy of the operating executive are the bases of success and if we do not speedily return to our earlier view, government's reputation may suffer in public approbation even more than it has. Production management not only needs to be reemphasized, but, equally, it needs to be renewed and revitalized because in too many cases it has become slothful and excessively bureaucratic.[4]

By the program manager, I mean, of course, the "line" executive, whether he is a bureau chief, a city manager, a department head who daily directs his own program, or—most numerous of all—someone who runs a field office of a widely distributed geographical enterprise. Such persons are commonly referred to as the "practical" executive, the one who knows how to deliver quality goods regularly and on time. If there were enough of these, the cost of government could be greatly reduced.

In the middle 1930s the orientation of American corporations was toward the following philosophy of management: the production manager needs all the factors at his command that determine production; he should control them and daily direct them; he should be in charge of personnel management and policy, make appointments, promotions, and the like, and confine the personnel staff agency to research and advice; the top management should concentrate on external relations, plan long-range strategy, and make all wide-scale

171

decisions, but the initial planning should be done by action segments, and the line people who do the planning should also control the execution. In other words, everything centered around the operations man, the direct producer. This has changed some in those companies that have become conglomerates and transnationals: they still pay lip-service to production management, but increasingly and inevitably they substitute remote thinking and decision for on-the-spot thinking and decision.

One of the results of this long-standing industry focus on production is that traditionally the staff function has been viewed with suspicion in business. The best staff man is a production man who is temporarily assigned to a position where he can think and consult, after which he will return to his normal line position. Accordingly, staff work is tied in with production organization, not placed at the apex of the pyramid as it has been in many state and federal governments the past 30 years. When the Brownlow Committee was considering the six administrative assistants for the president, for example, I was asked how many such assistants the top corporate executives had at the time. The answer was, "None, in terms of line of command. He has one or two personal assistants who handle his personal arrangements, but there is no staff activity until the departmental level is reached, where it is tied in with the line."

In some ways the Washington line executive's position was better in the 1930s and 1940s than it is now. The line executive got his mandate directly from Congress—his basic statutes were "his" and not someone else's. Similarly with his organization and his funds. Consequently the operations man was under a much greater necessity than now to deal with Congress in a direct and forthright manner. What was lacking in this set-up was a sufficient coordination and intermeshing of programs at the higher executive level, and it is this, of course, that the Bureau of the Budget and other central staff agencies have tried to supply. In business, this coordination would be supplied by the operating vice-president and the department heads, constituting a cabinet. In government it should be done this way, too, and eventually we shall have to come to it. Otherwise the production manager will gradually atrophy and our competitive potential as a nation will be weakened. The principal reason that size produces a deadening bureaucracy, as Peter Drucker was one of the first to enunciate and has been stressing ever since,[5] is that too many layers of coordination frustrate and literally strangle the production managers who require full resources and adequate freedom before they can perform.

By vitality I mean energy—not random energy but energy directed at a purpose.[6] Vitality makes it possible to tackle and solve problems vigorously. Equally, it is the urge to innovate and improve, to find better ways of doing things, of achieving superior results. It is both measurement and a philosophy. Vitality combines imagination with practicality to produce something new—in this sense entrepreneurship. Vitality has a certain steadiness combined with foresight and drive to seize opportunities when they appear, to make openings when they do not. Vitality is personal and motivated, flexible and resourceful, and it does not give up easily.

Managerial vitality is accordingly a balance between the systematic logic of bureaucracy and the innovativeness of enterprise. Here the analogy to the life sciences is that a combination of instinct and habit underlie group cooperation in the biological world and innovation resembles specialization and individualization required for the balance that assures survival.[7] Carried too far, each component in the blend becomes a pathology, an excess. When the reliance on system is too heavy, the advantages of bureaucracy shade off into a frustrating loss of initiative; and uncontrolled initiation, on the other hand, becomes deranged unless balanced by the steadiness that system provides.

Vitality also communicates itself to others, creating spirit and atmosphere within the program. To maintain vitality at a high level is a key problem of any society and when vitality begins to decline, it is essential to know why, and what must be done to renew it. Under the most favorable conditions, institutions do not necessarily begin to run down once they attain a certain age or size. Although the tendency is there, it is possible to control and reverse it. As organizations age, however, they do tend to resist change and hence if their executives would successfully maintain the vitality of the enterprise, they must fully understand the problem and devote their energies to solving it.

The Excesses of Bureaucracy

Certain unmistakable signs betray the fact that a given program is becoming excessively bureaucratic.[8] Instead of being outgoing and consumer-oriented, it is now introverted, oblivious to any but its own narrow concerns. The multiplicity of rules, exacerbated in recent years by the judicialization of the administrative process, creates a degree of rigid inflexibility that makes it hard for the program to adapt to change. This because discretion is the heart of change and the *sine qua non* of a developing managerial strategy, without which an operating executive is neutered. To the bureaucrat, change itself becomes a threat; only business-as-usual provides a sense of cocoon-like security. Excuses are found for not acting, and when action does not occur, the pace is slow. Employees behave as though doing business were a favor to the customer, and if something goes wrong, throw the book at him. They do only what their job descriptions require, are no longer obliging, and become officious to the point of sadism.

Passing the buck has become a game everyone plays, those at the service level passing it upwards to top management until at length top management is overwhelmed with a mass of petty decisions that are time-consuming and distracting. Quality is sacrificed to quantity. Things are measured instead of assessed ultimately as to their human and social import. Individuals "behave" instead of think. Minimum norms of employee performance are imposed but mean nothing in terms of service to the customer and the public. Rationality is defined as "what do I get out of it?," instead of "what does it do to the effectiveness of the program?" There is little pride of work, and esprit de corps vanishes as jealous cliques take over. And a weary management fails to renew itself.

These manifestations of excessive bureaucracy can be traced to four common pathologies. First is the tendency toward insulation (grooving, cloistering) as people try to protect themselves from system and impersonality, seeking a place to hide from the rigidities and frustrations that surround them. They resist cooperation outside their own small group, wanting only to be left alone. These are the same factors that explain the recent generation gap.

Second is a dislike of responsibility, for they are literally born into an environment where little is expected. As Maslow and others have said, they cannot develop their personalities and experience daily challenges. Play it safe is the attitude, avoid risk so you cannot be blamed. Motivation is reduced to drawing a weekly check and retiring early so as to begin to live.

Together with these two factors at the service level is the third, seemingly contradictory, pathology of empire building, encroaching upon others, which most often occurs at the supervisory level. This is intensified when compensation and promotions are gauged primarily by the number of those supervised instead of by the qualitative factors of social purpose, difficulty of performance, and social contribution. Jurisdictional infighting naturally becomes common under these circumstances, each fiefdom striving to profit at the expense of another. Reorganizations occur frequently, in the hope that combining existing agencies will miraculously infuse new vitality into them, whereas universal experience demonstrates that vitality generation is an internal thing —stand and fight, so to speak—in order to solve smaller problems before they become larger problems. Instead of doing their jobs better, therefore, in this third manifestation of bureaucratic neglect, competing units wind up doing a number of disparate and sometimes unrelated tasks less well. This is the basic situation from which the need for higher policy making and direction arises, not the lack of potential and resources in the operating unit themselves.

Finally, the fourth pathology is loss of personality and humanness, creating a deadening uniformity throughout the program. Employees are afraid to be different lest they be judged disloyal to worker and management norms. Instead of showing independence and enterprise, it is safer to conform to the mores of the system. The system itself develops a life of its own which continues from one generation of employees to the next, resisting change in the hope of staying comfortable. But since consumers often rate individuality and responsiveness higher than machinelike efficiency, the effort is self-defeating. A vitalized organization is a living thing and as such it develops personality.

The excesses of bureaucracy may be caused not only by internal factors but also external ones, and obviously it is easier to control the former than the latter.[9] Thus the external factor of environment—whether energetic or sluggish, alert or non-responsive—may be extremely influential. So also are social taboos and prejudices. Even the attitude of the press, power aggregations, and the American Bar Association has a decided influence on spirit and outcome, because if trust and respect are accorded line executives the production increases markedly, whereas if the atmosphere is antagonistic and the government is reviled, there are immeasurable losses of dedication and accomplishment.

In the government, as in firms, therefore, more is produced and more is enjoyed when autonomy is assured operating programs.[10] Competition and the freedom that goes with it benefit business associations: if government operating programs were given the same degree of freedom, the results would be similarly rewarding. Business and government are not all that different. Personal and organizational politics are found as much in one as in the other.[11] The common factor of advance is operations managers with a mandate. If one is inclined to doubt this, consider the difference in accomplishment when government is involved in a crisis such as war or depression: when "born" managers in government are given authority and commensurate freedom the resulting accomplishment changes for the better almost overnight. We credit this to the crisis, not to the fact that managers are given the ingredients of enterprise.

No nation, government, or firm ever stands still: it is either progressing or declining. Like the health of the individual, it is easier and more rewarding to maintain the vitality of the government action program—a positive approach —than to tinker with the chronic illnesses of bureaucracy.

The Life Cycle of Organizations

Understanding why these excesses of bureaucracy occur depends upon a knowledge of life-cycles, the cyclical gyrations toward excess and balance that Aristotle made so much of in his philosophy. On the basis of my comparative study of bureaucracy in big business and big government, I have come to some conclusions regarding the natural life cycle of such organizations. External forces cause change even when internal management is not ready for the test: centralization follows decentralization, internal emphasis on system and tidiness is eventually followed by enhanced public relations, computers are worshipped only to be followed later by the resurgence of human personality.

Of the four predictable stages in the life cycle of organizations, whether public or private, the first is entrepreneurship. An energetic individual has a new idea and quickly gets something going. Morale is high and people enjoy what they are doing, which is one reason why government so often creates a new agency for a floundering program instead of trying to breathe new vigor into an old one. The entrepreneur has a certain kind of personality: highstrung, self-confident, imaginative, bulldozing, and contemptuous of obstacles. Scientists and all true innovators have the same bundle of traits. But often the innovator is a poor manager, once the initial enthusiasm has passed. He often lacks patience and attention to detail. A true inventor will go on to something else as soon as he has got all the satisfaction he is going to get out of his latest invention.

The second stage is the administrative one. The executive who takes over from the entrepreneur is as orderly as his predecessor was temperamental. The peak stage in the enterprise often occurs at this point because it still enjoys the energy of innovation which is now joined by the logic of orderly procedure. Leadership here requires a personality that blends dynamism and steadiness, initiative and order. Most government programs, until they begin to slow down, are of this kind of course.

In the third stage, system has been carried too far and is now bureaucracy in the objectionable sense. The program's goals are obscured, subordinated to a concentration on means as ends in themselves. This is appropriately called the triumph of technique over purpose. Non-human factors such as organization, procedures, and especially rigid rules are elevated to a kind of pedestal and dominate the undertaking. The morale of employees and customers alike, once high, becomes progressively low, to the point of inertia. Innovativeness comes to a virtual halt and is outdistanced by more vigorous competitors. In many cases the social need still exists, but the service is not forthcoming.

The final stage is renewal, if renewal is to occur, for it takes a deliberate effort of will to bring it about. Again, there is an infusion of entrepreneurship, usually accompanied by the firing of the old leadership, while a new one is brought in. Bureaucratic pathologies are rooted out to be replaced with larger draughts of inventiveness and humanness. Taking risks and breaking with obsolete habit are rewarded. Some individuals have a genius for this kind of assignment, much as others have a genius for initially starting something. The creaking organization begins to shake itself and look up, to regain the energetic personality it had lost. In a word, entrepreneurship is personal and human, while pathological bureaucracy is automatic and colorless. In a struggle between the two in isolation, it is not difficult to predict which would win.

But even in this renewal stage it is necessary to work through others. The entrepreneur usually does three things: picks the key men with innovative ability he can work with harmoniously; develops a team of managers from all levels to update the goals and targets of the enterprise in terms of products and services as well as methods of operation, and then develops a first-rate re-training program for the enterprise as a whole in which the field managers (ultimate incidence of service) are given the main responsibility for training and indoctrination. In other words, the thing is turned upside down in more respects than one. This system has worked over and over again!

Bureaucracy or Enterprise

The trouble with bureaucracy is that it is too rational, and nothing else. As such, it appeals to the logician, the engineer, and the pedant whose stock-in-trade is categories and nothing else, but it is anathema to those who are productively oriented. Start with the assumption that each individual should be a specialist in his field, that it is a paper plan that is being administered, that no one should be expected to do more than his position calls for, and that the position is more important than who fills it, and you have the perfect prescription for bureaucratic excess. The operations man is interested in the opposite of such things, for he seeks teams and flexibility, strategy instead of logic, voluntarism instead of fear, and freedom from top-side domination. He is looking for people who can think and innovate and he does not trust those who use rulemaking only to enhance their own power and authority. Reduce everything to rules and you sap the life of any operating organization. The manager is holistic, the bureaucrat schizoid.

This mental set also affects those who are purely and simply staff-minded, which accounts for the reason that industry tries to get action men to do staff jobs. Although the staff man may pay lip-service to the idea that he has no authority and merely gives advice to the line operator, in practice it is rare to find a career staff man who does not seek to enhance his power at the expense of underlings in the line of command. It is a matter of mind-set. Every action must be reduced to rote, operations are to be made computerized and unvarying before they can be said to be efficient, nothing is left to chance, record-keeping is endemic. Such organizations are usually weak in two things: crises which seem to recur frequently and innovations which ought to occur but do not. The bureaucracy is also the offender when it comes to excessive layers of organization and communication, whereas an action agency has few levels because only then can it be hard-hitting. If the lines of communication are long and tortuous, if face-to-face relationships are rarer the higher you get to the top of the pyramid, and if the chief executive is thus unable to deal directly with his program directors who deliver the finished product, then that organization may look well on an organization chart but it is doubtful if it will produce very much or sustain its productiveness.

In short, the best in bureaucracy needs to be combined with the best in enterprise to produce a balanced, hard-hitting organization. The experienced man should be on top, not the pedant. The man who knows the substance and subject matter of the field should always be preferred to the man who merely knows technique and is deficient in subject-matter and a rounded philosophy of management.

Having examined one side of the coin, bureaucracy, let us turn to the other, enterprise. Other names for enterprise are initiative, freedom, self-determination.

The four components of enterprise which combine with those of bureaucracy to achieve balance in management are, first, an emphasis on person, because only the person can be innovative and creative. Thus the individual who serves and the customer being served are both of more concern than a machine being tended.

Second is an emphasis on ideas rather than procedures, because ideas are inherently innovative and potentially creative. Instead of management by rule, management is by objective. The attention of the organization is always on the ends sought, with the means figured out, flexibly, sometimes on the spot, in relation to the goals of the broad policy lines in the undertaking.

The third factor is motivation, of which the enterprising individual has a range that goes far beyond the weekly pay check. He wants the business to be profitable, of course, but people, ideas, service, altruism, patriotism, originality, and most of all creativity, are also important to him. He likes to do things his own way, even if it is an unconventional way. He is inventive and a good salesman. With enough of these motivated individuals, the whole undertaking begins to feel enterprising and people like it. Moreover, as creative executives keep rising to the top, the organization renews itself at all levels.

Creative men and women more often appear in small organizations than in large ones where their freedom is less and their potential more slowly developed. Large business corporations recognize this fact and have long been raiding the smaller firms for innovative leaders. Although big companies deliberately cultivate the image of themselves as innovators, the truth is that the atmosphere of large companies is less conducive to invention than is that of the smaller ones, where temperament plays as large a role as reason. The fact is that smaller firms and their creative personnel are the source of most significant invention in the business community.[12]

The fourth component of enterprise, and a close link to bureaucracy, is a sufficient degree of order and method to allow the creative person to be effective. He not only invents, he also understands the reason for it and how it can be used to advantage. A dreamer, he is also a builder, a useful combination of qualities, especially in the second stage of institutional growth when good management stabilizes the enterprise after the initial thrust. The same combination of qualities is also useful in the fourth stage when renewal is sought.

When the rationality of bureaucracy is blended with the initiative of enterprise, certain results occur naturally: employees act with human spontaneity; the personality of the enterprise becomes outgoing instead of being sullenly self-centered; and something like the multiplier goes to work so far as human acceptance and approval are concerned.

Institutional vitality continues so long as balance is maintained and it declines when it is lost. People enjoy their work instead of needing to escape from it before they can start to live. From this standpoint, both John Hobson and Thorstein Veblen were right in supposing that the instinct of workmanship may become one of the highest gratifications of the individual, for it lies in the same human areas as artistic talent.[13]

Various studies of creativity have turned up findings that point the way to how program directors may become more inventive and how they should be recruited and promoted. I shall mention four such examples. W. I. B. Beveridge, the British geneticist, reports in *The Art of Scientific Investigation* (1950), that there have been two types of discoverers in sciences, the A and B types. The A type recognizes significances that the B type overlooks: they see connections and implications more clearly than others do. The B type is more thorough, more painstaking, more fact-minded. Both are necessary, and their results need to be combined. Secondly, in our own field of management,

Chester Barnard, in *The Functions of the Executive* (1938) discovered that executive genius depends on the ability to combine diverse factors into a whole, a strategy that is successful at a particular time. The executive is intuitive and resourceful and is thus able to make broad policy that includes all the factors instead of only those that are obvious and hence easily measurable. Thirdly, L. L. Thurstone, the psychologist, discovered as a result of "factorial analysis" of executive traits that the successful executive is able to go immediately to the heart of complex problems and discover how they all add up. And, finally, Arthur Koestler, in *The Act of Creation* (1964), pulled all this research together and came to the conclusion that bureaucrats think characteristically on a single level whereas creative people think simultaneously at several levels of consciousness and hence come up with insights, programs, and inventions which involve intricate syntheses. There are universals in all discovery, from humor to affairs of state.

Toward a Renewal of Vitality

The composite picture that we get of the dynamic line executive is one who can see what needs to be done and how to do it at a particular time in the life of a nation; one who has the sense to involve others in thinking through and planning solutions; one who is expert at getting others to do their bit instead of trying to do everything himself; one who will delegate because he insists on being trusted himself if he is to get a workmanlike job done; one who plans a lot but is never content with plans that do not progress beyond the paper stage; one who leads by example and relies upon positive incentives instead of upon fear and compulsion; one who appreciates all the facets of executive skill but avoids the mistake of overstressing any one; one who respects the different ways others may choose to accomplish a given purpose and who trusts such individuals to do it their own way; one who believes in measuring production but realizes that social goods and services are qualitative as well as quantitative and that what everything adds up to is a life-style based upon values. In short, he is a practical philosopher. One who does not get bogged down in detail but understands its meaning and implications. He is a balanced person much like Plato's concept of the well-rounded individual.

Management is an art, not a science, and those who treat it as if it were a matter of categories and models that are remote from the real world of practical affairs merely play intellectual games, or, at best, suggest rigorous analyses that the practical executive might find interesting, assuming he can understand their complexity in the first place. But such abstractions from reality are never the whole of management and never can be, because skilled management is more like the power to make viable syntheses which is the hallmark of creativity. I must be content merely to suggest a few implications from this line of reasoning.

First, no matter what we may think of business and its ethics, we ought to realize that it is the production man who ought to be the center of our concern, for it is he who attains objectives the enterprise seeks: goods, services, efficiency, economy, employee morale. How much he produces depends upon how much trust and authority he is given and whether he is allowed to make an occasional mistake. Responsibility and accountability need not be bought at too great a cost in the form of frustration and stalemate. Most of the gifted people who seek high-echelon jobs in government could be more productively used if they aspired to become program managers.

Secondly, public programs should be planned for several years in advance, with the legislature accommodating itself to this requirement. The center of initiative should be the action agency, which advises the legislature and the chief executive what to do.

Thirdly, the public personnel system must be made more flexible from recruitment through to retirement, with the ultimate power of decision in most cases residing in the practical executive and not the staff agency. His idea of "merit" is often more reliable than what any colorless register is able to reveal. The successful program managers should be paid the highest salaries found in the government service. Their skills are far rarer than those in any other category.

Fourth, the universities should change their usual emphasis on training specialists to training executives. The universities have done the easiest thing, concentrating on courses for specialists in personnel administration, public finance, public relations, and other staff functions, but these—necessary within certain bounds—infringe on the rounded jurisdictions that line executives need. Every executive should learn enough about law so as to avoid being in bondage of the lawyer who knows nothing, or next to nothing, about management.[14]

And, finally, the greatest need is for a changed philosophy of management over what is commonly found in government. Management is not, in fact, a process, or what the lawyers call a procedure. It is a knowledge of what substantively needs to be done in a certain area of the economy, at a given time, to further the values and enjoyments of the citizens in a way that respects the concept of scarce and exhaustible resources. Management is one of the most positive things in life. Treat it as a process or a set procedure and the country will be stuck on dead center or actually decline.

If the worst faults of bureaucracy are to be avoided, the mental set of management must be shaken up, converted from an insistence on procedure by rule and rote to initiative in policy objectives. A creative philosophy of management recognizes that when an able executive understands what the objectives and the policy are, he should be given the freedom and discretion to attain results in a practical, experienced way. Only with a high degree of freedom to operate in accordance with a positive philosophy are the best operators attracted to their work and only as we produce more production leaders will we maintain our values and our high standard of living.

Notes

1. Also deserving of prominent mention is Marver Bernstein, *The Job of the Federal Executive* (Washington: The Brookings Institution, 1958). On the business side, Edward C. Schleh, *Managing by Results* (New York: McGraw-Hill, 1961).

2. Paul H. Appleby, *Policy and Administration* (University: University of Alabama Press, 1949), pp. 49-50.

3. David Granick, *The Red Executive: A Study of the Organization Man in Russian Industry* (New York: Doubleday, 1960).

4. See, for example, the remarks of Charles M. Hardin, *Presidential Power and Accountability* (Chicago: University of Chicago Press, 1974).

5. Compare the statements in Drucker's books, *The Practice of Management* (New York: Harper, 1954), p. 234, and his *magnum opus*, *Management: Tasks, Responsibilities, Practice* (New York: Harper & Row, 1973), Ch. 55.

6. Marshall E. Dimock, *Administrative Vitality: The Conflict with Bureaucracy* (New York: Harper & Row, 1959).

7. C. Brooks Worth and Robert K. Engers, *The Nature of Living Things* (New York: Signet Key Books, 1955), pp. 79, 146.

8. Dealt with more extensively in *Administrative Vitality*, op. cit., Chapter 8, "The Pathologies of Bureaucracy."

9. There is a good discussion of this in Peter Drucker's *Management: Tasks, Responsibilities, Practice*, op. cit., Chs. 24-26.

10. This theme is developed in Marshall E. Dimock, *The Executive in Action* (New York: Harper, 1945), and also in *A Philosophy of Administration* (New York: Harper, 1959). For business, Drucker, in Chapter 31, "The Manager and his Work," observes that the first task of a manager is "creation of a true whole that is larger than the sum of the parts" (*Management: Tasks, Responsibilities, Practice*), op. cit., p. 398.

11. This was commonly said by business leaders in the 1930s and 1940s when I studied bureaucracy in large corporations firsthand. As early as 1951, Harvard professors E. P. Learned, D. N. Ulrich, and D. R. Booz, found that "politics" ranks either first or second among the most needed executive skills in business. This in *Executive Action* (Cambridge: Harvard University Graduate School of Business Administration, 1951), and since then corporations have become vastly more political.

12. John Jewkes, David Sawers, and Richard Stillerman, *The Sources of Invention* (London and New York: Macmillan, 1958).

13. Thorstein Veblen, *The Instinct of Workmanship* (New York: Macmillan, 1914); John A. Hobson, *Work and Wealth* (New York: Peter Smith, 1914).

14. For the attitudes that produce this result, see Bernard Schwartz, *Administrative Law* (Boston: Little, Brown, 1976), Chapter 1; on the methods used to dominate the administrative process, Mark J. Green, *The Other Government: The Unseen Power of Washington Lawyers* (New York: Grossman Publishers, 1975).

Some Observations About Foreign Service Reform: "Famous First Words"

Under Secretary of State Elliott L. Richardson:

I might add, parenthetically, that after I had been here two or three weeks, I expressed to one of my staff assistants the hope that I would have the opportunity to spend a considerable amount of time in matters of personnel administration and reform—even at the cost of involvement in interesting current, substantive issues—and he observed to me, rather sardonically at the time, 'Famous first words.'[1]

The new Under Secretary of State uttered these words in May 1969, on the occasion of the reconstitution of the Board of the Foreign Service and the launching of a "major and comprehensive review of the new administration of the entire foreign affairs personnel structure." The review will be carried out under the auspices of the Board of the Foreign Service, which is composed of representatives of some of the more important foreign affairs agencies and which will henceforth—and for the first time—be chaired by the Under Secretary of State.[2] The study itself will be directed by the newly designated Director General of the Foreign Service.

Thus has begun "yet another" effort to reexamine and reform the personnel system of that corps of officers legally known as The Foreign Service of the United States and some of its siblings—Foreign Service Reserve and Staff officers, and the civil service in the Department of State, and the foreign services of some other agencies which operate overseas. This will be about the 12th such attempt in the last quarter century, but its setting, format, and problems are distinctive from its predecessors. Indeed, the variety of auspices and arrangements for the different inquiries reflects a high degree of administrative ingenuity. They have included: a presidential staff agency (Bureau of the Budget in 1945); a group of Foreign Service officers within the State Department (the Chapin-Foster study in 1945); a presidential-congressional commission (the first Hoover Commission in 1949); committees composed principally or entirely of "outsiders" and appointed by the Secretary of State (the Rowe Committee in 1951 and the Wriston Committee in 1954); a presidential ad hoc group in the White House (the Du Flon study in 1955); studies by outside organizations under contract with congressional committees (The Brookings

Institution in 1951 and 1959, and Syracuse University in 1959); a committee of "outside" but experienced persons sponsored and financed by private foundations (the Herter Committee in 1962); and a study by a professional association (the American Foreign Service Association in 1968).[3]

One can almost hear James H. Rowe, Jr., who chaired one of these studies and participated in two others (the Hoover Commission and the Herter Committee), saying: "Here we go again." For however much wisdom, effort, and ingenuity went into the various studies, few of them resulted in substantial change—whether or not regarded as reform. The Chapin-Foster study was the basis of the Foreign Service Act of 1946; and the Wriston report led to the entrance of a great many civil servants and Foreign Service staff employees into the FSO corps. Some of the others, such as the Rowe Committee and the Herter Committee, resulted in some changes in the internal operating procedures in the Department of State, but little that could be described as fundamental reform. Of the others, two were not even published, and most left no visible trace, though some may have contributed to subsequent modifications. Of course, the report published by the American Foreign Service Association last year,[4] is too recent to appraise in these terms; in fact, it probably contributed to the reconstitution of the Board of the Foreign Service in its present form, which it specifically proposed, and to the launching of the current study.

Lessons from Earlier Reform Efforts

This bleak history of efforts to "reform" the Foreign Service suggests some lessons. One is that the reshaping of a personnel system anywhere, but perhaps particularly in government, is a difficult and time-taking task. Very probably, a reorganization of an organization *structure* is a lot easier, provided it does not involve any basic modifications in the personnel system. It took nearly a half century of struggle, spotted by scandal and catastrophe, to establish the federal civil service system, and it took several decades to legitimate a professional Foreign Service in the Rogers Act of 1924. The civil service system has changed very fundamentally in the years since World War II through a series of what some might characterize as incremental changes. But some of the "increments," such as the Classification Act of 1949, the Training Act of 1958, and the labor relations policy of 1962, were of considerable dimensions. Most of these changes were responses to complaints and criticisms which began well before World War II and became increasingly strident during the '30s, '40s, and '50s. On the whole, the Foreign Service has been more successfully resistant to change in recent decades, perhaps because of its relatively small size, its self-containment, and its career system which assures that many or most of its most prestigious, influential members will be old-timers.

A second lesson of this recent history is that proposals for significant change are likely to flounder unless they have: (1) the support of the leadership corps of the Service itself, as in the case of the Foreign Service Act of 1946, or (2) aggressive, even ruthless, follow-through by the very top political officers in the State Department, as in the case of the Wriston recommendations, or (3) both. In this regard the current signals are hopeful. One lies in the "famous first words" of the Under Secretary and, more important, his assumption of chairmanship of the Board of the Foreign Service. The second lies in the takeover of control of the American Foreign Service Association by younger and middle-grade officers in 1967 and their evident concern about the Foreign Service, not only its status, prestige, and emoluments, but also its role and responsibilities in the whole foreign affairs community. This group, often dubbed somewhat inaccurately as "young Turks," organized a number of committees, which included representatives of foreign affairs agencies in addition to the State Department, to conduct studies and make reports on various problems of foreign affairs personnel. These reports were realistic and forward looking. They were appended to the master report, which itself was a summary of their recommendations, considerably modified.

A third lesson from the frequent studies of foreign affairs personnel is that there is evidently continuing dissatisfaction with our systems of employing professionals to represent and work for this country in its interests overseas; and that the focus of concern is the Foreign Service of the United States. I know of no body of personnel in the public service which is more intelligent and more dedicated than the Foreign Service. Yet, to my knowledge, no group of personnel, public or private, has so frequently been criticized, even abused, and reexamined. Over the years, the Service has been criticized by presidents and their staffs from Roosevelt to Nixon, by Secretaries of State and their political associates, by representatives of other federal agencies, by congressmen, by journalists, and by scholars. It would be impossible herein to document these various charges, but it may be noted that there is a good deal of agreement in the nature of the criticisms. They include alleged lack of responsiveness, inertia, resistance to change, emphasis upon form and process rather than substance, insufficient specialization, red tape, overconformism, inflexibility, lack of innovative thinking and initiative—in short, most of the popularly accepted shortcomings of bureaucracy. In defense of the Service, it should be pointed out that similar criticisms are, and long have been, directed at most other agencies of the national government. For a number of reasons, the Foreign Service is a particularly vulnerable target: it is accessible and peculiarly exposed around the world; it is a convenient whipping boy for politicians and particularly demagogues; it seldom is credited with "victories" in foreign affairs, but must often share the blame for mistakes and misfortunes. Its role within the Department of State and within the government as a whole has not been clear for at least a third of a century; and the cherished goal of an elite, unified "Foreign Service of the United States" has seemed a will-o'-the-wisp.

Beyond these factors, the Service suffers in a particularly sensitive way the abrasions normal to relationships between career or civil service personnel and political officials, elected and appointed. Foreign affairs have become so central a concern of American politics and of American presidents, and the Foreign Service has long been considered—or at least has sought to be considered —a principal adviser to secretaries of State and presidents on foreign policy and principal implementers of policies once decided. At the same time, if it is to serve succeeding administrations with equal effectiveness, it must maintain a stance of political neutrality—a difficult balancing act at best. For the same Service and many of its same members must serve not only successive presidents and secretaries, but a bewildering merry-go-round of lesser political officers in the White House, State Department, and other agencies, presumably with unflinching loyalty, devotion, and initiative. One facet of the problem was illustrated in Schlesinger's book on the Kennedy years.[5] In a chapter much of which was devoted to "standard" criticism of the Foreign Service, Schlesinger discussed the problem of Kennedy's encouragement of "dissent and daring" in his administration as it applied to foreign policy:

> But what if dissent meant opposition to the neutralization of Laos or to the Alliance for Progress or to the center-left experiment in Italy? This was a riddle which the White House, wishing free minds in the bureaucracy but at the same time demanding commitment to its policies—and the Foreign Service, proclaiming its loyalty to all administrations but at the same time reserving the right to defend old policies against new—never solved. Probably it was insoluble.[6]

One consequence of this problem has been that presidents since Hoover and their secretaries of State have relied to a great, though varying, extent upon political rather than career appointees for guidance and leadership in foreign affairs. Some career officers have won the confidence of presidents; the names of Welles, Kennan, Bohlen, and Thompson come to mind. But many, possibly most, of the most sensitive and responsible assignments have gone to "amateurs" like Hopkins, Harriman, Lodge, and Bunker. Last winter, President Nixon, speaking before a group of State Department, AID, and USIA officers, said that ". . . I do think we have the best career service in the world."[7] But a week later, he reorganized the machinery for managing national security and foreign affairs which President Johnson had attempted to center in the Department of State.[8] The effect of his action appears to be a transfer of primary initiative and leadership on foreign policy matters to the assistant to the president for National Security Affairs and his staff.

Dissatisfaction with the Service from the outside, which seems to be endemic and perhaps inevitable, has recently been paralleled by a growing dissatisfaction within. The latter is directed primarily to its role, its responsibilities, its capabilities, and to the respect and prestige which it commands. The best indication was the take-over of the American Foreign Service Association by the so-called "young Turks" on a platform of reform; their subsequent formation of study committees, the committee studies and reports, some of which were radical in terms of older doctrines; the publication of the general report, cited earlier; and the later (in 1969) specific recommendations submitted by the Association to the new under secretary of State. Although the general report stated that the morale of the Service was "surprisingly high," the very fact that it was written and the nature of some of its recommendations suggest that there is a fairly widespread disaffection. There is other evidence. In his 1966 questionnaire of a sample of Foreign Service officers (FSOs), John E. Harr found that topping a list of nine potential objectives of "concern" were: first, "How the State Department is managed," and second, "General condition of the FSO corps."[9] Both were considered to be of major concern to 40 percent or more of the officers.

Dissatisfaction appears to be keenest among the younger officers, especially the better ones. A 1968 article provocatively entitled "Is the Foreign Service Losing Its Best Young Officers?" which was based upon a study of junior officers who had entered during the years 1960 through 1964 and dropped out prior to 1967, suggested that, on the average, the answer was "yes."[10] The dropouts had more prior education and more fulltime pre-Service work experience than those who stayed in. A later study showed that the dropout rate (20 percent) within four or five years of appointment in the '60s was about double that during the period 1924-46, and that during the earlier period, there was no appreciable difference in education and experience between those who resigned and those who remained.[11] Further analysis of the speed of promotions of the dropouts in comparison with those who stayed in the service during the two periods indicated that, in the 1960s, the dropouts were superior to those who remained in the service; in the earlier period, the reverse was the case.

There are difficulties in the upper reaches of the Service as well as the lower ones. For some years, the number of senior officers—career ministers, Class 1s, and Class 2s—has been high, relative to the number of assignments for which they are deemed fit by assigning officers and relative to the total size of the Service. This has been a festering problem for State Department management as well as the officers concerned, and a source of restiveness for officers of lower rank who fear blockage to their own opportunities for advancement.

The top and most prestigious ranks in the Foreign Service are career ambassadors, who comprise only a handful of the most distinguished officers, and career ministers, who have normally served in one or more posts of ambassadorial level and who are judged by their superiors and peers on the selection boards to be worthy both of high distinction and of further assignments at that level. In recent years the number of career ministers has been between 60 and 70. In a recent article, Ambassador John M. Steeves, who was Director General of the Foreign Service from 1966 to 1969, deplored the relatively low, and declining, "correlation between career seniority and career responsibility" among career ministers.[12] In early summer of 1969, only 60 percent of the career ministers were serving as ambassadors, assistant secretaries of State, or in positions of equivalent responsibility, i.e., positions for which they are considered by their fellows to be preeminently fit. In fact there were about as many FSOs of lower rank serving as ambassadors as there were career ministers. This of course does not include the substantial number of ambassadorial posts filled by political appointees. Steeves attributes this situation in part to the currently popular "Accent on Youth" in top-level appointments. Most career ministers are in their 50s and 60s. In part he considers it a departure from the merit principle: ". . . I am convinced that choosing others in preference to those upon whom the system has placed its highest stamp of approval cannot be justified if merit is to be the sole rule."[13] Some presidents and some secretaries of State might question this equating of merit with the approval of the "system." But Ambassador Steeves' main point remains: two-fifths of the top officers of the Foreign Service are not fulfilling the roles anticipated for them for whatever reasons.

The Closed Career Principle

Most of the post-World War II studies of the Foreign Service have dealt with similar problems, though with varying emphasis. The hardy perennials among these problems have included: proliferation of the American responsibilities, tools, and requisite skills overseas; the leadership role of the Department of State in foreign affairs; the relations of foreign policy, foreign operations, and administration; the internal organization of the Department of State and especially the role of the Foreign Service; the government of the Service itself; the meaning and content of "diplomacy"; specialists and generalists; the needs and especially the limitations of lateral entry; the relations among the various "categories" of Foreign Service personnel; the relations between Foreign Service and civil service; the internal systems governing entry, assignment, evaluation, promotion, and selection-out.

It is not within the compass of this brief article to analyze and compare the findings and recommendations of these various study groups. What is noteworthy is that most of them have apparently assumed as a *given* the desirability of a personnel system based upon the closed career principle. Some would tinker with it, relax its strictures, or open it up temporarily (as did the Wriston Committee). But almost none have questioned whether the principle is the best guide to provide the leadership corps for American activities in the foreign arena. It should be recalled that the principle as applied to foreign affairs was first legally enunciated in the Rogers Act of 1924, when it may have been the best possible response to the patronage-ridden chaos of the old diplomatic service. It was somewhat modified, but also elaborated and reinforced, by the Foreign Service Act of 1946, which may also have been the best feasible response to America's enlarged overseas responsibilities following World War II. Its inflexibilities were temporarily relaxed by the Manpower Act of 1946 and, during the mid-'50s, by the Wriston program. A variety of legislation enacted over the last 20 years, of which perhaps most important was the Hays amendment to the USIA career bill of 1968,[14] has made it legally possible to change the application of the career principle fundamentally without further basic legislation. But there has so far appeared little disposition on the part of the Service or the Department to reexamine the principle itself and its viability in this increasingly turbulent society and turbulent world.

The closed career principle as here understood envisages a personnel system composed of people selected soon after completion of their basic education on the basis of competitive examinations who are expected and who expect: (a) to spend the bulk of their working lives in the same organization; (b) to be advanced periodically on the basis of competition with their peers and evaluation by their superiors to top grades in their organization; and (c) to be protected in such competition from outsiders. A personnel system based upon the closed career principle normally tends to be self-governing in the sense that the criteria for selection and advancement are determined by superiors in the system. And to the extent that intrusion and intervention by people outside the system can be prevented, the system becomes increasingly self-sustaining, homogenized, and conformist in accord with its own norms and criteria. If the environment around it and the subject matter with which it must deal change at a rate faster than its own norms and criteria, it tends to be increasingly insular—unable and unwilling to adapt itself to that changing environment. Thus it seems very possible that the allegedly declining influence of the Foreign Service over American foreign affairs, frequently deplored by members of the Service, derives in part from the closed career principle itself.

The Service and Social Change

It is here suggested that the current reexamination of the Foreign Service might properly start with a reconsideration of the closed career principle; and that, while the well-worn but real problems upon which earlier studies have focused should certainly not be ignored, the beginning question should be the *viability of careerism in relation to the rapidly changing nature of American society now and in the decades immediately ahead.* It is this society from which the Foreign Service will be drawn, by whatever system of employment; and it is this society whose interests the Service will be called upon to represent. This society is a far cry from that of the '20s and that of the '50s, and it will probably change even beyond the predictions of "futuristics" by 1980.

Space limitations do not permit an extended analysis of the evolving nature of American society. But I would like to give passing reference to a few features which seem both obvious and highly relevant to the kind of foreign affairs personnel system which will best serve the nation's needs.

1. *The Knowledge Explosion.* A number of observers of the current American scene have referred to it with such expressions as the "post-industrial society," the "scientific revolution," the "professional revolution." The accelerating accretion of new knowledge and its somewhat slower application to the problems of society are a significant mark of these times and are also a source of basic shifts of power and influence in our society. Several years ago Dr. Clark Kerr wrote that:

The basic reality, for the university, is the widespread recognition that new knowledge is the most important factor in social and economic growth. We are just now perceiving that the university's invisible product, knowledge, may be the most powerful single element in our culture, affecting the rise and fall of professions and even of social classes, of religions and even of nations.

Later, Dr. Daniel Bell affirmed Kerr's analysis:

. . . the dominant institutions of the new society, in the sense that they will provide the most creative challenges and enlist the richest talents, will be the intellectual institutions. The leadership of the new society will rest not with businessmen or corporations as we know them, but with research corporations, the industrial laboratories, experimental stations and the universities.[16]

The thesis may, for emphasis, be overstated. Certainly it is more immediately applicable to technological and material developments than to social problems. But even in the social area, the rapidly developing theories and techniques of the social sciences including those associated with operations research, gaming, simulation studies, systems analysis, PPBS, and organizational development will be increasingly relevant. The State Department, unlike the Defense Department and a few other agencies, has been notably deficient in conducting or sponsoring or promoting research of these kinds in the areas of its primary concern. And its potential academic counterparts have moved in the direction of grand or precious theories and techniques, little used or useful in the conduct of foreign affairs.

The personnel of the Foreign Service should include a growing number of persons capable, knowledgeable, and interested in keeping up with and applying the latest concepts and instruments relevant to our foreign problems. This will mean the employing on an equal basis of at least a few eminent scholars in many academic fields who are able, through their own knowledge and reputations, to deal with other American scholars and with distinguished foreign representatives. This suggests, too, a system which can attract accomplished experts in a great variety of disciplines for a number of years (though not necessarily for life), a system which can accommodate "in-and-outers," and a system which can afford to send a good many of its members back to educational institutions for purposes of bringing them up-to-date with their own specialized fields.

2. *Sensitivity and Flexibility.* It is a tired truism of our times that the only certain thing we can predict is that there will be change, probably accelerating. In foreign affairs we need and will need more and more a body of people who can anticipate change, can prepare for it, can respond to it, and can, to the extent possible, guide and influence it in directions deemed desirable by our government. I refer here not alone to the staccato of overseas problems and crises nor the more gradual shifts in mores, values, and economies of foreign peoples. They must also be keyed to the tonal shifts, the crescendos and diminuendos of our own society. And this will require a high degree of sensitivity

among our foreign affairs personnel and a flexibility encompassing both the quick transfers of persons from place to place and assignment to assignment, and also ready adaptability within the minds of the people themselves. It may also involve the ability to bring in from outside persons capable of dealing with specific situations and the removal of those who are unable to deal with new problems.

3. *Professionalism and Mobility.* More than half of the products of the nation's universities and colleges, graduate and undergraduate, are educated in specializations designed to prepare them for one or another professional occupation. Not including housewives, the majority of the others will later return for professional graduate training or will enter upon some line of work, such as the Foreign Service, wherein they will acquire the accoutrements of professionalism through training and experience. Ours is increasingly a professional society or, more accurately, a professionally led society. And American governments are the largest employers of professionals, not the least being those parts of the national government which concern themselves with foreign affairs. In fact, few areas of governmental endeavor are dependent upon as high a proportion and as wide a variety of well-qualified professionals as the conduct of foreign affairs.

The rise of professionalism bears important implications for the career principle as it has developed in foreign affairs. One is that, while professionalism may well inhibit movement from one kind of occupation to another, it encourages mobility from organization to organization (or to self-employment) whereby the professional may apply his special knowledge and skills at more and more challenging levels. This phenomenon is probably most pronounced among the best established and also the most esoteric professions—e.g., lawyers, economists, engineers, system analysts, scientists, public health doctors. And within each of them it is probably most pronounced among the best qualified, most ambitious, and most problem-oriented individual professionals. For them, movement in and out of government or between different agencies of government or between different assignments in the same agency is normal. They are more likely to pursue interesting problem areas where they think they can make a contribution than prestigious but stodgy organizations where their skills may be stifled or dissipated.

A second implication arises from the fact that professional behavior is conditioned primarily by the norms, the standards, and the workways of the profession itself rather than those that may be imposed by an organization structure. This is probably most true among well-established professions except where professional standards are approximately consonant with organizational objectives—as, for example, the strictly defined diplomatic profession within the Department of State. And professionals seek a considerable degree of individual autonomy and discretion in the application of their particular skills. They resist working *under* the close supervision of others, especially if those others are not members of the same profession. When they work on problems which require the application of a number of different professional skills—and these include almost all problems in the social arena—they prefer to work with other professionals on an equal or team basis, founded in mutual respect.

A final implication to be mentioned here is that the problems of foreign affairs are such as to call upon professionals with some years of responsible experience behind them. Few can be produced to the required level of competence only by university training. Except for those skilled in the more narrowly defined diplomacy itself, the foreign affairs agencies are not equipped to provide such qualifying experience. It must be gained elsewhere, prior to entry upon a foreign affairs career.

4. *The New Bureaucracy.* The discussion of professionalism above suggests the probability of profound changes in the patterns and styles of bureaucratic organizations. The changes are already well under way in many progressive institutions, both in the public and private sectors. They are a product of rapidly rising levels of education among an increasing proportion of the population, of deepening professionalism and the accompanying demand for individual autonomy, and of rising job mobility among educated persons. They are a product also of the growing turbulence of the environment within which most organizations must operate and of the growing complexity of problems with which organizations, particularly "thought" organizations, must deal.

In short, the old Weberian description of bureaucracy, the accuracy of which has probably been exaggerated in this country, with its emphasis upon formal structure, routinization, efficiency in the narrow sense, and hierarchy, is rapidly becoming obsolete. Organizations must become more responsive, more adaptive, more creative, and more innovative. This means, among other things, that they will be increasingly structured around projects, around problems to be solved, rather than as permanent hierarchies of offices, divisions, and sections. A growing characteristic will be temporariness, as old problems are resolved and new ones arise. And there will be a growing premium on problem—rather than status—oriented personnel. In the words of Warren G. Bennis: "People will be differentiated not vertically according to rank and role but flexibly according to skill and professional training."[17]

Already, the movement toward this style of organization is evident in the national government, particularly in research and development fields such as those of NASA, NIH, and the scientific laboratories. It is increasingly observable in the social fields, including foreign affairs, with the growing reliance upon inter-agency ad hoc committees, task forces, and similar problem-oriented groups. It is reflected also in the nature and the assignments of a large portion of the so-called "political" appointees, who are not politicians and whose party regularity is incidental if not, in some instances, totally irrelevant. A good many of these appointments appear to be predicated upon professional competence in an appropriate occupational field and demonstrated ability to apply their skills creatively to problems. Can a closed career system develop, to a comparable degree, such skills and such problem orientation?

5. *Youth.* A corollary and perhaps one of the consequences of the knowl-

edge explosion in science and technology has been the rebellion of college youth across the country, sparked and led principally by students of the social sciences and the humanities. One need not be misled by the well-televised sloganeering of the extremist agitators, much of which must have been stale stuff at the close of the 19th century. The foreboding facts are that so many other students, particularly in social and humanistic fields, have chosen to join in the movement and that they include a very high proportion of the best students, those whom the Foreign Service as well as other government agencies and private businesses have sought to attract. I do not pretend to understand the real sources of the current agitation, other than that the Vietnam War and the draft have certainly fanned the flames. But my own observations lead me to a few hypotheses which seem relevant to the career principle in the Foreign Service.

First is that there is widespread distrust and hostility to what is described as the "establishment," usually defined to include administrations of universities (mistakenly I think), big business, and government. Near the acme of the "establishment" must surely be the Foreign Service of the United States.

Second is a very high degree of idealism—idealism toward freedom, equalization of opportunity, preference for underprivileged minorities, and peace. Accompanying such idealism is a considerable skepticism about the values, norms, and criteria of the older "straight" generation and toward large-scale organizations and their accompanying hierarchy.

Third is a desire to be of direct and immediate service in pursuit of these ideals. The attractiveness of programs such as the Peace Corps and VISTA has very probably been greatest among the left-leaning student bodies of the more left-leaning universities.

Fourth is a reluctance to make commitments about lifelong careers. Among graduating student bodies, not already committed by undergraduate professional education, the question of "watcha goin' to do" usually prompts ambivalent answers.

It is anyone's guess how long the current malaise may persist. But there are other reasons to question a career principle predicated upon passing an academical examination at or soon after graduation from college. Written examinations are coming under increasing question, not alone by university students and faculty but also by recruiters of progressive business and even federal agencies. There is little evidence that the Foreign Service examination is a valid indicator of subsequent Foreign Service performance. One may at least hypothesize that a better criterion of future effectiveness in the Foreign Service would be the idealism and dedication demonstrated in organizations like the Peace Corps and VISTA plus accomplishment and leadership demonstrated in one or more other jobs. And, as discussed earlier, many of the better junior FSOs, working in routine assignments, quit within the first few years.

6. *Representativeness.* The current concern about preparing the underprivileged and particularly the minority racial groups with educational opportunities and progressively responsible and rewarding work has a special dimension

in foreign affairs. Our overseas personnel are seen by foreign peoples as representing us, not alone in their official capacities but as representatives of our people. The greatest proportion of those foreign populations are, by our standards, underprivileged; and they are not white. The Department of State in recent years has sought to attract more Negro applicants and even to help young blacks to prepare for its entrance examinations. But its success has been less than conspicuous. Despite a genuine and vigorous effort by Secretary Rusk and many of his subordinate officials to attract Negroes to the Foreign Service and despite a foundation-financed program to prepare promising young Negroes for the entrance examinations, the number of Negro officers in the Foreign Service increased only from 17 to 19 between 1961 and 1967—out of a total of more than 3,700 officers.[18] The Service has steadfastly resisted the "lowering" of its entrance standards and the modifying of its criteria for measuring them, even though neither the standards nor the criteria have been validated against subsequent needs and performance. Very possibly, an employment system which permitted the hiring of blacks and other minority persons on a basis of full and equal status at levels above the current entering level after they had significant employment experience elsewhere might help to correct the current imbalance.

Another group of our population which is severely underrepresented in the Foreign Service is that majority: women. Many brilliant young women who meet the current standards admirably are discouraged, or effectively barred, from a Foreign Service career because they must, in effect, "take the veil" upon entry. The current bias against married young women is, for administrative reasons, probably justified. But under a less rigorous career system, older women might be brought in, on an equal basis, at whatever appropriate grade, not only to add to the general resources of the Service, but also to provide informational and representational services abroad—as among women's organizations—not accessible to men. This might apply particularly to women who have had successful careers in the United States or who have been active in civic organizations and whose families have grown up.

* * * * *

A year ago in Great Britain a committee, appointed by the Prime Minister and chaired by Lord Fulton, published perhaps the most remarkable report about the British civil service system in the past century.[19] Among many other things, it proposed abolishment of the class system, including the administrative class, breaking of the public school-Oxbridge monopoly of the top civil service posts, elevating the rank and influence of professional, scientific, and technical personnel, and establishment of a Ministry of the Civil Service directly under the Prime Minister. The Fulton Report, which was supported by five thick volumes of studies and testimony, was accepted by the government, and many of its recommendations were immediately implemented—on paper at least. It will probably be some years before its full effect can be assessed. However effective it may prove, the Fulton Report is the product of a reexamination of a very old personnel system in the light of the changing nature and changing needs of the society which it serves.

The American Foreign Service system is about half the age of the British civil service system and is probably a somewhat distant descendant of it, at least ideologically. It seems hardly imaginable, however, that we wait another half-century to make a comparably intense reexamination of the Foreign Service system. The foregoing paragraphs were intended to suggest some—certainly not all—of the current and probable future developments in American society which should be considered in such a reexamination. It may be noted that most of them are equally relevant to other personnel systems in this country, public and private, and certainly not least the tenure system in academic institutions. The basic problems of the Foreign Service are difficult and somewhat different, but they are not altogether unique.

We may hope that Under Secretary Richardson's "last words" on this subject may prove, over the years to come, more famous than his first ones.

Notes

1. From a press conference of May 7, 1969, as quoted in the *Department of State News Letter,* No. 97 (May 1969), p. 3.
2. The Board includes four State Department officials and representatives of the Departments of Commerce and Labor, AID, USIA, and the Civil Service Commission. Conspicuous among the agencies not represented are the Departments of Defense and the military departments, Agriculture, HEW, and Transportation, and CIA and the Peace Corps.
3. For a review and analysis of these studies, see Arthur G. Jones, *The Evolution of Personnel Systems for U.S. Foreign Affairs: A History of Reform Efforts* (New York: Carnegie Endowment for International Peace, 1964).
4. Entitled *Toward a Modern Diplomacy: A Report to the American Foreign Service Association* (Washington, D.C.: The Association, 1968), the report was prepared by a committee under the chairmanship of Graham Martin. It was summarized in 17 specific recommendations designed to revamp the structure and machinery for Foreign Service management, unify the Service with those of some other agencies, better equip it for broader responsibilities, and enhance its status and prestige.
5. Arthur M. Schlesinger, Jr., *A Thousand Days: John F. Kennedy in the White House* (Boston: Houghton Mifflin Company, 1965).
6. *Ibid.,* chapter 16, p. 432.
7. *Department of State News Letter,* No. 94 (February 1969), p. 4.
8. Foreign Affairs Manual Circular, No. 521 (February 6, 1969). The actual effects of President Nixon's reorganization of the National Security Council system upon the locus of real power and influence in foreign policy are not yet clear. For a more thorough discussion of its probable implications, see the article by Dr. Kolodziej in this symposium.
9. John Ensor Harr, *The Professional Diplomat* (Princeton, N.J.: Princeton University Press, 1969), pp. 214-215.
10. The article by Elizabeth A. Bean and Herbert J. Horowitz appeared in the *Foreign Service Journal,* Vol. 45, No. 2 (February 1968), pp. 30-32, 44.
11. Carroll R. McKibbin, "Attrition of Foreign Service Officers: Then and Now," *Foreign Service Journal,* Vol. 46, No. 6 (May 1969), pp. 6, 8, 10, 12.

12. "The Predicament of the Senior Career," *Foreign Service Journal,* Vol. 46, No. 8 (July 1969), pp. 29, 40, 41. The quotation is from p. 29.
13. *Ibid.,* p. 40.
14. P. L. 90-404, which was signed by President Johnson August 20, 1968, established a career category of Foreign Service Information Officers. The amendment introduced by Congressman Wayne Hays authorized both the State Department and the USIA to establish a category of Foreign Service Reserve Officers with unlimited career tenure.
15. Clark Kerr in *The Uses of the University* (New York: Harper and Row, 1963), p. vii.
16. Daniel Bell, "Notes on the Post-Industrial Society," *The Public Interest,* Vol. 1, No. 6 (Winter 1967), p. 27.
17. Warren G. Bennis, *Changing Organizations: Essays on the Development and Evolution of Human Organization* (New York: McGraw-Hill Book Company, 1966), p. 12.
18. Idris Rossell, "Equal Employment Opportunity—Too Much or Not Enough," *Foreign Service Journal,* Vol. 46, No. 1 (January 1969), p. 12.
19. *The Civil Service,* Vol. 1, *Report of the Committee, 1966-68* (London: Her Majesty's Stationery Office, 1968).

CLARA PENNIMAN

Reorganization and the Internal Revenue Service

In the last quarter century we have moved from prescribing a model organization form for all agency ills to a skepticism that suggests reorganization is at best a palliative, possibly shifting pressures but without necessarily changing the underlying forces. And that moreover reorganization may disrupt both informal and formal work arrangements to the detriment of the effectiveness of the organization at least in the short run. It is true that both the national Hoover Commissions and the numerous state Little Hoover Commissions freely recommended reorganization as a solvent to numbers of problems. Many administration specialists saw in these reorganization proposals old, traditional views of reform and a failure to use new knowledge that reflected grave doubts of the efficacy of reorganization as a general prescription. The subsequent years have supported much of the skepticism. On the one hand, congressmen have refused to consider reorganizations that they believed might upset cherished relations such as the division of authority between the Army Corps of Engineers and the Bureau of Reclamation. On the other hand, reorganizations enacted have produced unanticipated results for their supporters and opponents. Frank Rourke found that the apparent presidential-labor victory in the transfer of the Employment Service-Unemployment Compensation functions to the Department of Labor was followed by a transfer of states-rights industry pressure not only to the new department but to Congress and action there that tended to restore the pre-reorganization status quo.[1]

If reorganization is not a remedy to be widely prescribed, neither is it to be entirely rejected. The need is to understand and to describe organizational symptoms with sufficient clarity and precision to recognize when and in what respects reorganization may be the appropriate prescription. This brief description of the reorganization of the Internal Revenue Service will not settle this controversy as to the role of reorganization in reform and change, although it may contribute to the understanding of that role. The questions raised are modest: What characteristics of the organization structure of the Bureau of Internal Revenue contributed to the problems culminating in open scandals? Has the new organization structure helped to meet the old problems without raising major problems of its own?[2]

196

Bureau of Internal Revenue, Post-War

On the eve of World War II, the reputation of the Bureau of Internal Revenue stood high with the Congress and the public. The known rectitude of Secretary of the Treasury Morgenthau sheltered the Bureau. And Roosevelt's Commissioner Guy Helvering had achieved for himself and the Bureau almost the imperial status of J. Edgar Hoover and the F.B.I. Helvering's unprecedented term (10 years of FDR's 12, 1933-43) as commissioner covered changes of importance—collection of taxes from the newly legalized beer and liquor industry (1933), decentralization from Washington to the field of the appellate function (1939), blanketing of all deputy collectors under civil service merit system (1942), extension of the income tax to all with incomes of $600 or over, and (just before he left) adoption of general withholding to aid in tax collection (1943). The fact that only the deputy collectors and not the collectors were placed under the merit system and that no institutional machinery for coordination was developed among the diverse divisions of Internal Revenue either in the field or at the Washington level left problems for the future.

The Bureau was both decentralized and highly centralized, and no sense of a single administrative organization, policy, and program infused the agency. All individual income tax returns reporting net income above $5,000 (by 1945, $7,000) and all corporate income tax returns were sent from the collectors' offices to Washington, examined, and referred to appropriate revenue agents in charge, if field audit was required. Washington alone could make many of the final decisions immediately affecting taxpayers. Separatism and independence characterized the field and Washington and relations between the field and Washington. Each of seven deputy commissioners in Washington supervised a major segment of tax administration. The deputy commissioner of Accounts and Collections through a staff of 13 field supervisors attempted to coordinate the offices of 64 collectors. The deputy commissioner of the Income Tax Unit coordinated the work of 39 district offices with Internal Revenue agents in charge. The deputy commissioner of the Miscellaneous Tax Unit (later renamed Excise Tax Unit) and the deputy commissioner of the Employment Tax Unit supervised field activities that were in part located in the collectors' offices. The deputy commissioner of Intelligence worked through 14 district offices headed by special agents. After 1939, the deputy commissioner of the Technical Staff (Appellate) had 12 field divisions checking 35 local offices.

In all, approximately 200 field officials reported to the seven deputy commissioners in Washington. There, cooperation took the form of a gentleman's regard for the proper amenities without prying or interfering. Cooperation in the field not only tended to be less in substance but also less in gentlemanly procedure. Almost no single office brought any group of field officials together. Frequently they were not in the same city. Distrust, or even disrespect for the competence of colleagues with differing responsibilities, reinforced the separatism. The 64 collectors were presidential appointees. Other field officials came under the civil service merit system. Normal career promotion lines ran in each of the specializations—collection, income tax, miscellaneous tax, employment tax, alcohol tax, intelligence, or appellate.

Weaknesses, tolerable perhaps with a prewar 1940 tax return load of 19.2 million, proved a serious strain when the tax return load had grown to 83.8 million in 1945 and continued to grow. Almost every working adult now filed an income tax return and individual income tax returns reached 43.6 million taxable returns in 1945 in contrast to 3.9 million in 1940. The Bureau of Internal Revenue faced the peacetime adaptation of an organization developed for less than one-fourth of the new work load and a staff grown approximately two and one-fifth times. Housekeeping details of handling returns, depositing money, and filing returns had assumed proportions unknown a few years before. Even the housing of additional employees stretched the already inadequate field facilities.

Appraisal and Reappraisal

With the end of the war, Bureau leaders raised their budget requests for personnel. The implication appeared that if the Congress would provide sufficient funds for more and more employees, the Bureau could wipe up the war backlog and continue operation much as usual. The Congress for fiscal years 1946 and 1947 responded generously to these requests. The Bureau added positions and in fact reached its all-time high (as of 1961) in personnel in 1947 with 57,386 net average permanent employees. The Eightieth Congress, through its appropriation committees, showed less sympathy for the Bureau's needs and more skepticism of its accomplishments. Deep budget cuts followed in fiscal years 1948 and 1949. The average number of employees dropped to 49,356 and 50,634.

Although maintaining that insufficient personnel created the greatest handicap, the Bureau on its own and at the instigation of the Treasury undertook some management studies. In October 1946, Secretary of the Treasury Snyder launched a "Management Improvement Program." Successively there were attempts at work simplification programs in the field, employee incentive awards, and special committees on administration appointed by the Commissioner or Secretary (in particular, the so-called Wiggins Committee reporting in November, 1948). In 1948, the first "audit control study" was initiated to assist in meeting the problem of selecting only those income tax returns for audit that were likely to contain significant errors (both in the taxpayer's favor and against him). With funds made available by Congress, the Bureau hired the management firm of Cresap, McCormick and Paget in 1948, first to make a comprehensive analysis of organization and procedure in the collectors' offices and later for a similar study of the whole Bureau—both studies to include recommendations.

The first Hoover Commission in its 1948 *Report* reviewed studies undertaken by Congress and the administration of the Bureau of Internal Revenue and added its own broad recommendations for a complete reorganization of the Bureau for economy and efficiency, elimination of presidential appointment of collectors, and an increase in the rank of the Commissioner of Internal Revenue to Assistant Secretary of the Treasury.

Congressional Investigation

Bitter words and political controversy over the cut in the 1948 budget increased normal congressional interest in Internal Revenue. The Joint Committee on Internal Revenue Taxation secured the services of four distinguished public citizens who reported formally on January 27, 1948. The subcommittee of the Committee on Appropriations of the House of Representatives initiated investigations by its staff in 1947 and 1948. Under a subcommittee of the House Ways and Means Committee, detailed investigations were carried on more or less continuously from 1948 into 1954. This subcommittee's most critical investigations occurred in 1951 and 1952 when Cecil R. King (Democrat of California) was chairman. Although the Senate left most of the investigating to the House, the Senate Special Committee to Investigate Crime in Interstate Commerce (the Kefauver Committee) and John J. Williams (Delaware) through the Post Office and Civil Service Committee, pointed up difficulties in tax administration. Other committees, especially the House and Senate Appropriation Committees, exhibited critical, questioning attitudes in hearings with Internal Revenue.

The investigations by congressional committees not only highlighted the fact of corruption in Internal Revenue but also the apparent inability of Bureau officials to identify and handle its problems. The center of criticism again and again revolved around the Office of Collector. The collectors' offices received and processed the 82.6 million (1951) tax returns. They collected most of the 50.4 billion tax dollars (1951) either initially on receipt of the return or subsequently when audit reflected additional taxes due. Although corporate returns and the larger individual income tax returns were audited by revenue agents in Washington or in the field, the bulk of the individual income tax returns were examined and audited in the collectors' offices. And there in 1951 worked more than 60 percent of all Internal Revenue employees.

The Collector's Office Stumbling Block

The collector's office was an old one, brought into existence with the Bureau in 1862 and continuously providing patronage to the party in power. The collectors were appointed by the president with the consent of the Senate. For most years until 1939, the deputy collectors in the office of the collector were appointed by the collector. (The class "deputy collector" covered most employees above the clerical level in the office so that they represented substantial patronage and control.) In 1939 appointment of the deputy collectors was vested in the Secretary of the Treasury, and in 1942 the deputy collectors were brought under the merit system. Merit system coverage did not convert immediately the deputy collectors from political appointees to neutral civil servants. Temporary, war service appointments after 1942 did not guarantee political neutrality for new deputy collectors where the collector did not wish it. The collector, usually a political figure of importance in his community (as a Chicago attorney expressed it, "a man who would be regularly seen at the prize fights") might or might not be knowledgeable in the technicalities of tax administration. He might have business interests that permitted only part-time attention to the work of the collector's office. He presumably did know his way around politically and would listen sympathetically to requests for delays in tax payments or other tax problems.

Since the collector not only was a presidential appointment as was the Commissioner of Internal Revenue but also normally had the endorsement of a U.S. Senator, there were both legal and practical political questions as to the reality of supervision and control from Washington. The Bureau charts showed a line of supervision running from the Commissioner to the Deputy Commissioner of Accounts and Collections to the collector, with a field force of Supervisors of Accounts and Collections under the direction of the Deputy Commissioner presumably supervising and coordinating the work of the 64 collectors. Evidence in Congressional hearings as well as stories in the Bureau recounted that individual collectors had thrown out district supervisors with whom they disagreed and at least one collector put through a direct call to the president when he disliked an order of the Deputy Commissioner who was visiting his office. In other words, each collector represented an island of power that could be and was directed at times against the headquarters office of the Bureau. Management changes, including adoption of punch card machine equipment, that might conceivably reduce personnel or shift control of work, met resistance. Not only did the collector's office in its own work pose a threat to headquarters, but it created difficulties in other divisions. Enforcement work that was not translated into effective collection efforts was worse than useless. Carelessness that permitted corruption, or collusion in corruption, in the collector's office did not always remain confined.

The position of the collector barred management changes unacceptable to the collectors and prevented serious consideration of field integration. Management recommendations to consolidate field services and reduce the number of separate field operations secured little Bureau attention where almost no one wished to bring the professionally and technically qualified revenue agents, intelligence agents, and others hired under merit system procedures into the collector's office and under the collector. Under the Statutes it was impossible to eliminate the collector or to consolidate the collector's office with other functions and place anyone but the collector in charge.

Other Blocks to Management Improvement

But the collector was not the only organizational soft spot. Everywhere work loads exceeded accomplishments. Washington could program, could secure appropriations on the basis of programs outlined, but generally could neither enforce program commitments nor always learn the progress made. Field reports were often late, incomplete, and inaccurate. Statistical comparisons from the forties to the fifties are hazardous except in grossest terms. Washington supervision, organized within each division, faced work loads impossible to handle under the old system and did not initiate adequate new means.

Until 1951, Bureau officials met defensively the recommendations of the studies initiated internally, by the Treasury, or by the several congressional committees, with the answer that given money and time they would work out the problems. Reorganization proposals that would involve remodelling the old collectors' officers, eliminating patronage, reducing specialization, tightening coordination in the field, and installing thorough-going management audit and internal security controls did not fit easily the interests of many of the long-time career men in the Bureau, nor of a substantial number of congressmen, nor of influential individuals in the American Bar Association and accounting societies. Many of the career men who were personally honest and ethical were unwilling to believe that all colleagues were not equally scrupulous. "Sure there's a bit of politics here and there, but that's the way the world works, and congressmen, especially Senators, would be the first to complain if it didn't." Or again, "Of course the organization needs some modernization but it would be unmannerly to rock the boat, and in time changes will be made."

Only the far-reaching disclosures of 1951 convinced most of the Bureau men that corruption had become a malignant growth that required early, drastic surgery. From the time John M. Dunlap became Commissioner, the Bureau adopted a number of expedients in direct reaction to congressional findings—including the creation in October 1951 of an Inspection Service to administer net worth questionnaires, audit personal income tax returns, and investigate charges of misconduct for Bureau employees—and "cooperated fully" in the investigation.

The Reorganization Plan

The 1951 findings had also convinced President Truman. On January 14, 1952 he submitted Reorganization Plan No. 1 of 1952 to the Congress. The actual proposal came as a surprise to most Congressmen and even to the Bureau. In four brief sections, the Plan abolished all presidential appointments in Internal Revenue except that of the Commissioner; provided for three assistant commissioners, a maximum of 25 regional commissioners and 70 "other officers" to be appointed by the Secretary of the Treasury under Civil Service merit system; and transferred all functions and authority from the Bureau of Internal Revenue to the Secretary of the Treasury for redelegation as he determined.

Public hearings and debates in both the House and Senate emphasized the variety of interests involved. Supporting the Reorganization Plan were the Administration spokesmen in the Treasury, the Bureau of the Budget, the Civil Service Commission. Citizens for the Hoover Commission *Report,* the American Federation of Labor, the Kiwanis International, the Junior Chamber of Commerce, and the National Civil Service League were among other groups that supported the plan. The American Bar Association Tax Committee gave its support, but the House of Delegates of the Bar reversed the Committee. No one supported corruption, but many found reasons for opposing the particular plan—some Senators for whom patronage was important, Republicans with hopes of 1952 victory who preferred to undertake their own reorganization, collectors and their friends and associates who had found the system satisfying, attorneys and accountants who did not wish to lose their knowledge of old Bureau ways, and skeptics of organization change as a solution.

The House with little discussion accepted the recommendation of its Committee on Expenditures in the Executive Departments and approved the president's plan. The Senate Committee on Government Operations under McClellan, spurred on by Senator George, disapproved the plan with Senators Humphrey, Monroney, and Moody submitting a strong minority report. The floor fight (led by Senators Humphrey and Monroney and joined by Williams of Delaware, Aiken of Vermont, and others) resulted in defeat (53-37) for Senator George and the Southern Democratic-Republican coalition and brought reversal of the Committee's recommendation.

With broad authority to reorganize, hundreds of decisions followed to bring about a new organization within the following months and to transfer the legal authority from the old to the new officials (new titles whether always new individuals or not). Ten task force committees worked to put the plans into operation by the statutory deadline of December 1, 1952. In addition a selection board was set up to recommend individuals for the 17 regional commissioner and 64 district director positions to the Secretary of the Treasury for appointment. The selection process combined factors of personal acquaintance, career experience, and open competitive examinations. With the Republican victory in the fall of 1952, efforts were made to assure that party's acceptance of the change. When the Cleveland Regional Office was opened with a public ceremony in December 1952, the newly designated Secretary of the Treasury, George M. Humphrey, sat on the platform and joined in the installation.

The Republicans Assume Command

The Eisenhower administration in January found an Internal Revenue agency reorganized but an organization just off the drawing boards, not yet tested for strength and durability. The administration named T. Coleman Andrews as the new Commissioner of Internal Revenue.[3] He began with important congressional support not only from the Republicans but from Democrats (notably Representative Vaughn J. Gary of Virginia, ranking Democratic member of the House Appropriations subcommittee handling Post Office and Treasury budgets). In an early step, Andrews appointed B. Frank White, management consultant, to review the new organization and to report to him as to its feasibility. A favorable report confirmed Andrews' view and brought only minor changes in implementation of reorganization, e.g., reduction in the number of regional offices from 17 to nine and the placement of alcohol and tobacco tax administration in the regional office with no operating responsibility under the district director. The change in number of regional offices from 17 to nine enabled Andrews to make some show of dissent from the Democratic reorganization and eased some personnel adjustments he thought necessary. The original "districts" now assumed the designation "regions" and the 64 collectors' offices became districts (the term used throughout this paper). And on July 9, 1953 the Secretary of the Treasury officially changed the designation of the Bureau of Internal Revenue to the Internal Revenue Service. Although the new Republican Congress, through the subcommittee of the Ways and Means Committee, pursued the question of corruption in the Bureau, the administration in the persons of the Secretary of the Treasury and Commissioner Andrews accepted the reorganization from the Truman administration. Andrews, for example, asserted to the Senate Appropriations budget hearing on April 7, 1953, ". . . I do think that fundamentally the reorganization was a sound thing."

Objectives of the Reorganization

Many individuals from time to time stated their view of the objectives of reorganization and, however different the emphasis, the list included: (1) elimination of patronage and establishment of a career service; (2) improved Washington coordination and control with decentralized service to the taxpayer and adoption of administrative techniques and methods necessary to meet an increasing and changing work load; and (3) restoration of the integrity of the agency to regain administrative, Congressional, and public confidence. Objective three had a status in its own right as well as representing a hoped-for result of (1) and (2). What has happened?

The New Organization Structure

From a loose congeries of specialist divisions in the Washington office, each with its own field office, the new organization structure sought hierarchy, pyramid, and consolidation. Instead of some 200 field offices reporting directly to the Washington office, nine regional commissioners report to the Commissioner of Internal Revenue. All of the older field operating offices, except appellate and alcohol and tobacco tax, were consolidated with the 64 district offices. General supervisory and housekeeping functions moved from Washington to the regions. All of the functions of collection, assessment, audit, investigation, and review for most taxes levied by the United States were placed in the hands of the district directors. Within the Internal Revenue Service, only alcohol and tobacco tax collection is administered out of the regional office through its own field offices apart from the district director.

The 64 (by 1960, 61) district directors report to nine regional commissioners who have functional specialists as assistant regional commissioners (e.g., intelligence, collection, audit) responsible for advising and assisting district directors and their staffs in the carrying out of their responsibilities under uniform policies established in Washington. In addition to alcohol and tobacco tax enforcement, the functions of appellate and of inspection in the regional offices do not have counterparts in the district offices. Regional appellate division opens opportunities for taxpayers to have a further administrative review of their problem by individuals who have not worked on the case earlier. Inspection has responsibility for internal audit and internal security, the first to assure management control and the second to check honesty. For final control and responsibility in the Commissioner of Internal Revenue, the line of authority runs from the regional inspector to the assistant commissioner (inspection) Washington to the Commissioner.

Although organization charts, as usual, tend to produce the tidy view from the air rather than the more ragged view at ground level, repeated reappraisals of the new organization have concluded that the broad line of command follows the lines of the chart and that the centrifugal factors of the past have been reduced. The district director brings under his purview the revenue officers (formerly deputy collectors), the revenue agents, and the intelligence agents. The former walls of separation among these specialists may not have disappeared, but the thickness of the walls has diminished. Difficulties, since reorganization, arise over the practical meaning of a functional and hierarchical authority. The alcohol and tobacco tax administration retains a separateness reminiscent of the old tax-by-tax structure. The three processing centers for mechanical handling of most returns and perhaps the new electronic computer center do not fit tidily into the pyramid.

Career Service

The adoption of the Reorganization Plan in 1952 formally removed the necessity for political approval of all employees in Internal Revenue except the Commissioner. The Eisenhower administration accepted and, over the years, strengthened the career system.[4] The Kennedy administration has continued to bring support.

From the point in 1953 when the Civil Service Commission withdrew earlier general authorization to Internal Revenue for final appointing and reclassification authority to the present there was a generally continuous improvement in career development terms. Job reclassifications both up and down, promotions, transfers, layoffs troubled the first years. A two-year experiment with a revenue agent training program at a midwest university proved mutually unsatisfactory in its original conception. Even in 1960, a House subcommittee inquiry into layoffs in the Des Moines District Office suggested ineptitude in personnel matters. Yet these and other difficulties lose importance in the broad pattern. Entry into Internal Revenue has followed merit system procedures. Emphasis on early advancement in key areas such as revenue officer and revenue agent has permitted since 1956 a normal promotion expectation from GS-5 and GS-7 to a journeyman level of GS-9 and GS-11 within three years of entry for all revenue officers and agents who meet the Service standards. Thereafter the individual secures promotion at his own rate of development.

General executive direction in Internal Revenue begins with the position of assistant district director. At this level the specialist needs to achieve a general management viewpoint. Assistant district director vacancies since 1956 have been filled by Revenue Service employees selected in national competition who have taken the six-months training in the field and in Washington under the Executive Selection and Development Program. The position of assistant district director is one of the major stepping stones to the higher management positions. In a period of five years 70 employees selected for the program began while they were in the following position grades: 33 in grade GS-13, 24 in GS-14, 13 in GS-15. These same employees at the end of December 1960 held position grades as follows: one in GS-13, nine in GS-14, 42 in GS-15, and 18 in GS-16. The classes of 1956 and 1957 naturally showed the highest promotions. The system of selection, training, and appointment to assistant district director positions assures a supply of trained candidates for almost every top position; discourages political interference; and dramatizes to personnel in Internal Revenue the lifetime career opportunities open.[5] Service officials in recommendations to the incoming Secretary of the Treasury in 1961 placed support of the Executive Selection and Development Program as their first priority.

Other tangible benefits have developed. The average grade level of employees has risen from GS-5.9 in 1951 to a GS-7.6 in 1960. The Service had available 157 supergrades (GS-16, -17, -18) at the end of calendar year 1960 and would have approximately 33 more with the fiscal year beginning July 1, 1961.

Integrity

The congressional investigations produced a continuous barrage of adverse publicity for Internal Revenue that hurt the morale of all employees and presumably weakened the voluntary compliance of taxpayers on which the agency depends heavily for much of the enforcement of tax laws. The scandals involved varied types of problems: petty theft and embezzlement on the part of individual employees or a few combined, individual acceptance of favors in return for adjustments, acceptance of favors and the granting of adjustments by a number of individuals including personnel highly placed in the field and in Washington, a standard in collectors' offices, especially, that permitted requests for delay and special attention to be honored simply as a part of a local political give-and-take or at times in return for more tangible favors, and personnel appointments designed to further some of the above activities.

Removal of presidential appointment of the collectors and consolidation of the field organization changed both the lines of control and the means to advancement in the organization. The establishment of an independent inspection service for internal audit and internal security, responsible only to the Commissioner, added to the institutional means for continuously checking the performance of field offices.

The problems of petty theft and embezzlement by individuals or employees in concert as well as individual acceptance of favors in return for a variety of "adjustments" have not been eliminated in the post-reorganization period. Just as, one might add, banks have never eliminated theft and embezzlement by their employees. Hopefully, the Inspection Service, the functional reviews, the layers of coordination discourage some employees who might be tempted and identify most of those who fail to resist temptation. The distinction between the late 1940s and today is the level at which corruption exists and its presumed absence up through the ranks of the Service. Even the uncovering of an especially large embezzlement ring involving individuals inside and outside of an Internal Revenue district office in 1959 was handled by the Internal Revenue Service without interference by the administration or the Congress and without serious adverse publicity. There was confidence that the Revenue Service could and would handle the problem effectively.

Congressional attitudes and action strongly reflect a return of confidence. Appropriation requests in the last five years or so have received increasingly sympathetic attention. Public praise has been bestowed during hearings. Approved appropriations have included support for the "Blue Ribbon career service program" and the addition of supergrades. Cuts in appropriation requests by the House have been restored in whole or in part by the Senate. One group of Senators has on two occasions written to the Senate Appropriations Committee requesting higher appropriations than the administration had asked.

Productivity

Has reorganization with its concomitant tightened national office direction, improved personnel selection, and increased integrity resulted in better tax enforcement and increased tax dollars per unit of administrative effort? Logically the answer should be "yes" and in fact the answer seems to be "yes," but the evidence is fragile. Statistically one can show that with 51,206 and 51,047 employees in 1959 and 1960, total taxes collected exceeded $79 billion and $91 billion in contrast to 54,411 and 56,262 employees collecting approximately $39 billion and $51 billion in 1950 and 1951. Additional assessments in 1950 and 1951 totaled $1,422 million and $1,576 million, respectively (exclusive of excess profits taxes) in contrast to additional assessments of $1,821 million and $2,052 million in 1959 and 1960 with several thousand less employees. Although such statistical evidence is in the right direction, no one familiar with tax administration would consider these figures conclusive nor would they accept comparative figures as to the cost of collecting $100 of revenue. (The latter comparison is frequently used in management firm reports and elsewhere, yet actually the result is conditioned probably as much by the tax rates and the economy as by the efficiency of the tax agency.) The detailed statistics that might serve more adequately to measure efficiency are considered unreliable for comparative purposes between the two periods.

The statistical "impression" of improved productivity is supported by other impressions. In the immediate pre-reorganization years, a sense of an impossible task in controlling the work load apparently permeated the organization. More recently the task has appeared more as a challenge than an "impossibility." Research efforts have been broadened and deepened not only to identify more accurately the gap between total taxes due and total taxes collected but to pinpoint the items that make up this gap. With the change in organization structure, the national office has assurance that audit, collection, intelligence, and other programs designed on the basis of this research will be put into effect at district and regional levels or explanations will be forthcoming. The establishment of service centers with mechanical means to handle faster and more accurately many former clerical operations and the adoption of electronic data processing equipment for an eventual master file of taxpayers are opening rich avenues for programs capable of meeting work loads.

Conclusions

The organization structure of the old Bureau of Internal Revenue failed to contain many of the "centrifugal tendencies" of a large decentralized field force that Herbert Kaufman identified and found well-controlled in the Forest Service.[6] Local influences were often more important to the collector than were national loyalty, policies, recommendations, and orders from Washington. Mutual respect through common professional training provided an *esprit* for revenue agents and occasionally for revenue agents and intelligence agents but emphasized the separatism from the personnel in collectors' offices and in alcohol tax administration. Differing lines of promotion and, of course, political endorsement for collectors, added to the divisive forces. The organization structure emphasized differences and failed to provide a unified view of the Bureau program to the field or in Washington.

The new organization and the removal of patronage have restricted the centrifugal forces at work in Internal Revenue. A career system draws the specialists into competing for advancement in the same channels. Controls built into the new organization provide a sensitivity to field conditions that did not exist. A frankness exhibited in management manuals and in discussions at joint meetings of the commissioner and his assistants with regional commissioners and district commissioners suggests mutual respect and understanding.

The Washington office places greater confidence in the field today with decentralization of most operating authority, but it exercises a vigorous leadership to maintain the reality of its confidence. But, again as Kaufman saw in the Forest Service, the victory is never finally won.

Notes

1. Francis E. Rourke, "The Politics of Administrative Organization: A Case History," 19 *Journal of Politics* 461-78 (August 1957).
2. On the assumption that there are innumerable possible organization structures to be paired with innumerable possible objectives (at least modifications of objectives), no attempt is made to establish whether the new organization is the best possible. See James G. March and Herbert A. Simon, *Organizations* (John Wiley & Sons, Inc., 1958), p. 176.
3. The author's collective impression of Andrews as commissioner from numbers of interviews with Internal Revenue staff members is that he showed an understanding of management and a "brassy toughness" in the years of 1953-1955 that contributed to the acceptance and strength of the new organization.
4. A story around the Internal Revenue Service and referred to in *The Bulletin* of NAIRE (National Association of Internal Revenue Employees), October 1955, suggests that strong pressures existed in the first years of the Eisenhower administration to shift a number of positions in Internal Revenue to "Schedule C," but that Commissioner Andrews resisted to the point of threatening to resign and announcing the reason.
5. Internal Revenue officials interviewed indicated that immediately following passage of the Reorganization Plan congressmen and other individuals observed a "hands off" attitude almost as if in fear of possible association with Internal Revenue. Not all have retained this view and from time to time there are those who will recommend "deserving" candidates. The selection and training system for high promotion permits the answer to recommendations: "Have your man apply for the Executive Selection and Development Program." The political recommendation then loses force in the succession of selection steps required.
6. Herbert Kaufman, *The Forest Ranger, A Study in Administrative Behavior* (Johns Hopkins Press, 1960).

Bibliographical Note

No attempt has been made to document this study in detail. The author interviewed most of the top officials in the Internal Revenue Service as well as a half-dozen individuals previously with Internal Revenue or the Treasury or knowledgeable in the problems of Internal Revenue. The following bibliography is representative but not complete.

John W. Snyder, "The Reorganization of the Bureau of Internal Revenue," 12 *Public Administration Review* 221-233 (Autumn 1952), an Administration description of the reorganization with a "Chronology" of Treasury and Bureau administrative improvement efforts from 1946 to 1952.

The *Annual Reports* of the Commissioners provide statistical data and a general history of the Bureau and the Revenue Service.

Of the large number of published Congressional documents covering the post World War II difficulties of Internal Revenue and the adjustments in the years immediately following the 1952 reorganization, the following were of particular use:

Advisory Group Appointed Pursuant to Public Law 147, 80th Congress, *Investigation of the Bureau of Internal Revenue, Report to the Joint Committee on Internal Revenue Taxation* (1948).

Joint Committee on Internal Revenue Taxation, *Hearing on Reorganization of the Bureau of Internal Revenue*, 83 Cong., 1 sess. (September 25, 1953).

Special Advisory Group (appointed by the Chairman, Joint Committee on Internal Revenue Taxation), *The Internal Revenue Service, Its Reorganization and Administration* (1955).

House Committee on Ways and Means, Subcommittee on Administration of the Internal Revenue Laws: Hearings, Parts 1, 2, 3, 4 (variously dated between September 10, 1951 and May 5, 1952); Report No. 2518, to the 82nd Congress (January 3, 1953); Hearings, Parts A, B, C, D, E (dated between February 4, 1953 and July, 1954); *Internal Revenue Administration*, Progress Report (April 22, 1957).

House Committee on Expenditures in the Executive Departments, *Hearings on Reorganization Plan No. I* of 1952 (Bureau of Internal Revenue) (January 18-23, 1952); Report No. 1271 (January 24, 1952).

House Committee on Appropriations, Subcommittee, Treasury and Post Office: Hearings, Investigation of the Bureau of Internal Revenue (including Preliminary Report of Subcommittee Staff, July 24, 1947), (July 25, 1947); Hearings, Treasury Department Appropriation Bill for 1949, Investigation of the Bureau of Internal Revenue (Boston), (December, 1947); Hearings, Treasury Department Appropriation Bill for 1949. Part II includes summary of Report of Subcommittee Staff, February 1948.

Senate Committee on Government Operations, *Hearings on Reorganization Plan No. I, 1952* (Bureau of Internal Revenue); Report No. 1259 (Majority), (March 10, 1952); Report No. 1259, Part 2 (Minority), (March 10, 1952).

In addition, the House and Senate *Hearings and Reports* on appropriations for the Bureau of Internal Revenue and Internal Revenue Service, as well as the *Budgets* frequently included relevant material.

ROBERT T. GOLEMBIEWSKI
ALAN KIEPPER

MARTA: Toward an Effective, Open Giant

Experience at MARTA (Metropolitan Atlanta Rapid Transit Authority) can be instructive to public managers, both those contemplating start-up efforts of their own, as well as those managers interested in specific applications of "organizational humanism" in public agencies.[1] Authorized by a 1971 referendum, MARTA sought to gear up quickly to launch a program whose estimated cost was $1.3 billion, and whose developmental phase was projected to cover the better part of a decade. MARTA thus qualifies as "the biggest game in town," and is in fact the largest regional public project since the early TVA days.

The Force-Field at Start-Up

MARTA was born in a context that was both intense and uncertain, with no prospect that things would get easier or more definite. Specifically, the challenges facing MARTA in 1973 reflected many aspects of both opportunity and danger, as well as of "hurry up" and "wait." Illustratively, MARTA more or less simultaneously had to:

- Manage and enlarge an existing bus company, using technologies that are well-established and straightforward, in general.
- Monitor and coordinate the design and construction of 69 miles of rapid-speed rail lines with associated stations, park-and-ride facilities, etc., involving technologies of sometimes substantial indeterminacy and complexity.
- Develop a broad range of design, development, and operating capabilities as a "strong" central staff, in contrast to a staff with a narrower mission, as is the case at BART.
- Aggressively develop a transit system when funding was highly dependent on grants from federal agencies whose level of appropriations were uncertain.
- Develop fluid working relationships among a senior staff recruited nationwide only over the past few months, none of whom had experience with projects of the scale or pace of the MARTA program, and some of

210

whom no doubt would learn relatively early that MARTA was not their cup of tea.

● Respond constructively to multiple constituencies—as represented by a MARTA Board whose directors were appointed by political bodies from four counties and from the city of Atlanta, with two counties having representation even though local elections there had rejected referenda to authorize a sales tax increment earmarked for MARTA

— as represented by the entire state legislature, which authorized a local sales tax increment to get MARTA started, as well as a blue-ribbon committee to oversee MARTA operations

— as represented by federal agencies which were variously regulators and dispensers of grants for mass transportation projects.

● Be open to the broadest range of local inputs as to design features, etc., within the context of the basic plan that was voted on in the referendum.

● Organize so as to effectively design and build a $1.3 billion system by 1978.

● Live within the limits of three awesome facts:

— the MARTA system would significantly determine major aspects of the development of metro-Atlanta for decades, physically, and economically, as well as in terms of the quality of life;

— any delay in developing the MARTA system would be costly, with as much as $250,000 per day in additional system costs attributable to inflation alone, not to mention the growing economic and psychologic costs of moving more people and more things with less dispatch; and

— MARTA had neither taxing power nor the right of eminent domain; only the state legislature could authorize taxes, and only the several local governments could condemn property needed by MARTA.

Toward an Organic Managerial System

Overall, the MARTA force-field patently was not congenial to a "standard operating procedure" approach. Considerable expenditure of socio-emotional energy at start-up thus was expended to help prepare MARTA officials to cope with certain uncertainty and permanent temporariness. The guiding model was an organic one, of MARTA as a dynamic and evolving organization with which its members and several publics could identify as an open and effective managerial system. There was no practical alternative, given that at least seven stages were envisioned in MARTA's development over a decade, beginning with the late-1972 appointment of its general manager. These stages are as follows:

● Immediately, MARTA would operate and radically expand an already-extensive set of autobus routes.

- As soon as possible, MARTA must develop its unique style and character, reflected not only in staff, policies, and procedures, but also in the way MARTA business was conducted.
- Over its first two years, MARTA would develop detailed designs of its integrated rail/bus system, evaluate any additions to the basic referendum plan, etc.
- In its second year, MARTA would get heavily into real estate acquisition, relocation of families and businesses, and possibly even into construction for such relocation.
- Within three years MARTA would transition to an emphasis on overseeing massive construction projects.
- Within six to eight years MARTA would begin an equipment-testing phase.
- Shortly thereafter, MARTA would have to develop into an integrated operating system of rail and bus transit.

In short, there would have to be several MARTAs, whose development would be compressed in a brief time frame. The smoothness of the unavoidable transitions would significantly influence the project's successful completion.

To help prepare for these necessary transitional shocks, learning designs based on the "laboratory approach to organization development"[2] were used to accelerate the development of the MARTA managerial team, as well as to influence the style in which that team would conduct its public business. Broadly, the goal had aspects of both avoidance and approach. As much as possible, the start-up goal sought (1) to avoid the closedness and ponderousness of large-scale bureaucratic programs which tend to be hierarchy-serving and emphasize stability, and (2) to approach the openness and agile proactiveness of an organic system which is oriented toward problem-solving and emphasizes timely change of complex, temporary systems.

Figure 1 provides substantial illustrative detail about what is to be avoided and that which is to be approached. The anti-goal was a "coercive compromise" system of management, and the thrust was toward enhancing the "collaborative-consensual" features of the MARTA managerial team.

Movement in MARTA toward the collaborative-consensual system of management was seen as requiring a long-term effort, the success of which was dependent upon behavior consistent with five basic ethical orientations characteristic of the "laboratory approach to organization development and change." These orientations could not only be "espoused," in Argyris' terms; they also had to be "operating" guides for behavior. Briefly, the five orientations require:[3]

- *Deep acceptance of inquiry and experimentation as the norm in relationships with others.* "It is what we don't know that can destroy our relationships" could well serve as a motto. The opposed meta-value is perhaps more common and is reflected in such maxims as: "Familiarity breeds contempt." The difference between these guiding values is profound. The true acceptance

FIGURE 1
Dominant Characteristics of Two Opposed Ideal Managerial Systems

Coercive-Compromise System	Collaborative-Consensual System
• Superordinate power is used to control behavior reinforced by suitable rewards and punishments.	• Control is achieved through agreement on goals, reinforced by continuous feedback about results.
• Emphasis on leadership by authoritarian control of the compliant and weak, obeisance to more powerful, and compromise when contenders are equal in power.	• Emphasis on leadership by direct confrontation of differences and working through of any conflicts.
• Disguising or suppression of real feelings or reactions, especially when they refer to powerful figures.	• Public sharing of real feelings, reactions.
• Obedience to the attempts of superiors to influence.	• Openness to the attempts to exert influence by those who have requisite competence or information.
• Authority/obedience is relied on to cement organization relationships.	• Mutual confidence and trust are used to cement organization relationships.
• Structure is power-based and hierarchy-oriented.	• Structure is task-based and solution-oriented.
• Individual responsibility.	• Shared responsibility.
• One-to-one relationships between superior and subordinates.	• Multiple-group memberships with peers, superiors, and subordinates.
• Structure is based on bureaucratic model and is intendedly stable over time.	• Structure emerges out of problems faced as well as out of developing consensus among members and is intendedly temporary or at least changeable.

Based on Herbert Shepard, "Changing Interpersonal and Intergroup Relationships in Organizations," in James G. March (ed.), *Handbook of Organizations* (Chicago: Rand McNally & Co., 1965), pp. 1128-31.

of inquiry and experimentation involves a mutual accessibility of persons to one another. Such accessibility also implies a potential vulnerability to each other, as well as a real commitment to the possibility of being influenced by the other. The opposed meta-value legitimates a more distant relationship and, if only in a superficial sense, a safer one.

Such an orientation is no mere humanistic luxury in organizations like MARTA, at least in its early stages of designing and constructing a system which has numerous one-of-a-kind features. An agency with a mass-production mission could well do with far less of this spirit of inquiry and experimentation.

● *Expanded consciousness and recognition of choice.* Patently, inquiry and experimentation would be sterile in the absence of a consciousness of the diversity of choices that exist. The linkages are direct: an expanded consciousness or awareness generates wider choices; choice permits experimentation that could lead to change or more informed decisions; and freely made choice also helps assure that the individual will own the change or decision rather than (at best) accept its imposition.

These subtle processes were seen as essential in MARTA. To suggest the point by contrast, many management teams have too narrow a view of the choices open to them, based on faulty feedback and disclosure processes. They can generate decisions that have to be constantly policed, enforced, or even continually redecided because of low commitment to them by the very decision makers who superficially acquiesced in them.[4] This implies a human tragedy, and only trouble for projects like MARTA.

● *Collaborative concept of authority.* This is meant in two senses. In laboratory learning situations, first, the role of the participant is a far more influential one than in traditional learning situations. Second, laboratory learning situations provide an experience with collaborative authority relations that can later be approached in the "real world." Even though extreme forms of mutual influence may be seldom applicable outside of designated learning situations, more or less extensive sharing in power and authority is usually possible and is often necessary.

Experimentation with collaborative authority is no mere curiosity. Complex projects typically require substantial and subtle sharing of power and influence by wide ranges of contributors at many levels of organization. The goal is that the problem and who has the competence to deal with it will be major determinants of who seeks to influence, and whose attempts will be accepted. .

"Collaborative authority" has a pleasant sound to many nowadays, but it raises a variously serious potential contradiction. In this case, for example, the general manager of MARTA stressed his *personal* responsibility for seeing that his general preference for collaborative authority did in fact work. But he also might sometimes act unilaterally—even against the consensus of those reporting to him—for various reasons, including the failure of collaborative efforts to bear timely fruit. The balance is clearly a delicate one, with intent being likely to differ from performance and with definitions of "timely" and "collaborative" probably differing in complex ways at various points in time.

· ● *Mutual helping relationships in social settings.* Helping is seen as perhaps the distinctive human attribute that requires cultivation and development. Relatedly, the social setting—in contrast to a one-on-one setting—is seen as an optimal (perhaps even natural) locus for mutual helping. This world view assumes the classical concept of man as a social animal. In addition, the emphasis acknowledges the extraordinary and perhaps unique capacity of groups to induce massive forces to reinforce learning or change.

Numerous social adhesives reinforce the helping relationships stressed by the laboratory approach. For example, its learning designs tend to generate substantial (even unparalleled) exchanges of warmth, or support, between members. Such exchanges can help cement a community of learners. Similarly, the laboratory approach rests on acceptance of the other person, on what has come to be called "unconditional positive regard." Acceptance does not imply approval, but rather a concern for the person. Relatedly, designs based on the laboratory approach attempt to stress the psychological safety of participants. As two careful students note:

People must certainly differ greatly in their ability to accept the guarantee of psychological safety. To the extent that the feeling of safety cannot be achieved—and quickly —the prime basic ingredient for this form of learning is absent. Its importance cannot be overemphasized, nor can the difficulty of its being accomplished.[5]

To be sure, much of life in organizations is narrowly self-interested and even destructive, rather than helping. The goal was to encourage greater attention to helping in MARTA than is common in many organizations. More specifically, the dual objective was to test the limits of psychological MARTA safety possible among MARTA managers, as well as to determine whether these limits could be expanded. The practical result is the exchange of minimally distorted communication which is the life-blood of effective managerial action. The main ethical product is a more humanistically oriented workplace.

● *Authenticity in interpersonal relationships.* A final value emphasizes the expression of feelings, as well as the analysis of the behaviors inducing them. The rationale for the meta-value of authenticity has two kinds of roots. First, there are the clearly moral precepts on the theme: "To thine own self be true; thou canst not then be false to any man." Second, authenticity is seen as critical in communication. Failure to be authentic in the sense of "leveling" and "expressing feelings" so as to elicit similar behaviors from others can accumulate so much interpersonal garbage as to overburden interaction and impair rational-technical performance.

Note that being "congruent" or "authentic" is a two-way street, to contrast these notions with the cruel narcissism associated with extreme forms of "doing your own thing." Specifically, Argyris urges thinking of authenticity as an interpersonal phenomenon rather than a personal state or characteristic.[6] He conceives of human relationships as "the source of psychological life and human growth," especially because such relationships are then those in which an individual enhances personal awareness and acceptance of self and others, in ways that permit others to do the same. Consequently, for Argyris, it is no more possible to be authentic independent of others than it is possible to cooperate with yourself.

In MARTA, the costs of inauthenticity could be enormous. For any derivative lack of communication and trust would be reckoned in terms of suspicion or overcaution, delay, and eventually huge costs of lengthening schedules. Witness the related emphasis in NASA on "zero defects" at the same time that the organization gospel was: that mistakes were understandable in complex projects, up to a substantial point; that mistakes could provide valuable learning opportunities; and that in all cases it was intolerable to hide an error, for the consequences could be profoundly serious.

Learning Designs and Some Consequences

This article basically details the early learning designs used in MARTA to move toward a collaborative-consensual system, and also sketches some of the consequences of those designs over the first year. Three major elements in the learning design can be distinguished:

A. a team-building experience for the general manager and seven aids who comprised the senior staff, a linkage between the first and second tiers of management,

B. an interface experience between the senior staff and the third tier of management, and

C. an interface experience between senior staff and the MARTA Board.

Each design element was the focus of a separate three-day session held at a university center for continuing education, and each element also involved various follow-up activities.

A. Team-Building by Senior Staff

Just as the last member of the senior staff had been recruited, and while others were still settling into new homes and offices, a team-building experience was held. Its thrust is suggested by Figure 2.

FIGURE 2
Brief Rationale for Team Building

1. Any management group can improve its operations.

2. Such improvement can be critical even for a management group that is well-satisfied with its present performance, as in preparing for unpredictable stress situations.

3. An audit of interpersonal and group processes is an important way of testing for existing effectiveness, as well as of inspiring improvements. Such an audit can:
   - aid in increasing mutual understanding and empathy
   - heighten awareness of interpersonal and group processes, and so generate more realistic and detailed perceptions of "what's going on"
   - help build identification, mutual goodwill, and comradeship borne of a sometimes intense experience
   - facilitate the development of shared perspectives and frameworks that facilitate communication
   - emphasize the importance of reality-testing based on the fullest possible expression of information, reactions, and feelings
   - build norms encouraging openness, candor, and face-to-face confrontation.

Basically, the first learning design encouraged senior staff to acknowledge and deal with the products of their interactions as persons and officials. The senior staff had only a brief interactive past, so there was little unresolved socio-emotional "garbage." The focus was on the present and the future-soon-to-be-present. Team-building at once encourages almost non-stop inter-action between participants, and also seems to speed up psychological time. One official reflected both aspects of the impact of team-building designs on time:

I've learned more in three days about you guys, and more about my place on the senior staff, than I probably would have learned in three weeks back at the office, for sure, or even in three months.

I also feel like I've been here forever, even though my calendar tells me it's only been some 50 hours spread over three days.

There is ample reason to believe that such speeded-up psychological time is particularly well-spent around start-up. Simply, start-up implies a set of issues having a substantial potential for polluting the rational-technical performance of an executive team. Illustratively, these characteristics include:

- Substantial confusion about roles and relationships.
- Fairly clear understanding of immediate goals, but lack of clarity about longer-run operations, which cumulatively induce wicked double-binds: a strong desire to get on with the task, and yet a pervasive concern that precedents may be set which can mean trouble over the long run.
- Fixation on the immediate task, which often means that group main-tenance activities will receive inadequate attention and individual needs will be neglected.
- A challenge to team members which will induce superior technical effort, but which may also have serious longer-run consequences for personal or family life and which in any case probably will generate an intensity in work relationships that requires careful monitoring.

Confronting and Contracting. The team-building design for the senior staff —which was based on a well-known technology for behavioral change[7]—had two basic features: confronting and contracting.

Confronting refers to a complex of attitudes and behavioral skills that are seen as enhancing a management team's rational-technical performance in two basic ways. Thus such attitudes and skills can make members more aware of their socio-emotional processes, as well as more effective in their management.

"Confronting" often has a colorful press, as in versions that advertise "tell-ing it like it is" or "letting it all hang out." As used here, however, confron-ting is a two-way exchange expressable in terms of four complex emphases:

1. Team members become more aware of their own reactions and feelings, as well as those of other members;

2. Team members become more aware of the stimuli inducing particular reactions and feelings in themselves and others;

3. Team members accept and maintain a norm which sanctions the expression of the full range of applicable information, reactions, and feelings;

4. Team members develop skills to share their concerns in ways that encourage similar expression by other members.

The basic vehicle[8] for focusing on confronting attitudes and behavioral skills is a simple one based on the development and sharing of 3-dimensional images. In this case, the general manager prepared three lists in response to these questions:

- How do you see yourself in relation to the assistant general managers?
- How do you see your assistant general managers?
- How do you believe they see you?

As a group, the AGMs, collaboratively also developed lists in response to three similar questions. The lists were prepared separately, and then shared. Figure 3 contains the two sets of 3-D images, edited here to clarify points unintelligible to outsiders.

Extended discussion of the two 3-D images, with the aid of a consultant, constituted the basic early experience with confronting, and also provided substantial skill-practice with appropriate attitudes and behaviors. Mechanically, the procedure is simple. The two sets of 3-D images, written on large sheets of newsprint, are taped to a wall, side-by-side. Participants survey the lists, and are urged to ask for examples where the meaning of some item is obscure or confusing. The basic ground rule to participants is that they seek to understand the image, and to acknowledge any feelings of defensiveness or resistance but not dwell on them. Such discussion and analysis can be both varied and intense, but it is typically accompanied by periods of explosive laughter and friendly commiserating, as in a mutual reduction-of-tension.

Such designs tend to "work" for several reasons. First, basically, participants need such information, discomforting or even initially hurtful though it may be. The senior staff's compelling concern about "the project" is implied in their agreement, even enthusiasm, to "build a better team."

Second, participants typically understand that the best—indeed, perhaps the only—way to raise the probability of receiving such needed information in the future is to be accepting of the 3-D images in the present. Acceptance does not necessarily mean agreement, be it noted. "I can understand how you see it that way," might go such a case of acceptance without necessary agreement, "but I hope you recognize there are many things about which reasonable people can and do differ."

Third, confronting with 3-D images is a shared experience that can build mutual identification and understanding, which is what many participants are seeking. The design is accepted and valued, consequently, and in a sense made to work.

Fourth, most individuals are uncomfortable if their verbal or non-verbal behavior is at some substantial variance with what they really know, believe, or feel. That lack of comfort increases sharply if the person suspects that relevant others are being similarly incongruent. The analysis of 3-D images usually helps to reduce such variance by encouraging a mutual escalation toward openness and owning. Participants typically are much concerned about what the other group or person is writing on their 3-D image in that other room, for example, for they realize that too much varnishing of the truth on their part will be painfully apparent when the 3-D images are compared. The intent is that this greater but still-tentative openness and owning will free for productive use sometimes substantial energies previously needed to repress information shared in the confrontation.

Hence confrontation designs usually leave participants with a sense that barriers are being lowered, and things are "really happening" with less effort. Consider the symbolism in these common reactions to a 3-D image exchange. "Well, that took the cork out of the bottle, and about at the right time," reports one participant. Another participant had this insightful perspective on the exchange of images:

That's quite a load off my mind, although I didn't quite dare to put down on paper all that concerned me. I'll look for an early opportunity to make some further mileage. It was a good start, and not as tense as I had expected. I guess all of us really wanted to get over the hump of mannerly closedness, but none of us knew how or was willing to risk starting what we all were clearly eager to do. We were off-and-running on the images almost before the instructions were completed.

Fifth, substantial agreement typically exists between pairs of 3-D images, as is the case in Figure 3. This agreement almost always increases the participants' sense of mutual competence and acceptance, by confirming that one person or group shares perceptions with another as well as by signalling that a real process of exchange has been begun. Especially for a managerial team, it is both critical and comforting that its members see some important issues in similar ways, and that they also characterize the same processes in similar terms. Moreover, the resulting mutual enhancement of self-esteem can provide powerful impetus toward, as well as a solid foundation for, future communication and collaboration. In sum, the inevitable areas of major agreement on pairs of 3-D images signal that the confronted other is like the self in significant ways, which can build a sense of identification and empathy. And these, in turn, can encourage further attempts to reach and understand the other in areas where agreement or even awareness does not exist on 3-D images.

Contracting is the vehicle that seeks to assure that the sharing of 3-D images does not merely dissipate into a kind of warm glow that is quickly forgotten. Based on the 3-D images, the general manager and the group of assistant general managers each prepared "shopping lists" directed at the other. The three lists constituted responses to three questions:

FIGURE 3
3-D Images that Facilitated Confrontation

3-D Image Prepared by Assistant General Managers	3-D Image Prepared by General Manager
I. How AGMs See General Manager 1. Unapproachable (closed door) 2. Not open 3. Dedicated 4. Determined 5. Cool under fire 6. Hard working 7. Priorities (not ordered) 8. Meticulous 9. Procrastinator 10. Too detailed 11. Sensitive 12. Organization above people 13. Tough 14. Poor delegator 15. Aloof 16. Formal 17. Highly structured personality 18. Programmed 19. Too busy 20. Violates chain of command 21. Fails to pinpoint responsibility	**I. How General Manager Sees AGMs** 1. Reluctant to share concerns and opinions, especially with GM 2. As disregarding opinions of others 3. Reluctant to take initiative 4. Dedicated to MARTA 5. As wanting some "answers" where none exist 6. As frustrated
II. How AGMs See Selves in Relation to GM 1. Insecure 2. Ineffective 3. Frustrated 4. Unable to perform effectively 5. Wasted and unimportant 6. Inhibited 7. Too willing to please	**II. How GM Sees Self in Relation to AGMs** 1. Spread too thin personally 2. As spending too little time with AGMs as group 3. As emphasizing brush-fires, without breathing room to focus on key issues 4. As too lenient with AGMs as to assignments, deadlines
III. How AGMs Believe GM Sees Them 1. Relies on group (reluctantly) 2. Trusts us, with reservations 3. Does not see us as team 4. Naive (and sometimes we are!) 5. Sees potential in us 6. As less effective than we should be, and less effective than we can be	**III. How GM Believes AGMs See Him** 1. As cautious, indecisive 2. Not trusting, due to newness of relationships 3. Expressed lack of trust via deadlines, detailed reviews 4. Busy-busy, not having time for at least some AGMs

1. What should you keep doing about as now?
2. What should you stop doing that you now do?
3. What should you start doing that you do not do now?

Participants were encouraged to be as specific as possible about the behaviors or attitudes in question. Not particularly helpful are such global injunctions: Be smarter!

The three lists become the bases for a complex exchange process. The key generic process follows such a form: If you want me to stop X behavior, are you willint to do more of Y which is on my list of behaviors that I would like you to start performing?

The intent of contracting is transparent. The intent is to model a process that can be used back home. More immediately, the goal is to build agreement among participants about a few exchanges for openers, as it were. The process of reaching this agreement often induces forces that can later reinforce any trade-offs that are decided upon in the contracting period. The potential social power implicit in such group decision making has been amply documented by much behavioral research, beginning with such classic experiments as that by Coch and French.[9]

The specific contracts entered into by the MARTA senior staff will not be reported here, but they focused around more substantial freedom of action for the assistant general managers, which was exchanged for several items on GM's "start" list. Overall, senior staff became more aware of how their past experiences in more stable and structured local government administrative situations limited their early and resourceful responses to the novelty and quick-silveredness of the MARTA program.

Tracking Effects of the Design. The effects of the confronting and contracting among the senior staff were judged by a series of semi-structured interviews as well as by periodic administrations of a paper-and-pencil test, the Group Behavior Inventory (GBI).[10] Only the GBI will be discussed here.

The GBI, whose basic dimensions are sketched in Figure 4, proved useful in two basic ways. First, several administrations of the instrument permitted a test of whether the expected consequences of the team building did occur, for specific members of the senior staff as well as for the aggregate. Figure 4 details the effects anticipated as results of a successful team building effort, and also summarizes the actual results, using the GBI dimensions. Note that "short-run effects" compare GBI responses immediately before the team building to responses obtained two weeks later; and "longer-run effects" involved comparisons of the benchmark GBI scores with an administration of the instrument some seven weeks after the team building began, at which time the effects of the team building become increasingly confounded by the rush of workday activities.

The GBI results are generally consistent with expectations about the effects of a successful team-building experience. Overall, that is, approximately two-thirds of the changes reported by participants are in the expected direction,

FIGURE 4

GBI Dimensions, Expected Effects of Team-Building Design, and Summarized Actual Effects

Group Behavior Inventory Dimensions*	Expected Effects of Team Building	Summaries of Actual Effects	
		Short-Run Effects	Longer-Run Effects
I. *Group Effectiveness.* This dimension describes group effectiveness in solving problems and in formulating policy through a creative, realistic team effort.	I. Increase in effectiveness is expected, but may be slow to build	I. 5/8 participants report increases	Ia. 5/8 report increases
II. *Approach to vs. withdrawal from leader.* At the positive pole of this dimension are groups in which members can establish an unconstrained and comfortable relationship with their leader—the leader is approachable.	II. Increase in approachability is probable, but may be slow to build	II. 6/8 report increases	IIa. 4/8 report increases
III. *Mutual influence.* This dimension describes groups in which members see themselves and others as having influence with other group members and the leader.	III. Substantial increase even in the short-run, which should persist; note that GM may perceive inroads on personal authority and power	III. 6/8 report increases	IIIa. 5/8 report increases
IV. *Personal involvement and participation.* Individuals who want, expect, and achieve active participation in group meetings are described by this dimension.	IV. Substantial increase even in the short run, which should persist	IV. 7/8 report increases	IVa. 6/8 report increases
V. *Intragroup trust vs. intragroup competitiveness.* At the positive pole, this dimension depicts a group in which the members hold trust and confidence in each other.	V. Increase is expected, but may be slow to build	V. 3/8 report increases	Va. 6/8 report increases
VI. *General evaluation of meetings.* This dimension is a measure of a generalized feeling about the meetings of one's group as good, valuable, strong, pleasant, as contrasted with bad, worthless, weak, unpleasant.	VI. Increase is expected, but may be slow to build	VI. 4/8 report increases	VIa. 6/8 report increases

*Based on Frank Friedlander, "The Impact of Organizational Training Laboratories upon Effectiveness and Interaction of Ongoing Work Groups," *Personnel Psychology*, Vol. 20 (Autumn 1970), p. 295.

and seven of the 12 aggregate comparisons achieve usually accepted levels of statistical significance. Note also that these substantial effects, if anything, understate the impact of the team building. That is, the weeks following the initial off-site session were traumatic and difficult ones that severely stressed all members of the senior staff. In addition, benchmark administrations of instruments designed to measure team-building effects often seem to reflect a kind of "rose-colored glasses" effect, either because respondents are truly optimistic, or are cautious in being open, or are simply not fully aware of the variety or magnitude of issues facing them. Post-experience scores thus often will understate actual change when they are compared to such cautious/optimistic/uninformed benchmark scores. Reinforcing this surmise is the general opinion of participants about one year later. One participant noted, to illustrate the dominant and probably universal reaction:

You didn't promise us a rose-garden, I know. But it was quite a shock to confront an array of issues so early in the game. It violated all my governmental experience, where such confronting was done at greater leisure, and probably not at all. But I'm increasingly glad we did the team building. MARTA cannot afford to let nature take its course. There is too much to be done in a short period to risk getting sand-bagged by hoping that issues will go away if they are neglected long enough.

Second, the GBI results were also used to indicate where follow-on activity might be appropriate for individual participants. To explain, all members of the senior staff identified their completed GBI forms, which were returned to the consultant at his university address. Only aggregate results would be discussed publicly. In the two cases in which senior staff indicated by their GBI responses that the short-run effects of the team building were for them ineffectual or negative, however, the consultant contacted the respondents and sought to verify their "deviant" GBI scores.

The GBI proved sensitive in both cases. In one case, the respondent saw the initial experience as more hopeful than impactful, but certainly not harmful to his relationship with other senior staff. The second respondent reported a significant worsening of his relationships with the GM, over the interval between the first and second GBI administrations. The team-building session reinforced the AGM's perception of this rift, and did nothing to resolve what was to him a one-on-one issue not amenable to discussion in that group setting. Consultant suggested a third-party design[11] to explore these issues, which suggestion the respondent accepted. Subsequently, the two parties got together at an early date to deal with their relationship.

Note that such transactions imply significant ethical issues. In this case, basically, consultant sought to create the sense and reality of his independence in that his commitment was to facilitate MARTA's effectiveness rather than to serve as an agent of the general manager. It is easy to be self-deluding in such matters, of course. Were the subordinates under duress to accept consultant's proposal? It is at least a good sign that one AGM felt free to reject that proposal. And it is the fact that the general manager, the co-author of this paper, still is unaware of the identity of the AGM who advised that consultant's suggestion was not appropriate. Finally, both the GM and the AGM who "dealt with their relationship" perceive the outcomes to have been positive, especially so in the case of the AGM whose performance until then was unsatisfactory to him and the GM because of the growing issues between them. That AGM is now a solid performer on the senior staff, perhaps in part because of the timely suggestion to both executives which was induced by the broader OD design.

B. Two Levels of Interfaces with Department Directors

Approximately one month after the team building among senior staff, another three-day experience sought to concentrate on two sets of interfaces:

1. Between some 25 department directors and the senior staff
2. Between each assistant general manager and the cluster of directors he directly supervised.

Directors and Senior Staff. 3-D images were used to explore the interface between the senior staff and the directors. Six sets of images were prepared: one by each of the five clusters of directors reporting to individual AGMs, and one by the senior staff. These were prepared in private, and then publicly shared in a large common meeting.

The sharing of 3-D images was an intense experience, in large part due to several major issues that had been generated in the early days of assembling a work force and of developing personnel policies and procedures. Illustratively, these items were included by one group of directors in their list of perceptions of the senior staff: ·

- Some autocratic elements—dictatorial
- Secretiveness—lack of communication
- They have a tough job, in a rough environment, and are making good progress
- Question competence level of some—admire competence of some
- They earn their money.

Examples illustrating these descriptors were emphasized in an extensive public sharing period, and the associated discussion centered around several major substantive issues, mostly issues introduced by the directors.

Contracting took place at two levels. Thus the senior staff agreed to study a long list of issues, many of which were criticisms of newly instituted personnel policies and procedures. Parenthetically, some quick changes in policies and procedures were made soon after; other issues were studied over longer periods, with some changes being made later. This responsiveness no doubt reinforced the impact of this second design element.

Directors and Individual AGMs. Moreover, substantial time also was provided so that each of the five AGMs with directors reporting to them could begin some rudimentary team building in the organization cluster each supervised. Again, mutual 3-D images were developed and shared in each of the five clusters of AGMs-cum-directors. Consistently, also, contracting was encouraged between the several clusters of directors and the individual AGMs to whom each cluster reported. In addition, each cluster was mandated to provide any additional detail about the substantive issues raised in the large public meeting.

Tracking Effects of the Design. The effects of this second-level effort to develop an effective and open system in MARTA were estimated by the two administrations of the Likert (1967) "Profile of Organizational Characteristics,"[12] a simple and useful instrument. The "benchmark" administration was immediately before the organization-building session, and the post-experience administration was approximately two work weeks later. The form of the instrument used contained 18 items.

The profile has several interesting features. First, its several items can be scored along a continuum of 20 equal-appearing intervals, which are differentiated into four major systems of management:

Scores		System Descriptions
(1-5)	System I	Exploitative-Authoritative
(6-10)	System II	Benevolent-Authoritative
(11-15)	System III	Consultative
(16-20)	System IV	Participative Group

Second, each item is anchored by four brief descriptive statements, one statement for each system. For example, one of the 18 items is: "mostly at the top"; and the System IV statement is "throughout [the organization] but well integrated." Intermediate statements anchor Systems II and III emphasizing "some delegation" and "more delegation," respectively.

Third, the 18 profile items are intended to tap six broad phenomenal areas of organizational relevance. They are: (1) leadership (items 1-3), (2) motivation (items 4-6), (3) communication (items 7-10), (4) decisions (items 11-13), (5) goals (items 14-15), and (6) control (items 16-18).

Fourth, each profile item is scored twice. A now score reflects an estimate of the *existing* level of each item, and an ideal score on each item provides data about the *preference* of the respondent. In addition to providing useful data, the exercise is seen as meaningful for the respondent in a team-building experience. Its goal, simply, is to alert organization members to any gaps between their preferences and the interpersonal and group relationships that actually exist in their organization. This alerting can help motivate early remedial action.

Figure 5 presents data from the directors reporting to one AGM, the criterion for selection being that the design seemed *least* impactful in this case. Overall, a successful experience should move respondents' scores toward System IV, whatever their starting point.

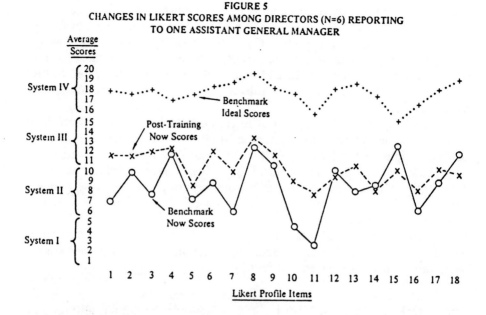

FIGURE 5
CHANGES IN LIKERT SCORES AMONG DIRECTORS (N=6) REPORTING
TO ONE ASSISTANT GENERAL MANAGER

Four points about Figure 5 deserve highlighting. First, existing interpersonal and intergroup relationships fell substantially short of where the directors preferred. See the contrast between ideal scores and the scores on the benchmark administration of the Likert Profile. A contrast of ideal scores with post-experience now scores gathered some two weeks after the team building supports a similar conclusion, although the gap has been narrowed somewhat.

The pattern is understandable. Most directors had been hired only recently; some had been on the job only a matter of days; and a few had just been hired. These were very early days, indeed, and hectic ones.

Second, the team building seems to have moved interpersonal and group relationships in the direction preferred by the directors, even in the least-impactful case illustrated in Figure 5. No statistical tests were run due to small sample sizes of the directors reporting to each AGM, but the conclusion holds for a variety of approaches to comparing scores. Grossly, 14 of the 18 now mean scores more closely approach the benchmark ideal scores after the training than before. The pattern is similar for "large changes," defined arbitrarily as ±2 points. There are seven such large changes that move closer to the ideal scores after the training than they were before training. Only one large average change moves away from the ideal.

Third, the zigs-and-zags in Figure 5 probably understate the degree of change if anything, for at least three reasons. As was noted, Figure 5 presents data from AGM/directors cluster for which the design was *least* impactful. Moreover, there apparently is a tendency for some respondents to provide benchmark self-reports that reflect the somewhat varnished truth, as they perceive it. Alternatively or even simultaneously, team building can make participants more aware of existing disagreements or unclarities. Illustratively, the largest deviant change in Figure 5 is for item 15, which solicits information about the degree of resistance to organization goals. This change can be explained in terms of the two possibilities above, or in terms of an actual increase in resistance generated by the team-building design. The last explanation of course, is less credible in this case because of the overall pattern of changes.

C. Linking the Board and the Senior Staff

The final design element in this first pass at institution building involved MARTA's board of directors and the senior staff. The board's members were appointed by elected officials in four counties and the City of Atlanta. The board of nine members—including two blacks—was clearly in transition. Earlier boards had been peopled by macro-prominents with independent power bases and a collective regional orientation. Over time, appointments were made from other tiers of leadership in the five jurisdictions whose political bodies named directors. Consequently, there was over time a growing responsiveness by board members to more "local" needs and aspirations. At the time of this OD design, the board had a quite substantial independence from local politics, but that relative autonomy clearly was being tested and would be substantially reduced as MARTA signed agreements with local governments and otherwise moved toward actual construction.

The board's style was to become increasingly active and involved in MARTA business as staff were selected and policies developed. Hence the especial importance of directly exposing board members to the kind of developmental experiences to which MARTA management had devoted some time and effort, with board knowledge. Moreover, the board had until then uneven but typically brief and sporadic exposure to the MARTA senior staff other than the GM. Board members desired far more contact with AGMs as a prime way of developing first-hand information about those AGMs whose policy recommendations and detailed design and construction proposals would increasingly come before the board for its action as MARTA moved toward construction. The importance of an early and mutual getting-to-know-one-another provided significant motivation for the third design element.

The design of the third stage in institution building had three prime elements, each lasting perhaps two-thirds of a day. Sequentially, the design emphasized:

● Separate meetings for board members and the senior staff, during which data about their respective internal dynamics were fed back by consultants who summarized interview and questionnaire information to serve as stimuli to encourage the two groups to evaluate their ways of relating to one another.

- Two integrative experiences, the first relatively gentle and the second far more threatening:
    - Board members and the senior staff independently developed verbal statements describing their concepts of MARTA's mission in some detail, which statements became objects for public sharing and comparative discussion.
    - Board members and the senior staff independently developed 3-D images, and these became central stimuli for public confronting and contracting activities.
- A work session, in which matters to be publicly presented in the immediate future were discussed by the board and the senior staff in common session.

The flow of the design involving the board is direct, then. The first element stresses internal dynamics; the second encourages limited integration, consistent with the differing roles of the board and the senior staff; and the third seeks to test the usefulness of the outcomes of the first two elements in a more-or-less normal work context. There were major elements of risk and threat in dealing with the board in the confrontive spirit with which the MARTA managers sought to deal with one another. But there seemed no viable alternative to the risk and threat, given the active board role and given the style which earlier design elements had sought to foster among MARTA management.

Tracking the Effects of the Design. No major effort was made to measure the effects of the third design element, but two conclusions are safe enough. First, the experience was a far more critical one for the senior staff than for the board, for obvious reasons. Basically, staff was still concerned that its concept of its job might conflict with the board's view of its responsibility; and staff was unclear as to board reaction to its overall performance.

Second, reactions of participants to the design were uniformly positive, and typically emphasized the useful beginning or acceleration of processes that required nurturing over the long run. The responses of the board chairman and vice chairman are typical. They were initially positive, and remained so after nearly a year. One official observed: "Unquestionably, I considered the experience worthwhile. It afforded us an opportunity to know one another better." The other board official had a similar reaction, but stressed the need for determined follow-up after the team-building experience.

In general, because of the difficulty in getting most people to listen, much less understand, I feel that such sessions are constructive, beneficial, and desirable. . . .

Specifically, I feel that this particular meeting gave me an opportunity to know our board and staff members better and to more fully appreciate the special relationship between the two groups.

I'd very much like to see these sessions repeated on an annual basis for two reasons: one, there are almost always personnel changes each year; and two, it appears that some participants have a tendency to forget the vital issues discussed and generally agreed upon. . . .

Conclusion

There is a revealing way of summarizing the thrust of the three-design effort toward making MARTA an open and effective giant. First, the goal was to help build more effective teams at several levels of organization: in the board, on the senior staff, and among directors reporting to the same AGM. This team building has an *internal* thrust, and seeks to make members of small, formal groups more cohesive and more aware of their own dynamics. The goal is to encourage members of these groups to be more willing to confront the differences that will inevitably exist among themselves, encouragement deriving from the similarities of experience and identification that are highlighted by successful team building.

Second, each of the three design elements had a major *relational* thrust. Directly, team building can be pernicious if it merely creates strong bonds of experience, identification, and affection between the members of some group. Team building in this sense can develop an intense sense of we-ness only at the expense of highlighting and perhaps manufacturing a they-ness to be distinguished from, or even opposed to. Hence the conscious effort to build cross-walk experiences into the design for a more open and effective MARTA; to utilize any forces deriving from successful team building to help bridge social and psychological and hierarchical distance rather than to merely exaggerate that distance which is variously normal or necessary or convenient.

This relational thrust is vital in MARTA for a very practical reason. Given its lack of taxing and independent condemnation power, MARTA had no reasonable alternative but getting and staying in the frame of mind that doggedly seeks the elusive reality of a complex sense of us-ness, not only inside MARTA but also (perhaps, especially) with various units of government and a wide range of interests.

Third, the three elements of the design also reflect an *institutional* or contextual thrust, in the form of a set of values which condition both the internal and relational thrusts distinguished above. In Selznick's terminology, the team-building experiences and the crosswalks between them sought to infuse MARTA with a specific set of values. These values imply partial answers to this critical question: To what social or moral purpose does the team building and crosswalking contribute?

This set of values is reflected at several levels. Thus the expectations that the design would have relatively specific consequences, as measured by the GBI or Likert's Profile, are at once predictions about what can be encouraged to exist as well as value judgments about the conditions whose existence is desirable in both instrumental and ethical senses. For example, movement toward System IV is desirable in at least three distinct senses. Thus participants overwhelmingly prefer System IV, as the ideal scores in Figure 5 testify, hypothetically because respondents conclude the System IV will meet their needs more than System I. Moreover, evidence seems to indicate that successful large-scale projects in fact require substantial doses of System IV philosophy and relationships.[13] Finally, System IV more closely approaches a variety of ethical guides than does System I.[14]

Care is necessary to avoid overrepresenting the narrative above. Consider the "success" of the efforts above. Several indicators imply that expected things did happen:

- Changes in the Group Behavior Inventory, overall, were not only expected but imply that a range of more effective relationships among senior staff were developed and maintained over time.
- Changes in the Likert Profile, overall, were not only expected but also move in the direction of presumptively greater effectiveness of the organization level reporting to senior staff.
- Interviews with both directors and managers, overall, indicate that most personal definitions of "success" were met.

But this article is also limited in basic ways. Thus it does not report on a "complete OD experiment," but rather a description of the character and some of the consequences of initial steps to develop a team consciousness. Relatedly, the results of the OD interventions are not expressed as *direct* management or administrative results; those results are not related to the bottom-line context of work. Those management or administrative results have to be inferred from statements of how people feel about their work and each other.

So this study reflects a pervasive in-betweenness. Some results imply that OD as a social technology has a range of predictable consequences, and hence is potent. But much still needs to be learned about the fuller range of work-related consequences of OD interventions.

Notes

1. Stephen R. Chitwood and Michael M. Harmon, "New Public Administration, Humanism, and Organization Behavior," *Public Management*, Vol. 53 (November 1971), pp. 13-22.
2. Robert T. Golembiewski, *Renewing Organizations* (Itasca, Ill.: F. E. Peacock, 1972).
3. *Ibid.*, pp. 60-68.
4. For some chilling details from the highest government levels, see Irving Janis, *Groupthink* (Boston: Houghton-Mifflin, 1972).
5. John P. Campbell and Marvin D. Dunnette, "Effectiveness of T-Group Experiences in Managerial Training and Development," *Psychological Bulletin*, Vol. 70 (August 1968), pp. 73-104.
6. Chris Argyris, *Interpersonal Competence and Organizational Effectiveness* (Homewood, Ill.: Dorsey Press, 1962), p. 21.
7. For details and supporting rationales, see: Golembiewski, *Renewing Organizations, op. cit.*, esp. pp. 142-155, 327-386, and 455-484; Wendel L. French and Cecil H. Bell, Jr., *Organizational Development* (Englewood Cliffs, N.J.: Prentice-Hall, 1973), esp. pp. 112-146; and

Newton Margulies and John Wallace, *Organizational Change* (Glenview, Ill.: Scott, Foresman, 1973), esp. pp. 99-121.

8. As important preliminaries and reinforcers, members of the senior staff spent approximately 40 hours at off-site learning experiences being exposed to exercises/concepts relevant to group dynamics, as well as to appropriate skill practice. Most of this learning time was scheduled in one three-day period. The exercises/concepts dealt with: decision making, interpersonal openness, giving and receiving feedback, functional roles, and interpersonal orientations of senior staff. In addition, a process observer attended approximately 10 worksite meetings of the senior staff during the three-month interval following the three-day session to help reinforce real-time effort consistent with the off-site experiences.

9. Lester Coch and John R. P. French, Jr., "Overcoming Resistance to Change," *Human Relations*, Vol. 1 (December 1948), pp. 512-532.

10. Frank Friedlander, "The Impact of Organizational Training Laboratories upon Effectiveness and Interaction of Ongoing Work Groups," *Personnel Psychology*, Vol. 20 (Autumn 1970), pp. 289-307.

11. Richard E. Walton, *Interpersonal Peacemaking: Confrontations and Third-Party Consultation* (Reading, Mass.: Addison-Wesley, 1969).

12. Rensis Likert, *The Human Organization* (New York: McGraw-Hill, 1967).

13. Leonard R. Sayles and Margaret K. Chandler, *Managing Large Systems* (New York: Harper and Row, 1971); and Harvey M. Sapolsky, *The Polaris System Development* (Cambridge, Mass.: Harvard University Press, 1972).

14. Robert T. Golembiewski, *Men, Management and Morality* (New York: McGraw-Hill, 1965).

LARRY KIRKHART
ORION F. WHITE, JR.

The Future of Organization Development

Our purpose here is to assess the future direction of organization development (OD) against what we see to be the major issue of our advanced industrial society—"technicism." In doing so, we will show that grid OD and situational/emergent OD[1] constitute two contrasting paradigms, and that when the differences between them are distinguished, the *meaning* of and social implications that are inherent to the future evolution of OD are more clearly revealed. After differentiating between grid and situational/emergent (S/E) approaches, we will discuss current patterns of innovation and development in the field and suggest a line of emphasis for future development which we see as desirable.

In order to see the dilemmas faced by OD in proper perspective, we must note the overriding societal issue of which all trends to the future are a part. This issue is most commonly termed "technicism"—i.e., the rise to predominance of mechanistic process over substance, the reign of routine, the tendency to set policy by viewing technical capability as opportunity, the pervasive systemization and control of human existence.[2] Perhaps the most probable future we face if technicism proceeds unabated is "technological libertarianism."[3] In the cybernetic society of the future, complete libertarianism would be possible because the ability of the state to organize stably the expression and satisfaction of a mass and variety of individual desires would be tremendously enhanced by cybernetic technologies. The price for this freedom would be individual privacy, since in order to correlate, integrate, organize, and control the processing of such a vast array of needs and wishes, the state would have to possess virtually total information about individuals.

In view of the conceptual history of OD—especially its early ties to "mental health/illness" concepts—a plausible case can be made that OD is simply an aspect of the trend toward technicism and the libertarianism of satisfaction that accompanies it. The emphasis that is placed on some OD techniques on open communication, a general posture of self revelation, and an implicit promise that this will bring some sort of organizational utopia where we are all going to be *happier,* certainly lends itself to the uncharitable interpretation that what OD is really doing is conditioning people to give up their privacy to organizations in return for "happiness and freedom" in a libertarian sense.

A further aspect of this argument is that OD is and will become even more a means for providing the controlling elites of organizations with an enhanced capability to manipulate organization members. To what extent is this interpretation of OD valid? While the answer to this question is not completely clear, the question on which the answer hinges does seem rather obvious—namely, can OD provide a plausible alternative (as well as technique for realizing this alternative) for the concept of *analytical rationality* that is the foundation stone of the current organizational world? It is on the basis of this industrial view of rationality that people have come to be viewed as means, objects to be manipulated, as problems in "technical" engineering.

Rationality based on the means-ends concept of analytical expertise is essentially an industrial idea—it is the paradigm of the industrial production process. The alternatives which face all change-oriented technologies, especially OD, is whether they shall address themselves to this fundamental problem of change, or simply assume the industrial model of rationality as their own framework and become a device for making institutional adjustments within it.

The stark question which advanced societies like ours face for the future is whether they shall make a transition into a post-industrial condition or remain, unable to reconstruct their institutions, in the increasingly unviable condition of aging industrialism. What this means is: Will we be able to shift our institutional culture and structure to fit in the economy to a *services* base? This is a question of highest importance. It is becoming clear that the industrial model of rationality is in the long run incompatible with the continuing existence of the human race on our planet. The most serious problems which we live in the midst of today are no more than the side effects or "diseconomies" that have occurred *external* to the boundaries traditionally employed as the frame for "rational" decision making in the past—e.g., the pollutants dumped outside the industrial plant and the social problems attendant to the "rational" sorting of human beings into competitively arbitrarily graded status systems. It is not obvious, however, that recognition of the problem inherent in the industrial rationality model will yield enough insight to allow us to go beyond it. The idea that "technology got us into these problems, technology will get us out" is a powerful one, as is any idea based in the existing paradigm of a society. Hence we could very well see the industrial model brought even further (than, say, it has been in the area of education) into the emerging services economy.

We can escape the pathologies of industrialism only if an alternative to its model of rationality is persuasively offered. This is the overriding dilemma which OD faces: it must either accept the industrial model or offer an alternative to it. OD, in this sense, shall be either part of the solution—or part of the problem.

The specific dilemmas which OD faces are but a variety of manifestations of this larger problem. In this light, we can note that the issue most often discussed in regard to OD, i.e., the difficulty of diffusing and giving permanence to the effects of OD programs, is probably superficial and transitory—attributable to the youth of the field. In addition there seems little question that OD could be shaped along lines that would be consistent with or conducive to existing patterns of power in organizations, and as such completely overcome the problem of "effectiveness." The deeper question is whether or not OD can solve its specific dilemmas in a way that will make it a true change philosophy and methodology.

Thus, the predicaments which OD confronts are simply forms of the question of how an open, relatively unbounded view of organizational reality—structure, process, and "rationality"—can be conceptualized and brought into being. Some of the main forms this question is taking are:

1. What philosophies of knowledge and research methodology are appropriate to OD if it seeks to construct truly open organizations? (As a corollary, how shall these be legitimated—or even communicated?) There has been clear recognition in parts of the OD community that conventional social science models of knowledge are not suitable: a good deal of work has been aimed at critically delegitimating closed views of science and asserting instead the "action research" and other more "phenomenological" views.[5] Still much OD practice remains based in and presents itself in terms of traditional social science research findings about organizational behavior.

Part of this dilemma concerns whether or not OD can maintain a firm base in academic institutions. In academia OD can expect much resistance both to "open" or "subjectivist" views of knowledge and to any close or extensive linkage of knowledge production to "application" or "action" in the "real world"—a linkage which open views of knowledge seem to entail.

2. A related enigma is what to do with efficiency. The cornerstone of the current organizational world is the evaluation that takes place under the rubric of efficiency. OD has not yet formulated a method for organizational evaluation that transcends the efficiency standard employed within the industrial paradigm. Further, it seems difficult to do so, since the idea of anything but person-centered (non-institutional) processes of evaluation seems inconsistent with an open, unbounded view of organizations. What seems implied therefore is for OD to present a perspective on organizations which does not rely on institutional evaluation—and to make this view plausible to a world currently relying on the efficiency standard.

At another level the efficiency problem is the problem of "participatory technology." Where should the line between technical parameters and participatory inputs be drawn? At present we lack even an adequate philosophical answer.

3. A third dilemma concerns the "politics" of the relationship of the OD professional to his clients: How shall the client be induced to step across into the new non-manipulative world of more open communication represented by OD—without manipulating the client? "Try it you'll like it" is not enough. Most often clients are not free to reject the OD message without some fear of

punishment. And they may somewhat justifiably feel that the entreaty to "come on in" (i.e., "open up" and "level") is unfair, since the trial experience itself alters the situation, and one cannot "go back," even if one feels more oppressed (as some do) in the "open" context than in the closed. What seems demanded here is a theory and method for change which is not based on the "health-illness" model for the personality, so that the client could not charge that he was being evaluated, manipulated, or enticed into a "healthier" state of being. This means OD needs a psychological perspective based on the idea of dealing with people *as they are*.

4. A most pervasive and powerful set of boundaries that must be faced by OD is made up of the system of rewards within the organization and within which the OD practitioner works. That is, the OD message about open, un-boundary laden, non-evaluative organizational processes is contradicted when OD does not speak of how to change the most basic fact of organizational life: i.e., that people are evaluated and rewarded differentially in the pay scale. The OD practitioner participates in legitimating such evaluative schemes insofar as he participates in the economic system in his own professional role—as he clearly does. This is probably the most difficult problem OD faces. Economic evaluation and the competitiveness it entails stand as a negation to the changes OD seeks. Either the economic boundary must be removed, or OD must make its message neutral to it.

5. A last problem that must be dealt with by OD is the relationship between the organization and its environment. As in the case of differential economic rewards, a crippling contradiction has existed between the world view pre-scribed by OD for inside the organization and the one for the outside of it. It is difficult to justify the humanistic arguments that OD makes because *coopera-tive* behavior is confined within the organization and is to be sought so it can better *compete* with other organizations. What is needed here are *inter*-organizational OD theories and strategies of collaboration and conflict media-tion.

Two Contrasting Paradigms

Our position is that the apparent entrapment of OD in the dilemmas we have just described is more a result of a rather general ambiguity that surrounds the field concerning its philosophical stance than it is a true contradiction of ideas, purpose, and practice. In order to resolve some of this ambiguity, we shall de-scribe what we see as the two main paradigms which are currently associated with OD, indicate how they contrast, and suggest that one offers greater hope of overcoming the technicist mind-set than the other.

Situational/Emergent OD

Within the past decade the field of organization development began to dif-ferentiate identifiably into two distinct orientations. The development of one

of these orientations, situational/emergent (S/E) OD, can best be characterized in terms of the familiar Lorenz curve. Its formative years, primarily
1960-1965, showed much ambiguity and slow evolutionary change. This is followed by a second period (the next five to seven years) in which a dramatic
shift upward in development occurs—a period of accelerated and sharply increasing rates of change. This process of development which is important to
understanding present-day conceptualization and practice of S/E OD was extremely complex, with many separate but often parallel lines of thought and
practice converging at various points in time. However, it is beyond the scope
of this essay to portray adequately these events and processes. Instead we shall
note only a few well-known individuals and theories that helped to shape S/E
OD.

One such person is Douglas McGregor who formulated the Theory X and
Theory Y perspectives of administration. These theories are commonly regarded as descriptions of the traditional authoritarian view of management
(Theory X) and the more recent development of humanistic management
(Theory Y). According to this interpretation, they represent two extremes of a
continuum of industrial management. At one end is Theory X which over-
stresses short-run production at the cost of human morale, resulting in excessive economic cost in the long run. On the other end Theory Y portrays a uto-
pian overemphasis of the human element in organizations at the cost of productive efficiency. It follows from this logic that the only "real" possibility is
for management to give *adequate* consideration to the efficient use of people
necessary to secure minimal cost and high-level production.

However, this is a gross misinterpretation of McGregor's ideas and is the
epitome of "enlightened" Theory X.

McGregor asserts that Theory X and Theory Y are two different management *cosmologies*—two distinct postures toward managing—and *not* polar
ends of a "continuum."[6] His primary message is that a manager's orientation
toward his work role affects significantly the definition of problems, the shaping of action, and interpretation of events. In other words, *no human behavior
is neutral.*

*The emotional and rational aspects of man are inextricably interwoven; it is an illusion
to believe they can be separated[7]* (emphasis in original).

The idea of a detached, impartial, uninvolved, and highly "scientific"
manager expresses the ideology of "technicism" and is a myth of the most
perverse sort: one that denies *how* organizational reality is shaped by managerial beliefs and *what* managers do to maintain the very problem they seek to
solve.

It is this myth that McGregor attacks through his Theory X and Y; he is
challenging the tightly bounded technicism and analytical rationality (Theory
X) of the industrial paradigm. His alternative, Theory Y, is a more unbounded
and relatively open way to view organizations, and especially management's

role in organizations. This theory places emphasis upon contextual or situational analysis. From the viewpoint of Theory Y, this entails minimizing bias through involvement and awareness of intentions, taking responsibility for self and being responsible to others, and focusing on the various action possibilities that exist or can be created—rather than *a priori* subscribing to a singular approach to problems.

A second early contributor to S/E OD, who in many ways placed the issue of technicism more starkly, was Chris Argyris in *Personality and Organization*.[8] When this volume was published it was regarded as a radical posture supporting humanistic individualism. Whereas McGregor considered the impact of technicism upon managerial views, Argyris explored the consequences of technicism on non-managerial personnel. Conceptually McGregor and Argyris supplemented and complemented each other, and along with other texts like *The Dynamics of Planned Change*[9] and *Personal and Organizational Change Through Group Methods*,[10] they helped to develop the early foundations for situational/emergent OD.

During this formative stage the field went through a time of more and more intense fermentation. The chief uncertainty was how to bring the emerging orientation of S/E OD to bear upon the problem of technicism and organizational functioning, i.e., *how to change total systems*. While changing total systems became more and more clearly the goal, the chasm between the goal and the practice was uncomfortably apparent. The existing interventions, available from the laboratory model of learning, were decidedly and understandably feeble. T-Groups designed to bring together strangers for the purpose of improving interpersonal skills and learning about self were for many reasons an inadequate strategy for affecting the total organizations. First of all, only a few executives from an organization could participate in this particular learning situation at one time. Secondly, the stress T-Groups placed on the here and now tended to make it difficult to relate the learning to the participant's organizational setting. These programs seldom explored how the learning could be related to formal organizations. In sum, the problem of translating and transferring behavior and action in the T-Group's organic culture to the typical mechanistic organizational culture was virtually insurmountable.[11]

By the early 1960s the "classic" T-Group was displaced in importance by a different intervention—team building.[12] Realizing the weaknesses of the T-Group, team building was created and intended as a more direct intervention into organizational processes and structures. Its primary focus was (and still remains) on a group of people who work together in an organization. The team normally consisted of 8-12 people who were an "organizational family" —a boss and his/her immediate subordinates. Central to the concerns of a team-building program was how well the members were achieving team goals and what they were doing to achieve them.

The format of this intervention had many positive features. By bringing together individuals who comprise a work group, the changes and learning that these people developed with each other had a greater probability of being sustained in their organizational setting. Team building was designed as an on-going process. The final part of the program looked at problems which were identified but not explored during the training program and which would be addressed at a later date. Also, team building usually entailed a follow-up, off-site training session approximately six months later. This second session was usually shorter in duration—two instead of three days—and was concerned with how the learnings and changes developed during the first session were applied, how the unsolved areas were approached—especially what could be learned from how these were dealt with—and what additional issues were not impinging upon the team's functioning. Lastly, the session ended with a list of other problems to be solved and identification of who would take responsibility for pursuing them.

This intervention is now basic to S/E OD. It is an important part of the repertory of action research activities that can be undertaken. However, from the perspective of total system change, team building has a rather obvious and sharp limitation—it involves only a small part of the total organization. The recognition of this limitation, concomitant with a surge of experimentation in interventions, brought forth a whole series of new strategies. It is virtually impossible to place these new interventions in a historical chronology. So, they will be treated in terms of their increasing impact upon the overall organizational system. Each of them is designed to assess and explore different aspects of the way an organization functions.

Intergroup building, patterned along lines somewhat similar to team building, enabled representatives from groups or departments to explore their *relationship* and invent ways to strengthen their capacity to interrelate each other's activities. It is a strategy for creating more effective relationships and, possibly, interdependency between two subsystems of an organization.[13]

Another intervention, the organizational mirror,[14] examines the effect one particular subsystem in an organization has on other parts of the system. Data are gathered from the points in the environment most affected by the focal system and upon which the system depends for its effectiveness. How the focal system is regarded by the other parts or subsystems is fed to the focal system, and strategies for improving relationships are explored and, where necessary and possible, created. The format for this exploration is similar to team building except that the orientation is toward the other segments of the organization, rather than the internal activities of the team.

A third intervention is deep sensing. Deep sensing expands the parameters of the organizational mirror to include the functioning of the total internal system. Designed to gather data about the organizational climate or culture, this strategy begins by interviewing a representative cross section of organizational members to find out how they see the overall functioning of the organization. Then this information is given to the appropriate points in the organization and ways of bringing about change are considered. This intervention produces an index of the internal dynamics of the total system.

Force field analysis[15] is an example of another intervention used widely during this time. It is a heuristic device that facilitates the consideration of problems and circumstances that are *blocking* or restraining the organization from functioning more effectively. It involves inventing strategies to reduce these circumstances. The impact of this strategy can vary considerably; it can be focused on a small part of the organization, the organization as a total system, or any range of scope in between. Members of the organization that would be involved in this intervention vary accordingly.

All these interventions are good examples of contextual analysis and its concern with the actors involved in the situation. They have been incorporated into the field of situational/emergent OD and are now practiced with more frequency.

For the most part, S/E approach to consulting has moved beyond the commitment to the prescriptive ideologies of personal well-being and "mental health" reflected in the T-Group movement. Currently, a different tone is evolving in S/E consulting and intervention theory. More emphasis is placed on the idea of working with systems in ways which would assist them in becoming more effective at solving their own problems. Also, there is a more strictly "here and now" concern with organizational functioning, a belief in the efficacy of working with what *is,* rather than what should be, taking people and situations as they are.

Grid Organization Development

More or less simultaneously with the early developments in S/E OD, another perspective was emerging—grid OD. Initially limited to the issue of team leadership, grid was an obvious and logical extension of Fleishman's leadership studies conducted in the early 1950s. Fleishman postulated that the effective leader manifested a high concern for both *initiating structure* (defining and facilitating group interactions toward goal attainment) and *consideration* (the leader's consideration of the feelings of those under him).[16] Changing Fleishman's terminology slightly, Blake and Mouton formulated the managerial grid[17] theory which states that the most desirable management style is one which maximizes *concern for production* and *concern for people—the 9/9 management style.*

This correspondence with Fleishman is one of the two reasons why the grid is an extrapolation of the human relations movement which was in vogue in the 1950s. The second reason is that both the grid and the human relations movement had an unequivocal commitment to traditional behavioral science research theory, practice, and findings. This literature provides the underpinning for managerial grid which undoubtedly is one of the best documented theories in the behavioral sciences. Implications of the behavioral science posture are amply portrayed in grid methodology, especially the team-building strategy.

Grid OD specifies a comprehensive set of *labels* for different management styles, establishes *categories* of behaviors associated with each style, and offers a *moral injunction* for the most desirable of these management styles regardless of context. And these labels, categories of behavior, and moral injunctions are carried forth into the team-building situation through an *instrumental action research approach*. Semi-structured experiential exercises, carefully designed on the basis of grid theory, are administered by means of paper and pencil tests to the team-building participants. Test scores are calculated and provide each member of the team with an "objective" definition and evaluation of his management style. Thus, at the end of the team-building session each person has been carefully labeled by himself and the group; each knows, as do the other members of the team, what he must do to become an "effective" 9/9 manager.[18]

Unlike S/E, the evolution of grid OD followed a more or less linear pattern. Soon after the formulation of the grid team-building strategy, a series of additional interventions was introduced. These measures are intended to provide the grid orientation with a greater probability of impacting upon the total organization and moving the organizational culture to the ideal of a 9/9 system. Taken as a whole, the six different interventions are very sophisticated, rigorously designed and instrumented learning strategies. Each strategy occupies a logical position in relation to the others; each builds upon the previous one(s) to maximize the probability of cumulative effects.

Phase 1 of the six-phase approach involves studying the Managerial Grid as a theoretical framework for understanding behavior dynamics of the corporation's culture. In Phase 2, the behavior dynamics of actual organizational teamwork is studied and tested in settings of actual work against the Grid model for the perfection of problem-solving methods. The same kind of application is made in Phase 3, but to the interworkings between organized units of the company where cooperation and coordination is vital to success. The top team in Phase 4 engages in a study of the properties of an Ideal Strategic Corporate Model necessary to bring corporate profitability logic to a maximum-thrust condition. Phase 5 involves implementation tactics for converting the corporation from what it has been to what it will be under the Ideal Corporate Model. Phase 6 measures changes in conditions from pre-phase 1 to post-phase 5 for the evaluation and stabilization of achievement and for the setting of new goals and objectives of accomplishment for the future.[19]

Because grid OD features instrumented and routinized procedures, its training program can be performed without an experienced OD consultant. Early in a grid OD effort a training program is given to some personnel of that organization to teach them the methods of administering the grid training designs. Afterward the organization simply contracts for the appropriate, copyrighted training materials and then conducts its own program.

One of the reasons the grid orientation is attractive to an organization considering an OD effort is the coherent, rational plan it offers. Costs, time investment, and action steps are definable and predictable, and the role of top management is abundantly clear in phases five and six where the "top team" is responsible for devising and implementing an ideal strategic corporate model. Grid OD appears to be an objective package and helps make the decision to undertake OD clear-cut and unambiguous. Finally, a very compelling promise is made:

When a company enables its members to manage themselves and one another in a 9/9 way, it is utilizing what appear to be basic facts of human behavior. It is creating sound conditions in the relationships among men which have two fundamental consequences. One is that men can be mature, adult, and ready to accept the challenge to achieve objectives to which they can openly commit themselves. The other is that since these objectives to which they have committed themselves are identical with the profitability purposes of the firm, the company is mobilizing human resources in such a way as to realize its aim as well. Self-interests and corporate interests are meshed.[20]

A Comparison of Situational/Emergent and Grid OD

Taken as a whole, both branches of OD are quite different, but they do share two weaknesses. Neither has well-developed theories and interventions for two very important areas: organizational design or structure, and organizational/environmental relationships. Grid OD does have a rather precisely defined approach to organizational design. Apparently it has never been implemented, as no studies of the result of this approach can be found in the literature. To our knowledge grid has not been implemented beyond Phase 3— Inter-Group Relations. S/E OD can claim only one example of an intervention aimed directly at organizational structure. While this intervention was successful, and resulted in the emergence of an organizational design that goes beyond centralized or decentralized bureaucracy,[21] much refinement of the theory behind the intervention as well as assessment of results in other settings need to be undertaken.

Both orientations to OD discuss how the external environment of an organization affects organizational performance, but neither has taken the issue seriously enough to develop a coherent theory and strategy for affecting this relationship. Recently, S/E OD has made an effort in this area with the intervention called environmental mirror—which is described further on in this article.

That the culture or climate[22]—the values and norms—of an organization have an important bearing upon the functioning of the social system is a matter of concern for both S/E and grid OD. In relation to this concern, they both assert that training can be denied or supported by the culture of an organization and that training will not necessarily be transferred to the work world. Since organizational culture is regarded as dynamic and determined by multiple variables, such as individual behavior, interpersonal relationships, leadership, small group behavior, integroup relationships, organizational design, technology, and the environment, each branch of OD has developed multiple ways of intervening in the processes of an organization.

In all of its efforts to affect organizational culture, grid organization development operates from the viewpoint that a desirable pattern of organizational relationships and processes is known irrespective of context; thus what *should be* can be rather exactly prescribed and universally generalized. Situational/emergent OD, drawing from a different orientation to the world of management and organizations, is more open-ended in its mode of operations, more keyed to exploring the possibilities of action and emergent processes which might support new patterns of behavior.

Both forms of OD employ a type of action research, although in each case it is very different in theory and practice. The S/E orientation leads to gathering and interpreting action data from the viewpoints of the actors involved in the situation, rather than from an externally imposed and instrumented definition of what "should be." In short, S/E OD uses an organic[23] strategy for research; grid OD does not.

The total depth of the differences between the grid and situational/emergent approaches can be seen only when they are viewed as *action approaches to reality*—i.e., as ways of "constructing" a social world. In another context, this is the classic issue of "participation" as it has been dealt with in democratic theory: shall participation be structured and result in representation; or shall it allow for direct individual expressions of will?[24] In our view, fresh and important insight is brought to this traditional issue by the work of phenomenologically oriented sociologists, who view social reality basically as a complex verbal consensus.[25] The human world is a world of words, and human institutions (e.g., "marriage") are simply distinctive types of conversations through which the world is "named" (i.e., evaluated or bounded). From this view organizations have traditionally functioned as institutions where elites (management) converse and allocate generic economic-professional names to the people within (and, more and more, outside of) their organization. (Only educational institutions rival formal organizations in this regard.) However, as organizations have become more professionalized and hierarchy is ameliorated, the process of naming has become more and more ambiguous. The managerial elite have come into a position of in effect naming themselves through a complicated and uncontrolled multilateral competition for career success. Each person is out to "make the best name for himself" that he can. The consequence is that organizations lose control of their fate to the mysterious force of technicism. Decisions are made on the basis of elite stakes, but in the name of the organization. Hence we are beginning to see the modern anomaly of the mobile, successful executive who moves (upward) from one organizational disaster to another.

It is by this sort of dynamic that it has come to pass that no one is any longer in control of our organizational world. It is being driven by its own logic. We can only bring it back under control by reverting to blatant hierarchical controls at the top or opening it up to participative processes, by which it can be controlled in a different way and by a different type of rationality.

We see many reasons why a reversion to hierarchy is neither feasible nor desirable. Our hopes are placed on efforts that will extend the participative processes of naming in our institutions. We see such a potential in the situational/emergent approach to OD because it operates from the basic principle that the "facts" of a situation are to be defined (i.e., the situation is to be named) as all the people involved in the situation see them through a process of open participation. One need reflect only briefly on the implications of this method to see that it holds the possibility for truly innovative or novel lines of action. Also, it should be obvious that a basically different idea of rationality is implicit in this approach. When people are released from the artifact of means-ends objectivity, the suppressed elements of intuition (situational application of an objective analysis) and feeling (ethical judgment) can enter their calculus of rationality. What results is a more complete, *organic* form of human rationality. More structured approaches to OD which presuppose end states to be realized through processes of standardized evaluation and feedback cannot allow the full development of these organic processes of rationality in organizations.

New Situational/Emergent Interventions

While the S/E orientation has not fully developed its potential for bringing about the complete sort of participation which is implied by the naming process, developments seem to be occurring which head it further in this direction. By having made the distinction between technicist and non-technicist approaches to OD and by now reviewing some of the more recent elaborations of the S/E orientations, we hope to make this possibility clearer.

These strategies are presented in a sequence according to an increasing capacity to affect the total system of an organization. We describe and discuss both the potentials and limits of multi-team building, trans-team building, organizational devolution, environmental mirror, and Gestalt-team building. Gestalt-team building is placed at the end of this sequence because we believe it introduces a new conceptual perspective for S/E OD and is likely to be the beginning point for yet another series of new interventions.

Multi-Team Building

The purpose of multi-team building[26] is to provide a context in which teams from various organizations have an opportunity to learn from each other and to work intensively upon ways to develop further the effectiveness of each individual team in its own environment. Multi-team building is normally a one-week, off-site program. Working time is apportioned equally to two different sets of activities. The first activity is organized to bring each member of a specific team together with persons who are not members of his/her own work team. These "stranger" teams have the assignments of exploring and diagnosing each member's learning needs, doing a life planning exercise, and strengthening awareness of individual skills in small group interaction. The second phase of the program involves team building of the conventional sort. Each of the work teams reassembles and develops a list of needed changes in the team, sets priorities, and studies ways to improve on team effectiveness. At least one trained OD consultant works with each of the teams during this final phase of the program.

Overall, a multi-team building program helps individual members of a team to develop a sharper awareness of their strengths and weaknesses in the team setting. It provides a carefully constructed basis for interaction during the actual team building efforts. Its design facilitates the incorporation of data from various other teams into one's own team and promotes a higher level of risk-taking behavior during the last phase of the program.

The limitations of this strategy are essentially the same as conventional team building; that is, the team itself may have changed its patterns of behavior and ways of doing things during the program, but they return to a more or less stable organizational environment. How well the team is able to apply its learning and manage relationships with its environment are the factors that determine the effectiveness of the training effort.

Trans-Team Building

Trans-team building concentrates totally on work groups from the *same* organization. In this way it is a strategy that can have a widespread impact on the operating culture of an organization. Trans-team building is a one-week, off-site training program that is equally divided into two types of activities. The first part involves a conventional team-building program with periodic digressions in which teams share information on their own development. Once the internal issues in each team have been explored and strategies for change developed, the focus shifts to the relationship between the teams—inter-group building. In these sessions, teams examine both the positive and negative elements that affect each other's performance and efforts are made to construct better working relationships between the teams.[27]

This is one of the most difficult interventions to undertake because in most cases an organization is not willing to release three to six teams for a one-week period. Furthermore, it is difficult to assemble three to six trained S/E consultants to work with the teams. Nonetheless, trans-team building has great potential. Because the program deals with a large number of people—mainly subsystems of the same organization—agreements worked out within and between teams, thoroughly shared and discussed with each other, are likely to be sustained in the "back-home" environment. But like any other team-building venture, the problem of implementing the changes and managing the work environment remains the ultimate test of the effectiveness.

Organizational Devolution

A third new intervention is organizational devolution.[28] This method tests for the kind of *structure* a subsystem *needs* to function effectively. It is most usefully applied in either a context where an existing organizational structure is regarded as blocking more effective performance or when a new organization is being created.

Clearly this is a very complex issue and involves a rather complex implementation strategy. To date organizational devolution has occurred in only two settings, and in the two cases the intervention has not been exactly similar. Therefore we will limit our description and discussion to the generic considerations necessary for the strategy. First the members of the organization develop a definition of what subsystem(s) of the organization are the most important determinant of organizational effectiveness. Once this has been established and agreed upon, the next step is to negotiate with the focal subsystem and establish a reciprocal arrangement in which the larger organization grants the subsystem as much power and autonomy as possible. This grant of autonomy is as comprehensive and all-embracing as can be provided by the organization. It is subject only to the limits imposed on the organization by the external environment. In return for this power and autonomy, the subsystem must fulfill its part of the arrangement. It must develop and secure approval of a program statement that includes: (1) a definition of the environmental need for the whole organization, (2) a description of the purposes of the whole organization, and (3) an explanation of the goals that the subsystem intends to pursue during this experiment.

Also, there is a mutual agreement that the larger system will provide services on an actual cost basis and that the subsystem will feel free to call on the larger organization on the basis of need. This clause in the devolution agreement is non-restrictive and involves *all* external relationships—budget, financial, personnel, training, information services, etc. Through an agreement of this type, the extent and actual role that the larger organization can play in relation to the subsystem can be identified more completely.

During the experiment the subsystem has the authority to restructure itself and invent new strategies that will improve its internal operations and relationships with the environment or client served. It can allocate monies without budgetary constraints except in cases where it is limited by its agreed-upon goals and/or the restrictions imposed on the overall organization by the external environment.

Periodically during the experiment information is shared with the overall organization on the development of events and circumstances. This is simply for the purpose of helping the whole organization maintain an awareness of what has been happening. These sessions are not meant as an opportunity for evaluation or advice giving.

At the end of the experiment in devolution, representatives from the total organization meet with the experimental subsystems to explore the results. Then they decide the kinds of interrelationships that will promote the most effective performance and structural changes necessary for the attainment of effective performance.

This is the only known example of an intervention aimed directly at the structure of relationships between components of an organization. It is unlikely that it would be undertaken by an organization that has not developed a climate in which change carries minimal threat. It is important to bear this fact in mind, as the consequences of the experiment itself may drastically change the kinds and types of roles within the organization.

Environmental Mirror[29]

The aims of this intervention are to assist an organization in creating more effective ways of relating to its environment. For this reason data gathered from the external environment of the organization and feedback to appropriate points in the organization are essential components of this device. In many ways the environmental mirror parallels the procedures of the organizational mirror; its distinguishing point is that it centers on the world *outside* the organization itself.

The environmental mirror entails action research activities with the segments of the environment which have the most immediate bearing upon the focal organization, especially the clients who are served by the organization. Data are collected through semi-structured interviews. The subject matter of these interviews must be approved by the focal organizations with the agreement that if any additional themes emerge from these interviews, they, too, will be presented to the organization. After the interviews are completed, careful consideration is given to the compilation and amalgamation of this information in ways that will minimize, within reasonable costs, information distortion and/or loss. Next, the appropriate points in the organization to receive this data are identified; assistance is given in both the processing of this information and the designing of means that will improve relationships between the organization and its external environment.

This type of intervention has many benefits. It promotes an understanding of the way the organization is regarded by its environment; it elicits information which can identify the most pressing problems in the environment/organization relationship; and it can usually provide the specifics around which new programs are needed. However, these benefits are contingent on a critical criterion. That is, the data gleaned from the outside environment must be as accurate as possible.

Also, the environmental mirror can be done effectively only by persons who are trained in active listening, research design, confrontation skills, and instrumentation procedures. And it is important that they have a capability for providing information to an organization in such a way that the organizational members can use it to orient their own actions.

Gestalt-Team Building

Finally, a new approach to OD team building has been developed. For some time, team building has been the mainstay of most OD efforts and the most widely practiced intervention. Previously we presented the now classical form of team building as it has evolved with time and as it has become considerably more sophisticated. While this has been happening, a new approach to team building has been introduced. This strategy has developed from the pertinent features of modern Gestalt psychology. Stanley Herman of TRW Systems in Redondo Beach, California, has done the most to introduce this orientation to the field of OD. Conceptually, this strategy is consonant with the underlying paradigm of "conventional" OD, but involves a different implementation strategy, one which involves placing the members of the organizational team in a Gestalt learning situation. Personal data generated by the individual is neutrally reflected back to him in order to reveal personal restrictions which he or she is bringing to the organizational setting. The idea is that by bringing out more of the individual intentionality of the members of the team, it is possible to provide a work climate which has less distortion within it and which is more directly related to the actual possibilities of action within the team. Heightening the degree to which individual members of the team take responsibility for the way they shape the performance of the team is encouraged. The Gestalt approach is based on a radicalized individualism which places emphasis upon the capacity of the individual to react naturally to situations and to be able to proceed effectively even though the basis of action may not be amenable to "rational" description.

The main importance of the Gestalt approach, however, is that it frees OD from the residual ties to the simple prescriptive humanism on which it has too heavily relied in the past and which has been mainly accountable for the confusion of the grid OD paradigm with the situational/emergent paradigm. The worst contradiction of situational/emergent theory was that it seemed to rely on the development of individuals into an ideal personality state. The Gestalt approach is completely different, as the following words from Herman indicate:

In the model of the consultant's role I advocate the primary step is not to help people embark on self-improvement programs. Rather, it is to encourage them to recognize and appreciate where they are now. Then the consultant may help them find their own unique paths forward to change and growth. It is also important to recognize that this change and growth, at best, will occur naturally rather than being forced either by external pressure or internalized models. Paradoxically, natural change in an individual does not preclude his boss or others from exerting power or expressing their wants strongly or explicitly. *What is explicit and up-front is seldom harmful, though it may be difficult to deal with.* Covert, withheld or truncated expression is harmful. In most circumstances the consultant will do best to encourage in both individuals and organizations the full recognition and completion of their negative feelings rather than a premature objectivity or problem-solving approach. The consultant will also do best in setting an example through his own clear and explicit statement of *what* he wants and *how* he feels.[30]

What the Gestalt approach offers, then, is removal of presuppositions about desired personality patterns (and the didacticism that goes with such presuppositions) from the situational/emergent paradigm.

A Future Direction for OD

Warren Bennis has pointed out the main problem OD faces is that it asserts itself as a change strategy, but does not attempt to comprehend or impact upon the large, imponderable, and inexorable forces that have always determined the course of history.[31] The major one of these forces seems to be the "technological imperative," and the future of OD must be wrought in confrontation with this issue.

In a way, there is a truth to Bennis' point that cannot be either denied or answered. A large part of our fate may be beyond our conscious intervention. However, if OD can resolve the dilemmas it faces, it does seem that it may have a discernible impact in shaping the post-industrial future along lines that we desire as a society—rather than having our future unfold as it did in the era of industrial development, simply in unison with the elaboration of technical capability. If OD can act as a force to loosen the pervasive grip of the concept of industrial rationality which underlies our society, it will be able to produce real and deep change.

We feel that if the situational/emergent paradigm is emphasized in the future development of the field of OD, there is at least some real possibility that OD can become a force for social evolution of historical importance.

Notes

1. The concept of situational/emergent OD can be found in Larry Kirkhart, *Organizational Development in a Public Agency: The Strategy of Organizational Devolution* (unpublished Ph.D. dissertation: University of Southern California, 1973).
2. Jacques Ellul, *The Technological Society* (New York: Alfred A. Knopf, Inc., 1964).
3. Manfred Stanley, "Technicism, Liberalism, and Development: A Study in Irony as Social Theory," in Manfred Stanley (ed.), *Social Development* (New York: Basic Books, Inc., 1972), pp. 274-325.
4. For a more complete elaboration of this idea, see Orion White, Jr., "The Concept of Administrative Praxis," *The Journal of Comparative Administration,* Vol. V, No. 1 (May 1973), pp. 55-86.
5. Chris Argyris, *Intervention Theory and Method* (Reading, Mass.: Addison-Wesley Publishing Company, 1970), esp. chapters 4 and 5; Robert Rapopart, "Three Dilemmas in Action Research," *Human Relations,* Vol. XXIII, No. 6 (1970), pp. 499-513; and John Friedmann, *Retracking America* (Garden City, N.Y.: Doubleday, 1973).
6. Douglas McGregor, *The Professional Manager* (New York: McGraw Hill Book Company, 1967), chapter 1.
7. *Ibid.,* p. 18.
8. Chris Argyris, *Personality and Organization* (New York: Harper and Row, Publishers, Inc., 1957).
9. Ronald Lippitt, Jeanne Watson, and Bruce Westley, *The Dynamics of Planned Change* (New York: Harcourt, Brace & World, Inc., 1958).
10. Edgar Schein and Warren Bennis, *Personal and Organizational Change Through Group Methods* (New York: John Wiley and Sons, Inc., 1965).
11. Herbert Shepard, "Personal Growth Laboratories: Toward an Alternative Culture," *Journal of Applied Behavioral Science,* Vol. VI, No. 3 (July/August/September 1970), pp. 259-266.

12. William Crockett, "Team Building—One Approach to Organization Development," *Journal of Applied Behavioral Science,* Vol. VI, No. 3 (July/August/September 1970), pp. 291-306.
13. Jack Fordyce and Raymond Weil, *Managing WITH People* (Reading, Mass.: Addison-Wesley Publishing Company, 1971), pp. 124-130.
14. *Ibid.,* pp. 101-106.
15. *Ibid.,* pp. 106-109.
16. Edwin Fleishman, "The Description of Supervisory Behavior," *Journal of Applied Psychology,* Vol. XXXVII (1953), pp. 1-6.
17. Robert Blake and Jane Mouton, *The Managerial Grid* (Houston, Texas: Gulf Publishing Company, 1964).
18. Robert Blake and Jane Mouton, *Building a Dynamic Corporation Through Grid Organization Development* (Reading, Mass.: Addison-Wesley Publishing Company, 1969), pp. 84-87.
19. *Ibid.,* p. 16.
20. *Ibid.,* p. 74.
21. Kirkhart, *op. cit.*
22. Renato Taguari and George Litwin (eds.), *Organizational Climate* (Boston: Harvard University, 1968).
23. Sheldon Davis, "An Organic, Problem-Solving Method of Organizational Change," *Journal of Applied Behavioral Science,* Vol. III, No. 1 (1967), pp. 3-21.
24. For a discussion in this context, see Carole Pateman, *Participation and Democratic Theory* (Cambridge: The University Press, 1960).
25. See Peter Berger and Thomas Luckman, *The Social Construction of Reality* (Garden City, N.Y.: Doubleday Publishing Company, 1970), and Hans Dreitzel (ed.), *Recent Sociology,* No. 2 (New York: The Macmillan Company, 1970).
26. E. J. Jones, Jr., "The Prospects for Organizational Development Through Multi-Team Building," in *An Approach to Executive Development: The Federal Executive Institute Experience,* Paul C. Buchanan (ed.) (Washington, D.C.: National Academy of Public Administration, 1973), pp. 132-139.
27. Originally conceived by R. T. Williams of the Denver Institute for Court Management and implemented with the Air Force Systems Procurement Command in the summer of 1972—with the assistance of E. J. Jones, George Lener, and others. More recently trans-team building has been undertaken under the leadership of Paul Buchanan at the Federal Executive Institute in Charlottesville, Virginia.
28. For a more detailed discussion and documentation see Kirkhart, *op. cit.*
29. Further background and description can be found in Neely Gardner's article in this symposium.
30. Stanley Herman, "A Gestalt Orientation to Organization Development" (unpublished paper delivered at the NTL Conference on New Technology in Organizational Development, New York City, October 8-9, 1971), p. 25.
31. Warren Bennis, "Unsolved Problems Facing Organizational Development," *Business Quarterly* (Winter 1969), pp. 80-84.

JAMES S. BALLOUN
JOHN F. MALONEY

Beating the Cost Service Squeeze:
The Project Team Approach to
Cost Improvement

It's a rare day that doesn't see some public body under fire for rising costs or declining service levels. Witness these recent typical headlines:

Los Angeles Times: "State Deficit May Hit $100 Million"

New York Times: "State Retrenches as Revenues Lag—$130 Million Cut in Spending"

San Francisco Examiner: "Board OK's a Record City Budget"

While to some extent escalating public budgets are the result of today's continuing inflation, to a much greater degree they stem from unabated public demand for services—in welfare, health, education, transportation, to name a few. Only in the unlikely event of a decline in such demands or a change in public policy will the upward trend be reversed. Nonetheless, most informed observers in and outside government believe that not all this cost escalation is beyond control. They are convinced that there is a vast untapped potential in public agencies for cost improvement on a wide front—for increasing productivity, in the broadest sense of the term, by making more effective use of men, money, and materials.

However, managers of public agencies have been hard-pressed to come up with solid, really successful ways of cutting costs and making more productive use of their resources. Departmental cost surveys are commissioned, "scientific management" techniques hopefully are turned to as an answer, and budgets are cut more or less arbitrarily. But despite these flurries of activity, the cost/service squeeze persists. Comments such as these, typically made at the conclusion of cost studies, are red flags indicating that tangible results are not likely to be forthcoming:

- "The Committee deserves a great deal of credit for coming up with a lot of good ideas . . . [I will] take them under advisement . . . [after] careful study and review . . . hope to implement many of the group's ideas."
- "There will be no immediate reduction in costs . . . [but] it is anticipated

250

that the team's recommendations will be helpful in avoiding continued cost escalation.''

● "In conclusion, our recommendations focus on making fundamental improvements in procedures and policies, which should lead to a more efficient operation in the future.''

Management may well be discouraged when cost studies conclude on such indefinite notes. More often than not, their lack of specificity represents euphemistic glossings-over of an unsuccessful effort—and, unfortunately, they are much more the rule than the exception.

By contrast, some managers are receiving reports in a much more positive vein: ". . . opportunities have been identified to reduce costs and/or increase revenues by approximately $1.1 million . . . [of that] management has agreed to implement recommendations with potential annual savings of over $700,000." And six months later: "Attached is the regular [monthly] progress report . . . accepted recommendations have moved up to $900,000, tangible realized savings up to $433,000." (Quotations are from a cost-effectiveness improvement study team report and follow-up report in the Division of Bay Toll Crossings, Department of Public Works, Business and Transportation Agency, State of California.)

The case cited need not be exceptional. Indeed, the history of U.S. industry is one of continuing productivity improvement. Our experience indicates that even in apparently well-managed public and private organizations, the potential exists for a substantial cut in operating costs—as much as 20 percent—without a decrease in service levels. Clearly, such potential is well worth the effort to find a more effective approach to cost reduction.

Why do the majority of cost-improvement efforts yield insignificant or nebulous results while others (a small minority, it is true) lead to tangible, tough-minded action? Recent experience in California's Department of Public Works, built around a tested industrial approach, suggests what we believe are constructive answers to this question. This article will describe this approach, which has been used to identify and realize cost-reduction opportunities amounting to more than $2 million per year in the conduct of several successful projects in the department. Significantly, career civil servants played a major role in identifying and implementing these opportunities; and the program is designed for an ongoing series of similar efforts, all conducted by civil servants trained in the approach.

Parenthetically it might be pointed out that while the specifics of our approach will be illustrated by hardware-oriented or routine-oriented applications (e.g., bridge painting, toll collection), it will be obvious that the approach is more widely applicable than might be inferred from these examples. Even at the other end of the spectrum (e.g., the provision of education, case work services), where performance and results are less measurable, the methodology of the approach can be applied effectively to procedures, schedules, materials, etc.

Barriers to Public Sector Cost Reduction

In our experience, three major barriers block the achievement of significant cost reductions in public agencies: (1) lack of incentive for managers to cut costs, (2) skepticism of senior managers as to their ability to make substantial improvements, and (3) lack of a sound approach.

Lack of Incentive for Managers

Managers in public agencies rarely benefit from reducing costs; if anything, they often lose ground or are penalized in one way or another. While the profit motive encourages managers to take risks in private enterprise, thus far no adequate substitute has been found for motivating public sector managers.

There are two underlying causes for this condition: First, measures of cost performance in the public sector have not yet been refined to the levels of sophistication now common in leading private companies. One attraction of business performance measures like "earnings per share," "return on equity," and "residual income" is that they are composite measures of both how well and how cheaply goods and services are supplied. In the public sector, however, a two-month delay on a construction deadline, a payment error, or a pavement failure can be perceived and measured, but the tremendous cost built into the system to prevent such occurrences typically is not noticed to the same degree.

Example: In one agency a routine audit revealed a $2,000 error in contractor payment calculations. To prevent recurrence, a $12,000-a-year junior engineer was added to make a third check before disbursement. Had the error recurred without the additional check, the manager would have been criticized for not taking corrective steps—but the even higher cost of checking went unnoticed. Clearly, performance measurement in this example does not adequately reflect cost performance.

A second and obvious case is that public agency managers don't get promoted or rewarded for cost reduction. Meeting budgets and schedules is important, but cost reduction and capital recovery are not.

Example: A policy decision centered around the opportunity to save as much as $150,000 per year by more precise scheduling of project activities. Such refined scheduling would, however, have reduced flexibility and increased the risk that deadlines might not be met and that construction contracts might be delayed. Since the manager would have to bear the onus attached to delayed contract awards, and since his risk was not offset by an appropriate reward for cost reduction achievements, he naturally opted to stick with the present schedule.

In short, an ambitious public sector manager finds little that is attractive about cost reduction—and understandably so. It will not be measured, it will increase his risk of failure, and even if successful, it will have little impact on either his pay or his promotion.

Genuine Skepticism

One typical senior-level manager commented: "I just don't see how a cost reduction effort can result in any substantial savings in my organization. We are already highly cost-conscious. Every year we review our budgets carefully and argue long and hard over their levels." Unfortunately, tough negotiations over cost levels at budgeting time cannot ensure that an organization will be run most economically. Truly substantial cost reduction is accomplished not by negotiation but by significantly modifying the way in which things are done, by eliminating large areas of activity, or by fundamentally changing policies concerning the appropriate level or quality of service. These basic policy questions rarely come up for discussion in the budget review, and as a result, managers fail to appreciate the opportunities that may be uncovered by a careful study of their operations.

Lack of a Sound Approach

Last, though obviously not least, of the barriers to cost improvement is the lack of a sound, really workable approach—or, conversely, the plethora of ineffective approaches. As one manager put it: "Another study? We've been studied until it's coming out of our ears. We've had special citizen task forces. We've installed work standards. Little has come out of any of these efforts, so what makes you think a new study will be any different?" Here are some approaches that he may have been subjected to in the past:

1. *The across-the-board cut* in costs (e.g., a dictum to "cut overhead by 10 percent") creates numerous disruptions and yields few lasting improvements. It results in curtailing efficient as well as inefficient or dispensable activities, which of course hurts the best managers most because they are already "close to the bone." Deferred expenses must be reckoned with later on, and managers have little motivation for further improvement. Departments with high personnel turnover (e.g., data processing) tend to be hit hardest in a common accompanying feature—the hiring freeze. The across-the-board cut ignores the areas of permanent improvement (i.e., changing the way in which things are done). And it encourages padding against the possibility of another such cut in the future.

2. *Scrubbing up forms and procedures* is a somewhat more fruitful approach, emphasizing reforms in office procedures, form design, layout, etc., to permit reductions in personnel and costs. While some improvements do occur with this approach, it focuses primarily on minor, superficial aspects of the problem and obscures the larger opportunities with its flurry of activity.

3. *Making cost reduction the "job of every manager"* sidesteps the issue and rarely leads to substantial improvements. While the individual manager should of course be concerned with cost improvement in his bailiwick, the routine

pressures of his job leave him little time to stand back and systematically analyze opportunities for cost-cutting. A targeted, systematic effort is required to eliminate the unnecessary or to make major changes in how things are done. Furthermore, most managers have little training or experience to equip them for rigorous cost-improvement efforts. Finally, and obviously, the easiest course and the natural inclination is to accept the status quo and not to pursue opportunities for improvement aggressively.

4. *Total reliance on cost-reduction specialists* is likely to end in disaster. Certainly an outside expert with broad experience can perform a key role in launching an effective cost-improvement program, since he can bring to bear an objective viewpoint and a knowledge of what other organizations are doing. However, he lacks the intimate knowledge of the details of the operation that is essential to changing it, and for this he must rely on the middle managers involved. Sound implementation requires the active involvement and support of middle management. Total reliance on the unsupported recommendations of outside specialists, without the involvement and commitment of the managers affected, typically results in no action being taken; instead, the managers may devote their energies to proving the expert wrong rather than seeking opportunities to apply his recommendations.

Small wonder there's lack of enthusiasm for cost reduction in public agencies. First, to mount such an effort entails substantial risk with little or no chance for reward. Second, because of tremendous budget pressure, it's a short trip in logic to conclude that operations are already "bare-bone." Finally, the history of unsuccessful approaches—across-the-board cuts, superficial "scrub-ups," exhortations to "make every manager cost-conscious," and unsuccessful "expert" efforts—tends to make most good public managers highly skeptical about the outcome of cost-reduction efforts or campaigns.

A Tested Approach

While these major obstacles to cost reduction exist to some degree in most public agencies, they are by no means insurmountable.

The approach we have used to overcome them is essentially a simple one. It consists of setting up a team of operating managers (usually three to five in number) and assigning it to a specific, well-chosen, cost-improvement project —under an entirely new and different value system that encourages and substantially rewards success in cost reduction and, conversely, spotlights failure. For a period of eight to ten weeks the project team devotes full time to a fact-based analysis of cost-improvement possibilities in a specific area, operation, or activity. Critical to success of the approach, of course, is top management's sponsorship and wholehearted support, but there are several other essentials: First, team members must be relieved completely of their operating responsibilities for the duration. This not only gives them the time needed, but prevents their citing the pressure of regular work as an excuse for failure. Second, they must be provided with a definite plan to follow during the course of the project. Third, management must insist on a challenging, measurable objective (e.g., $400,000 yearly savings in an organization with an annual budget of $2 million). Fourth, while management may be unable to make specific promises of reward, it should be made clear that results will count decisively in each man's next promotion or assignment. Fifth, use of facts and objective analysis, instead of subjective opinion and argument, should be insisted upon. And finally, management must sustain the confidence of team members throughout the project with bold, competent leadership.

The project team approach incorporates methods proven effective over a number of years in private industry. It entails these seven steps: (1) choosing the project, (2) selecting a project team, (3) conducting systematic in-depth analyses, (4) developing improvement opportunities, (5) evaluating all improvement ideas systematically, (6) documenting recommendations in a final report, and (7) following up aggressively to ensure implementation.

Step 1: Choosing the Project

Judicious selection of the first project will to a large extent determine the ultimate success of the approach. A typical single project may cover a selected procedure across departmental boundaries, all activities in one department, a large purchase cost, or a particular overhead cost. The activity or area selected for study should have a fairly sizable annual budget (e.g., $500,000 to $5,000,000) so that the project can make a substantial impact, but it should not be so large or complex as to exceed the team's ability to deal with it in depth in the eight- to ten-week project period. It may be most logical to start out in an area where management has reason to believe there is room for improvement. However, the approach also pays off in apparently well-managed departments—what a well-managed area may seem to lack in potential, it is likely to make up in a high degree of staff cooperation, respect for facts, and speedy implementation. Finally, it is often most fruitful to choose an activity that is duplicated in other areas. (For example, in a state motor vehicle department, a relatively minor cost reduction in one branch's processing of license applications can have a major total impact when repeated throughout the state.)

Step 2: Selecting a Project Team

The project team technique enables management to bring to bear a diversity of skills and experiences appropriate to the problem at hand, as well as a range of motivations for conducting and implementing the study. Careful selection of a well-balanced, strongly motivated team—consisting of a leader, team members, and a group of "observers"—is a prerequisite to success.

1. *The team leader* sets the tone for conduct of the project, and to a large extent his skill and enthusiasm determine its degree of success. He should be a strong, mature middle manager, action-oriented, comfortable in the respect

and support of line managers. This respect, coupled with high motivation and commitment to action, will go far toward ensuring successful implementation. Ideally, he should understand the mechanics of the approach and be completely "sold" on it, and hopefully he should have had experience in applying it in at least one previous such project. (Where it is his initial project, it is important to include on the team a man already trained in the techniques of the approach.) Team leadership is a tough role, since the skills required are not those typically needed in most managers' regular work. The team leader must plan the project, develop team members in the use of analytical techniques, guide the documentation of the study, and ensure top management's support and interest throughout the project. Moreover, his is the challenging task of maintaining a positive attitude among the team, since men participating in a project for the first time generally become discouraged when they encounter their first apparent blind alley or roadblock. In return for this demanding performance, top management must assure the team leader that successful efforts will be clearly rewarded by eventual promotion opportunities—and it must see that it sticks to its word.

2. *Team members* should be selected from representative areas of the organization and should possess a mix of skills to ensure cross-pollination of viewpoints. At least one member should have specific knowledge of the area under study. (For example, a financial analyst could make an important contribution to a cash management effort; or an engineer might be included for seeking opportunities to reduce maintenance costs.) Team members should all possess demonstrated analytical and problem-solving abilities, and they should have a predilection for facts rather than opinions. Finally, they should be willing to work hard, for such studies demand long hours and intense concentration.

3. *Observers from the area under study* should be assigned responsibility for reviewing the findings. These are supervisors who will be asked to act on the team's recommendations, and their involvement during the study tends to assure that the team will come up with practical recommendations that are capable of being implemented. The supervisory observers are encouraged to be constructive in their criticism of the team's work, which lessens the likelihood that recommendations can be ignored or shelved following the study without really valid reasons.

Step 3: Conducting Preliminary Analyses

The team starts out by developing a fact-founded familiarity with the operation, activity, or area under study and by planning and scheduling its subsequent work. Team members should observe and prepare a description of the activity, cost out its key steps, and begin to develop some indicators of improvement potential by reviewing past trends in the major cost categories or by spotlighting major differences among similar units in separate organizations.

Rough quantitative measures (e.g., number of invoices processed per clerk, ratio of toll collectors to cars serviced) are useful indexes. (For example, an analysis of seven toll bridges indicated that reducing manning on four of the bridges down to the average number of toll collectors per million vehicles per year would result in a $400,000 annual saving.) A helpful adjunct to this basic analysis is a questionnaire administered to foremen and middle managers to solicit ideas for improvement. For example, in one recent project such a questionnaire drew more than 100 suggestions for improvement, some of which proved useful to team members in focusing on the most promising opportunities.

At the conclusion of this initial brief analysis period—usually the first week —the team must commit itself to an ambitious objective for cost reduction. Typically, for a large public agency this target will be in six figures. While the team may be reluctant to make such a commitment early in the project, setting a specific goal is absolutely essential to assure top management that the project is likely to pay off. First, it provides a gauge by which to determine whether to proceed with the study; it makes no sense to tie up a team of highly talented individuals for eight to ten weeks if the effort is going to accomplish little or nothing of a tangible nature. Successful cost-improvement projects yield annual savings of at least $10,000 to $20,000 per man-month of effort. Thus, if a study team includes four men who must devote ten weeks to a problem, the payoff should total a minimum of $100,000 a year. Second, a team that is committed to a substantial, tangible objective is far more likely to achieve significant cost reduction than a team with no specific goal. With such a set goal, the team's attitude will be: "What must be done to achieve X savings?" rather than "How much savings can we comfortably achieve?"

Step 4: Developing Improvement Opportunities

The team's next step is to challenge rigorously every aspect of each activity under study. Members should ask the purpose of an activity or operation, questioning whether this purpose is essential or whether it might be achieved in another way. One fruitful device is to conduct "brainstorming" sessions that focus on how a suggested change might possibly be effected rather than on questioning its feasibility. Use of a checklist of key questions (e.g., can we eliminate steps? combine or centralize operations? simplify operations? change timing?) often is helpful in generating ideas. The following are typical examples of ideas engendered in such sessions:

- "Use higher quality paint, and paint less frequently."
- "Deposit checks locally, not by mail."
- "Use part-time toll collectors at peak hours."
- "Eliminate typing of statistics."

During these sessions the team leader insists that the group withhold all judgments—that team members resist the strong temptation to brush aside new ideas with such statements as: "We've tried that before," "We've always done it this way," "It won't work," "Management will never agree," or "It costs too much." (For example, a practical-sounding, but nonetheless superficial, response to such a specific suggestion as "paint less frequently" might be "sandblasting costs will skyrocket." While sandblasting costs will obviously increase, the real issue is whether these costs will be exceeded by the savings realized from painting less frequently—an issue that shouldn't be resolved by a pat response without the relevant facts.) Worthwhile ideas are likely to be discouraged if quick, premature judgments are permitted; evaluation of ideas follows later. The end product of this stage is a long list of ideas that vary widely in their potential impact and practicality—two important questions that await detailed evaluation.

Step 5: Evaluating Improvement Opportunities

The team next proceeds to subject this comprehensive list of possibilities to rigorous, fact-based analysis. The first step is to place the ideas in order of priority by posing the basic question: *"If this idea worked, how much would it save?"* It will be evident from this exercise that many ideas, even if successfully applied, would have such minor impact that they would not justify the effort involved to test them. On the other hand, it will be apparent that some ideas would have a very substantial impact if successfully implemented.

After identifying the high-leverage ideas, the team then determines what facts and analyses are required to prove or disprove the practicability of each idea, and it organizes its information-gathering efforts accordingly. It is essential to identify *all* the facts needed in each instance. (For example, the data required to test a suggestion to paint bridges less frequently included the cost of longer-lasting paint, labor cost for application, and estimated wear—and therefore sandblasting cost—at varying ages for both higher and lower quality paints.)

Once this analysis is reasonably well along and the team has formulated what appear to be sound recommendations, the analysis is reviewed at a weekly "observers' session" attended by at least one man from each affected department. Here the observers have an opportunity to question the feasibility of each idea before a final recommendation is made. Observers may oppose the recommendation altogether, request additional facts, or approve the recommendation and agree to implement it. When a recommendation is opposed, the chief executive of the organization is the final arbiter to approve or disapprove it. Where further facts are needed, the team obtains them and presents the supplementary analysis at a subsequent observers' session.

Step 6: Documenting the Recommendations

As a final step to confirm results, the team prepares a report to management presenting its recommendations, the rationale for each, and action plans for implementation. The report typically contains:

1. *An introduction* describing the project, summarizing what was done, the significance of the results, and the basic steps to be taken.

2. *Detailed recommendations,* including descriptions of past practice, specific recommended changes, and the rationale for each change, including estimated savings.

3. *Detailed action plans* laying out a track for implementing every change, specifying each step to be taken, the person or department responsible, and starting and completion dates.

4. *Exhibits and appendices,* including charts, calculations, and detailed procedural descriptions that might be helpful for occasional reference.

Step 7: Following Up to Ensure Implementation

Emphasis on commitment and action before the study is completed is a *sine qua non* of the project team approach. Implementation should start as soon as the observers are satisfied an idea is feasible and worthwhile. Reinforcing this concept, a high-level sponsor (e.g., an agency or department director) should sit in on an observers' session at about the midpoint of the project and insist on action on those ideas that appear practical by that time.

Following completion of the formal team effort, management makes sure that implementation proceeds as scheduled by requiring monthly progress reports from the line managers responsible for applying the recommendations. Detailing the status of each recommendation (i.e., savings thus far projected, implemented, and realized), these reports go to the top executive who initiated the study—enabling him to check regularly on responsibility assignments and planned timing and to take action where halfway execution and foot-dragging are evident.

Keys to Ensuring a Favorable Atmosphere

Critical to success of the project team approach is the atmosphere in which the study is conducted. To ensure a favorable climate for the project, it is essential to:

1. *Stress the concept of top-management involvement throughout the project.* The knowledge that management solidly supports the teams' efforts should provide a strong incentive to achieve significant results. Team members should be informed of their selection at the outset by a letter from the chief executive of the organization. He or one of his closest representatives should introduce the project at the first team meeting, indicating that the criterion of success is *action* and not merely a well-conducted study. Progress reports should be demanded during the course of the project, and the chief executive himself should participate periodically as the opportunity arises.

2. *Counter anticipated resistance.* Concern for the fate of those whose jobs may be eliminated is commonly encountered at the outset of a cost-reduction project. This may be dispelled by explaining that attrition is usually sufficient

to offset any reduction in staff and by clearly setting forth guidelines for placement of people whose jobs are dispensed with.

3. *Involve line managers during progress of the study.* Observers' sessions are critically important to assure practical, acceptable recommendations, as well as to get line management committed to action early in the project. In addition, starting implementation of some ideas during the study will further involve line managers in the effort.

4. *Insist on action before conclusion of the study.* Many cost studies end in failure because they are "sandbagged" by supervisors after the team has disbanded. The two weapons for preventing this are: (a) the chief executive's insistence on some action before the project is completed; and (b) the observers' sessions that focus on facts and afford the team an opportunity to work with its potential critics and remove roadblocks in advance.

Conclusion

In these days of $100 million budget deficits, an approach that has saved the State of California more than $2 million per year ($900,000 of which was realized in the Bay Toll Crossings Project) may seem unimpressive. We believe it is not, for these compelling reasons.

First, the project team technique generates savings through productivity improvements—not through program cutbacks or increases in employee work loads forced by arbitrary cuts in staff. Accordingly, it does not reduce program effectiveness, and service levels remain high. Second, these productivity improvement opportunities can be identified and achieved by career civil servants after brief introductory training. Accordingly, while the potential of a single project may be relatively modest, there is tremendous leverage in the technique; multiplied throughout an organization, the savings can become sizable indeed. The team members we've observed, while certainly capable, are no more so than other men and women in public service. Once trained, they can train others, thus greatly augmenting the potential savings. (For example, a trained group of five project leaders with 15 additional team members should be able to generate $2.4 to $5.0 million annual savings over a series of projects lasting a year—using the rule of thumb of $10,000 to $20,000 payoff per man-month.) And finally, because the approach is built around single teams concentrating on a manageable area or activity, it can be applied to both large- and moderate-sized government units—the only variation being the number of teams and the need for a formal process of overall staffing and assignment.

While the project team approach demands hard work and concentration and is not particularly glamorous, *it gets results.*

DAVID A. TANSIK
MICHAEL RADNOR

An Organization Theory Perspective on the Development of New Organizational Functions

The Advent of the planning-programming-budgeting system (PPBS) in the civilian agencies in 1969 brings into focus a continuing interest in the management and utilization of new, innovative managerial tools in the civilian sector of the government. Although PPBS was not the first new and innovative managerial tool to be introduced into the government in the 1960s, it certainly was one of the most well-known of recent such innovations, no doubt due in part to its method of introduction via presidential directive.[1]

Other new managerial tools such as systems analysis and operations research/management science (OR/MS), to name only two, had been finding usage in many government agencies long before President Johnson's August 1965 message. Indeed, Bureau of the Budget Bulletin No. 66-3 (October 12, 1965) directed to the heads of Executive Departments and Establishments specifically referred to the use of systems analysis and operations research in PPBS analysis: "Whenever applicable, this effort [PPBS analysis] will utilize systems analysis, operations research, and other pertinent techniques."[2]

It is perhaps still too soon to evaluate the overall success or failure of PPBS and its associated approaches and technologies (which could succeed even though PPBS per se might not). A period in excess of five years transpiring two administrations does, however, provide at least a tentative basis for reviewing the PPBS experience thus far. To date, PPBS has been applied via BOB directives to nearly all branches of the Executive Department. Numerous congressional hearings on PPBS have been held. Books have been written on the subject. Whole issues of journals have been devoted to PPBS symposia. In addition, sessions of professional society meetings have been forums for debate relative to the merits (or absence thereof) of PPBS. Congress, however, has yet to receive a "PPBS budget"; that is, the budget sent by the Administration to Congress is still a line item document even though most agencies have filed PPBS budgets with the Office of Management and Budget (formerly the Bureau of the Budget). Within the Executive Branch, while some agencies have developed quite sophisticated PPBS systems, others have been noticeably behind in making PPBS a routine part of agency operations. In addition, much comment has been directed at OMB itself regarding what some people feel has been insufficient and often conflicting guidance to the agencies regarding the PPBS system.

It is not the purpose of this article to either extol the virtues of or to condemn the PPBS system. It is, however, the purpose of this article to put the evolution of the PPBS system over these past more than five years into an analytical perspective which can be used to understand and perhaps explain the events that have occurred.

The Innovation Function

PPBS, along with OR/MS, systems analysis, and perhaps other similar techniques, represent today's new managerial tools for decision making, just as some years ago the new tool was scientific management. Next year, the new "thing" might be something else, such as futuristics. At any rate, PPBS and for that matter OR/MS are but several contemporary managerial approaches and technologies which are, in spirit, similar to other such innovations introduced in years past.

The problems faced by PPBS and OR/MS in becoming fully integrated into the organizations they are intended to serve are similar to the problems faced by these older managerial technologies. Did not scientific management in its day face worker (and manager) fears and even congressional scrutiny? What is different are the *disciplines* inherent in each technology, but what is not so different is the *process* by which they come to be integrated into organizational settings.

For instance, just as did scientific management, OR/MS is developing a new breed of professional specialists. The Operations Research Society of America (ORSA) has many similarities to the old Taylor Society (now the Society for the Advancement of Management), albeit with a mid-20th century perspective.

. . . Change the setting from Bethlehem, Pennsylvania, to Madison Avenue, the time from 1910 to 1962, the costuming from overalls to gray flannels, and the tasks from simple muscular labor to complex scheduling decisions. Recast worried laborer Schmidt with worried media executive Jones. Then replace time and motion study with linear programming or PERT, and replace the stop watch with a computer. The story line can remain intact.[3]

Recognizing what appears to be a degree of commonality between these various developments, a framework for analyzing the organizational integration of such new functions as PPBS or OR/MS has recently been developed. What is involved is the conceptualization of several "life cycles" through which any new organizational function is thought to pass during its development.

The specific forces behind the development and organizational introduction of these new innovative managerial tools will not be analyzed here. Suffice it to say that these new tools have been and are being developed and that the leaders of many organizations often see fit to introduce these new tools into their organizations in the form of discrete organizational functions. Thus, PPBS was introduced into many of the civilian agencies by President Johnson via a Bureau of the Budget directive establishing agency PPBS "offices."

Life Cycles[4]

In studying new organizational functions such as PPBS, a major concern is with the conditions which might significantly affect their introduction, growth, and effectiveness in the organization. Below are identified several phases which are believed to represent milestones in the life history of a new organizational function that enters as a gross departure from traditional modes of organizational functioning. Following Radnor and White,[5] we term this a revolutionary as opposed to an incremental or evolutionary pattern, which takes place when organizations either succeed in keeping pace with technology or are content to follow behind in an obsolescent manner. Within each of the following revolutionary life cycle phases there may be important differences in the conditions necessary for effective operations, and since this appears to be a frequently encountered pattern whose operation does not seem to be well understood, it would seem useful for us to describe this process in some detail.

Penetration-Missionary Phase

Various forces from both within and outside the organization usually combine to provide an opportunity for the entry of a new technology into the organization as an important major change-producing development. Such forces may well result from factors such as environmental changes which place pressures on management, from advances made by competing or allied organizations, or from pressures exerted by certain organizational members who for reasons of their own wish to see such a function established. The presence or absence in an organization of an established subunit capable of absorbing or "hosting" the new technology may well foster or inhibit the penetration of the new technology. Thus, the prior existence of accepted OR/MS or systems analysis functions in an agency may have provided an initial refuge (or dumping place!) for a new PPBS activity.

The penetration of a new technology can take place via the casual exposure of certain managers to the new technology or through attempts by certain organizational members to acquire (by themselves, by training other organizational members, or by hiring new personnel) the necessary skills to practice the new technology. Thus, the new technology often tends to fall into the hands of key personnel who then have the opportunity to exploit it to their own or the organization's benefits (or both). In any case, the new technology tends to fall into the hands of potential missionaries—persons who see the chance to achieve personal and/or organizational objectives by effecting the organizational utilization of the new technology.

264 | APPROACHES TO ORGANIZING

In this penetration-missionary life cycle phase there tends to be a concerted selling effort by the missionaries as they attempt to make other organizational members aware of their (the new technology's) existence and capabilities. The name "missionary" comes from the observation that the proponents of the new technology often tend to act like religious missionaries as they attempt to ingratiate themselves in the organization and "convert" natives (other organizational members) to the "faith" of the new technology.

I don't know why these people are so stupid. You have to almost get down on your knees and plead to sell these idiots on the benefits to them of using you [PPBS][6]

For a similar concept, see Anthony Downs' description of the zealot.[7] Especially common is the attempt by the missionaries to gain a sponsor—a person usually in the top management level who will actively support the new technology in the organization. This top management support can then be used by the missionaries to lend an air of legitimacy or credibility to their actions. In addition, this top management support can be used in the form of an implied threat of top management sanction for those not "converting to the faith."

PPBS hits people where it hurts. You get in there and look down their throats. But [top manager] is backing us so we haven't been having too much trouble.

Given that the missionary efforts are at least partially successful, the new technology will tend to become a recognized, although usually not as yet, permanently endowed organizational component. Such activities may or may not go on from within a formal organizational unit. The point at which the new technology becomes a recognized organizational component has been referred to as the formal birth of the new function in that organization. This formal birth, depending on starting conditions, may take place before, during, or even after the missionary phase. Of course, the missionaries could be unsuccessful, and the new technology may face an untimely death in the organization during this period.

Organizational Resistance and Difficulties

Assuming that the new technology successfully penetrates the organization, a new phase in the development may occur. In many cases the new technology does not meet with complete and unequivocable acceptance and supportiveness in the organization. Most students of organizational behavior are well aware of the problems inherent in introducing and effecting organizational components. When these changes occur in essentially bureaucratic organizations not designed for or even used to the adaptiveness often required to accept a new change-producing technological function, these problems may even compound themselves.

The reasons for these problems seem to stem from three basic sources.[8]

1. *Interpersonal:* Fear of the unknown and an *a priori* lack of trust by mem-

bers of the organizational establishment in regards to the new technologists may well lead to an absence of support or even outright hostility toward the new technology. Insofar as members of the organization do not control the new technology, do not understand it, or have no built up credit with the new technology, they most likely will tend to at least passively resist its introduction.

Several authors have attempted to analyze an aspect of this phenomena in terms of the motivational base of the parties concerned. Merton uses the professional versus the organizational dichotomy to characterize the innovative *professional* spirit of the new technology as it clashes with the more locally oriented, *organizational* identification of many other organizational members.' Downs makes a similar distinction between the zealots who desire to capture or invent new functions and play a key role ". . . in the formation of new bureaus" and the conservers who seek to ". . . maximize their sincerity and convenience" and who ". . . have an asymmetrical attitude toward change."[10]

In addition, it is often found that the new technologists tend to bring with them new and special purpose languages or argot not readily understood by other organizational members. Thus, not being able to express themselves in simple language (at least as far as other organizational members are concerned), the new technologists are often shunned by the more entrenched organizationals who seem to express the feeling that they would rather not go out of their way to learn about the new technology.

A couple of times I got all these fellows [high-level managers] together in a room and they promised to stay a half hour. All I wanted was to explain in simple English what a matrix was and some other things like that so they could understand us. Fifteen minutes after we started maybe one or two were left. I think they told their secretaries to "save" them after we got started, so they got convenient phone calls.

2. *Organizational:* The ability to develop organizational legitimation is a task facing most all new functions. How quickly a new function can build up a record of successes in contacts with other organizational components, the extent of top management support, the organizational location of the new function, as well as many other factors all combine to influence the visibility, perceived credibility, and the overall perception of acceptance by members of the organization of the new function.

A new group like ours is only as good as its last project.

The allocation of sufficient budgetary resources to enable the new function to acquire a necessary working staff also enters as a crucial variable. This phenomena has been referred to as the need to acquire a "minimum critical mass" before significant impact can be made on the organization.[11]

How can we do 'good' PPBS? I can't even get the money to hire a decent secretary, much less a good staff.

In addition, the degree of reorganization, if any, required of other organizational components before they can utilize the new function enters the system. Such reorganization is often not only painful to established organizational members, but must sometimes be effected even before the introduction of the new function itself. Thus, hostilities toward the new function may well be brewing even before it actually enters the organization.

3. *Environmental:* Of no small importance are such exogenous factors as the ability to acquire needed personnel for the new function, degree of external pressure to adopt the new function (e.g., Office of Management and Budget insistence on PPBS usage), the current state-of-the-art of the new technology, and the general level of acceptance of the new technology in competitive and allied organizations. These forces from outside the organization which come to bear upon various organizational members can often pressure (or hinder) the organizational integration of the new technology. Such environmental forces have sometimes been used to explain variations in the rates of adoption of new technologies between organizations, industries, and even between nations.[12]

Why are our PPBS and OR/MS efforts going over so well? [The agency director] got a phone call a couple of months ago from somebody in the Bureau of the Budget, that's why.

Organizationalizing and Deprofessionalism

Given an initial successful penetration by the new technology and a successful weathering of organizational resistance to it, members of the new technology and other organizational members are often found entering into what might be called a period of "bargaining." This bargaining essentially revolves around attempts by members of the new technology to show what they can and desire to do in the organization and attempts by other organizational members to prevent the new technology from overly impinging upon their actions. Thus, a pattern of give and take whereby members of the new technology seek to exert themselves upon other members of the organization and whereby these other organizational members often seek to rebuff or limit the activities of the new technology often occurs. This pattern of give and take has been labeled the organizationalizing life cycle phase.

Very often, the result of this bargaining process is that the members of the new technological function go through a period of deprofessionalism. That is, the level of application or sophistication of the new technology often becomes less than that originally intended by the new technologists. This may often be the result of having a highly professionally oriented new technology leader removed from office or by accommodation on behalf of the new technologists as they adjust to the practicalities of the given organizational situation, and from the progressive loss of the more professionally oriented personnel who find the compromised environment unacceptable.

If and when I can, I'll go somewhere else. It's too bad, but I really thought OR/MS could go places here. Instead, all we do is push pencils through L.P. problems. We don't even have to use a computer anymore!

The level of active top management support of and usage of the outputs of the innovative function may well act as leverage for the parties involved in the bargaining process. So long as top management supports and uses the innovative function, less deprofessionalization and more of an organizational adaptation to the new function may occur as it gains credence from top management as well as an ability to influence organizational functioning via top management usage of its outputs.

So long as [an assistant to the agency director] keeps backing us, we'll do fine. People know we have his ear.

Things are going O.K. We win a few and lose a few, but by next year, we'll be the best OR/MS shop in the District. We just have to age a little.

Specialist and Maturity

The result of the organizationalizing process is not easily determinable on an *a priori* basis. Many factors, such as top management support of the new technology, the level of organizational resistance to the new function, the ability of the new technologists to acquire several successes in dealings with other organizational members, etc., determine the eventual outcome.

The deprofessionalization process could lead to a low-level technique application function. For instance, an OR/MS activity may become, after deprofessionalization, merely an applier of certain linear programming models to redundant problems arising in the organizatiaon. In the extreme case, the deprofessionalization process could even lead to the organizational dissolution of the new technological function.

Alternatively, the new technology function may well emerge from the organizationalizing process with little deprofessionalization having occurred, either because the technology is supported and protected, or because there arises a dissatisfaction with the deprofessionalized activity as the value of the new technology begins to be appreciated. In this case, certain members of the organization may well come to demand the services of the new technology in an improved (or reprofessionalized) form. Thus, rather than deprofessionalization a specialist-type period emerges in which the new function may mature. Maturity is defined as the full and routine organizational acceptance of the function. Given this maturity status, our new function (although not so new anymore) may well become an organizational subunit capable of absorbing in an evolutionary manner even newer technologies (see discussion relative to the penetration of a new technology) and thus the cycle may start anew.

OR/MS in [agency] is here to stay. Why not? They help us. (Comment by a user of OR/MS.)

We're an accepted agency function now. Only I'd be ashamed to have my old college teachers [of OR/MS] see what I do all day.

It's like [staff member] told me the other day. We're not lepers anymore. Management actually trusts us now.

Thus, a stable, or equilibrium, state for a new function can be achieved in the guise of one of several evolved states ranging from the deprofessionalized low-level technique applier to a highly specialized practitioner of the innovative technology. The precise state is, of course, dependent upon the unique factors inherent in each organization.

It must, of course, be recognized that the new function may fail at any given point during this evolutionary cycle. The life cycle stage of death thus may be entered from any point along the penetration to maturity continuum. The time range from penetration to maturity varies with each organization. Some OR/MS activities have been found to reach maturity in between 18 and 24 months, while others have taken eight to ten years.

Implications of the Life Cycle Approach

The applicability of the life cycle approach is not limited to OR/MS and PPBS. However, the visibility and contemporary nature of OR/MS and PPBS activities make them convenient vehicles to use to elaborate many of the concepts expressed here.

If the life cycle approach is a viable descriptor of one important common form of the development of new organizational functions, it is not surprising that different government agencies have shown varying degrees of success in their PPBS efforts. Variations in top management support of PPBS, level of organizational resistance to (or compliance with) the PPBS effort, ability of agencies to acquire and keep qualified personnel, and other similar factors all enter at various life cycle stages to influence eventual success or failure. Also, not all agencies' PPBS efforts began at the same point in time. Thus, the beginning of the progression through life cycle stages differs among various agencies. In addition, some have moved through the alternative evolutionary pattern of development mentioned earlier.

Some agencies had, prior to undertaking PPBS, organizational components doing work similar to that required by PPBS.[13] Perhaps partly a response to the need for OR/MS and systems analysis in PPBS work, many PPBS activities were given to existing OR/MS or similar organizational units. In some cases this may have lessened or even eliminated the birth pains and need for missionizing on behalf of PPBS. Some agencies, namely the hard data ones, were perhaps better able to initially embark on the quantitative aspects of PPBS, and thus were perhaps able to develop several early successes. Elizabeth Drew, in commenting on the HEW experience with PPBS, makes the point that a lack of hard data in certain areas initially limited that agency's PPBS efforts.[14] The existence or lack of hard data—which is a crucial PPBS input—

would therefore seem to be an important mediating factor in any organizational resistance to a new PPBS activity as it attempts to acquire several successes in its work efforts.

In a recent survey of 16 federal civilian government agencies' experiences with PPBS by Harper, Kramer, and Rouse,[15] a number of factors similar to concepts discussed under various stages were used to classify agencies according to their relative usage of the PPBS analytic effort. While perhaps appropriate as a point-in-time estimation of PPBS integration in the various agencies, such analysis may well be benefited by considering the dynamics of the development (movement through life cycle stages) rather than taking a static measure of overall, to date, impact. The classification of a PPBS activity as having little impact on agency operations may occur in the case of an activity which has penetrated an organization and regressed to a deprofessionalized state, or death; or such a classification might occur in the case of a newer activity only recently established or still engaged in the give-and-take organizationalizing process.

We must recognize here that while the former case may well be one of failure, the opportunity or potential in the latter should cause it to be viewed in a different light even though a static comparison of the two cases may lead to similar conclusions.

A Crucial Variable—Top Management Support?

The concept of top management support was mentioned quite often as being relevant in the various life cycle states. In the penetration-missionary phase the benefit of a top management sponsor was mentioned. Top management support to counteract interpersonal resistance, to aid in acquiring organizational legitimacy, and to aid via the budgetary process in acquiring a qualified staff was also mentioned as being pertinent during the organizational resistance stage. The level of top management support and usage of the new function's outputs was mentioned as being a potential lever in the bargaining processes inherent in the organizationalizing stage. And in the specialist-maturity stage, regular top measurement usage of the new function's outputs may act as an incentive for lower-level management to use the new function so as to be in on what is occurring in the organization as well as to acquire and retain top management's favor.

There are several key variables controlled by top management which may have a significant influence upon the functioning of new organizational activities. First, the organizational location of the new activity may in large part determine the focus of the activity's first efforts, and top management might wish to consider how location will affect early as well as long-term development. In addition, location may well influence the legitimacy or credibility afforded the new organizational function by other organizational members.[16]

Secondly, resource allocation decisions by top management may help determine the scope of the effort expended by the new organizational unit. Size and quality of the staff and resources such as computer availability are often important ingredients for the success of new organizational activities. Often, too, the initial resource outlays must be rather significant in order to generate sufficient momentum to sustain the new activity. A dilemma may result, however, in that such large resource outlays may bring organizational suspicions and hostilities which could hamper the development of the new activity.

A third top management variable is of a more intangible nature. The general level of support exhibited by top management for the new function is often tied to the willingness of other organizational members to accept (or at least not resist) the new organizational unit. Admittedly, top management support is related to the location and resource variables; however, support is often evidenced in other forms. Top management usage of the outputs of the new function, public praise of the new function, or overt requirements or suggestions to other organizational members concerning usage of the new function, are but several possible manifestations of top management support.

In an analysis of both business and government OR/MS activities, Radnor, Rubenstein, and Tansik[17] found a relationship between top management support and favorable client relations (both as perceived by OR/MS practitioners). In addition, Radnor, Rubenstein, and Bean[18] found a strong relationship in business organizations between the organizational fortunes of top management OR/MS sponsors and their OR/MS groups.

A major factor which may influence top management support and usage of the new organizational function is top management's knowledge and understanding of the new function. This knowledge and understanding could seemingly be acquired by many top managers through their contacts with the new organizational function. As an indication of this top management learning, Tansik has shown that top managers in charge of OR/MS activities in advanced life cycle stages tend to evaluate the activities more on the basis of OR/MS contributions to organizational goals than do top managers over early life cycle activities.[19] The implication here is that through contacts with OR/MS as the activity develops, the top manager may be able to develop an understanding of what OR/MS can do in his organization. Thus, to evidence their support, the top managers in charge of many early stage life cycle activities may have to accept the activities' outputs on faith rather than with a thorough understanding of what they are actually doing. It is not inconceivable that this will not be an acceptable course of action for many top managers.

However, the data we have collected on this relationship between top management knowledge, support, and use of OR/MS technology has led to ambiguous findings. Thus, White found only low or even negative correlations between these variables in government agencies, which seems to indicate that the obvious simplistic assumptions as to the effects of top management behavior which seem to be held by both theorists and practitioners cannot be accepted at face value, and that the clearly complex nature of relationships must be the subject of considerably more research.[20]

White's findings may thus be at variance with, for example, the previously mentioned report on PPBS by Harper *et al.*, and the report of Drew, both of whom mentioned support by agency heads of PPBS efforts as being the primary aspect of PPBS success.

The most important factor determining the relative effectiveness of an agency's PPB efforts was the active support and use of PPB by the agency head. If the agency head was interested in using PPB, he saw to it that the agency developed the other factors that aided the development of the PPB effort.[21]

Additionally, Drew in her review of PPBS states that:

How well PPB has worked, agency by agency, has depended more than anything on how seriously the man at the top has taken it, how hard he worked to attract good people to do the job, how much he lent his authority to the adoption of a system of hard analysis.[22]

More useful may be the attempt to integrate the type and form of top management support with the changing conditions over the various life cycles discussed above, to determine the likely effects. Thus, perhaps top management support is not a "save all." Perhaps it is a very important parameter or catalyst which helps other things happen at opportune times—the opportune time being highly influenced by conditions arising in various life cycle stages.

Conclusion

The increasing development of large complex organizations and the recognition of the openness and vulnerability of the organizations to developments in a changing environment pose pressures on management to not only introduce new technological advances into organizations, but also to develop processes for managing the introduction of these new technologies. The life cycle approach is intended as an aid to this latter pressure.

Insofar as the PPB system is concerned, the usefulness of the life cycle approach lies in its applicability to the events surrounding PPBS development in many organizations. To the extent that this scheme, where applicable, aids individual managers in assessing their PPBS development relative to other organizations, and to the extent that the scheme can perhaps serve as a guide to action, it would seem to serve a useful function.

Notes

1. "Introduction of New Government-Wide Planning and Budgeting System: Statement by the President to Members of the Cabinet and Heads of Agencies," *Weekly Compilation of Presidential Documents*, Monday, August 30, 1965, Vol. 1, No. 5, pp. 141-142.
2. Bureau of the Budget, "Bulletin No. 66-3," October 12, 1965, p. 8.
3. Harold J. Leavitt, "Applied Organizational Change in Industry: Structural, Technological and Humanistic Approaches," in James G. March (ed.), *Handbook of Organizations* (Chicago: Rand McNally and Co., 1965), p. 1150.

4. Much of the discussion in this section draws upon the notes and thoughts of the authors as members of the Co-operative International Program of Studies on Operations Research and the Management Sciences, headquartered at Northwestern University and directed by Michael Radnor. The concepts expressed here are the result of long discussions attended by many program members, especially A. S. Bean, State University of New York at Albany; Michael White, Northwestern University; and D. Hardin, Loyola University of Chicago, in addition to the authors. In particular, the work on life cycles has been considerably developed by Radnor and White, and a full description of these processes will appear in a forthcoming paper, "Patterns of Institutionalization of Innovation in Modern Organizations," Northwestern University Working Paper, October 1970.

5. Radnor and White, *ibid.*

6. This and ensuing similar quotations are drawn from the authors' research on PPBS and OR/MS in the federal civilian agencies which began in 1967 as part of the aforementioned Northwestern University research activity. This research has involved in-depth studies in almost 50 agencies and close cooperation with the Washington Operations Research Council and the American Society for Public Administration. The field work was carried out by D. Tansik and M. White with the cooperation of H. Welsch. For a full report on these studies, see *Management Science in Government*, M. Radnor, D. Tansik, and M. White (eds.) (Chicago: Aldine Publishing Company), forthcoming volume. Due to confidentiality promises to all respondents, these quotations must remain anonymous.

7. Anthony Downs, *Inside Bureaucracy* (Boston: Little, Brown, and Company, 1967).

8. These ideas are largely drawn from Michael Radnor, "Stages and Indices of the Evolution of Management Science in Organizations and Their Environments," paper presented at the XVI International Meeting of The Institute of Management Sciences, New York City, March 1969.

9. R. K. Merton, *Social Theory and Social Structure,* revised edition (New York: Free Press, 1957).

10. Downs, *op. cit.,* pp. 96 and 110.

11. Radnor, *op. cit.*

12. *Ibid.,* p. 9.

13. For example, the TVA and USDA by the end of World War II had moved away from the traditional object accounts toward what the Hoover Commission later called performance or program budgeting.

14. Elizabeth Drew, "HEW Grapples With PPBS," in Amitai Etzioni (ed.), *Readings on Modern Organizations* (Englewood Cliffs, N.J.: Prentice-Hall, 1969), p. 173.

15. Edwin L. Harper, Fred A. Kramer, and Andrew M. Rouse, "Implementation and Use of PPB in Sixteen Federal Agencies," *Public Administration Review,* Vol. XXIX, No. 6 (November/December 1969), pp. 623-632.

16. This issue of location is discussed in some detail in Michael Radnor, Albert H. Rubenstein, and Alden S. Bean, "The Integration and Utilization of Operations Research and Management Sciences in Organizations," *Operational Research Quarterly,* June 1968.

17. Michael Radnor, Albert H. Rubenstein, and David A. Tansik, "Implementation in Operations Research and R and D: In Government and Business Organizations," *Journal of the Operations Research Society of America* (November/December 1970).

18. Radnor, Rubenstein, and Bean, *op. cit.*

19. David A. Tansik, "Influences of Organizational Goal Structures on the Selection and Implementation of Management Science Projects," unpublished Ph.D. dissertation, Northwestern University, June 1970.

20. Michael White, "Top Management Response to OR/MS: Booz-Allen-Hamilton Project Report," Graduate School of Management, Northwestern University, April 1970.

21. Harper *et al., op. cit.*

22. Drew, *op. cit.,* p. 173.